新国标应用型本科商务英语系列教材

总主编　王立非

商务谈判实训

（双语）（第二版）

Simulated Training for Business Negotiations

(Second Edition)

主　编　廖国强　艾湘华
副主编　张　春　赵　军
王姝绘　王景洁
秦筱婉

U0950408

对外经济贸易大学出版社
中国·北京

图书在版编目（CIP）数据

商务谈判实训：双语：英文 / 廖国强，艾湘华主编. —2 版. —北京：对外经济贸易大学出版社，2023.9

新国标应用型本科商务英语系列教材 / 王立非总主编

ISBN 978-7-5663-2545-7

Ⅰ. ①商… Ⅱ. ①廖… ②艾… Ⅲ. ①商务谈判–英语–双语教学–高等学校–教材 Ⅳ. ①F715.4

中国版本图书馆 CIP 数据核字（2023）第 191981 号

商务谈判实训（双语）（第二版）

Simulated Training for Business Negotiations (Second Edition)

廖国强　艾湘华　主编

责任编辑： 杨娇娇

出版发行：对外经济贸易大学出版社

社　　址：北京市朝阳区惠新东街 10 号

网　　址：www.uibep.com

资源网址：www.uibepresources.com

邮政编码：100029

邮购电话：010 – 64492338

发行部电话：010 – 64492342

E-mail：uibep@126.com

成品尺寸：185mm×260mm

印　　张：17.5

字　　数：404 千字

ISBN 978-7-5663-2545-7

印　　刷：北京市泰锐印刷有限责任公司

版　　次：2023 年 9 月北京第 2 版

印　　次：2023 年 9 月第 1 次印刷

定　　价：58.00 元

“新国标应用型本科商务英语系列教材”
编　委　会

出版说明

党的二十大报告指出，中国积极参与全球治理体系改革和建设，践行共商共建共享的全球治理观，推动全球治理朝着更加公正合理的方向发展。中国呼吁世界各国弘扬全人类共同价值，促进各国人民相知相亲，尊重世界文明多样性，以文明交流超越文明隔阂、文明互鉴超越文明冲突、文明共存超越文明优越，共同应对各种全球性挑战。

习近平总书记强调，要大力培养掌握党和国家方针政策、具有全球视野、通晓国际规则、熟练运用外语、精通中外谈判和沟通的国际化人才。

教材是实现人才培养的基本工具和载体。"新国标应用型本科商务英语系列教材"是应对全球挑战、有效进行国际商务沟通、顺应国家现代教育改革的必然要求。2014 年 6 月 22 日国务院发布《关于加快发展现代职业教育的决定》(以下简称《决定》)，全面部署加快发展现代职业教育。《决定》指出要"采取试点推动、示范引领等方式，引导一批普通本科高等学校向应用技术类型高等学校转型，重点举办本科职业教育。"

截至 2022 年 8 月，全国有 429 所高等院校开设了商务英语本科专业，其中多数院校属于应用型本科院校。本系列教材结合商务英语语言和教学的特点，融合多年商务英语教学实践，由长期从事商务英语教学一线的专家倾力打造，适用于全国应用型本科商务英语专业和财经类本科专业学生。

本套教材具有以下特色：

一、吸收二语习得和现代教育的最新理论，体现《商务英语专业本科教学质量国家标准》的最新要求。教材编写上注重提高学生的语言技能、让学生掌握相关的商务知识与实践技能，培养学生的跨文化交际能力、思辨与创新能力，以及自主学习能力。

二、秉承应用型本科教育"优化理论，突出实践"的理念。应用型本科教育注重技术但不能完全抛弃学术，其人才培养是学术性与职业性的有机统一，其基本特征是"本科底蕴+突出应用+专业特长"。体现在教材上，它强调"优化理论，突出实践"，优化理论基础，注重理论与专业技术的相关性，以培养目标与从业要求为依据对基础理论进行优化整合，介绍与专业相关的必要理论，重点强化行业知识的讲解；突出实践方面，强调教材的编排设计从教学目标到内容的组织，练习题的设计都环环相扣、注重培养学生的职业适应能力，突出实践教学的内涵。

三、贯彻“任务引领、项目导向”的指导思想。本套教材以“任务驱动”为理念，强化了教材的任务驱动效应，突出作业流程的可操作性；以真实企业业务经营为主线贯穿始终，从而保持教材内容前后的一致性和连续性；通过具体任务的设计和实施，使学生能够掌握业务技能。

对外经济贸易大学出版社

2023年6月

前　言 Preface

全党深入开展学习贯彻习近平新时代中国特色社会主义思想主题教育，是贯彻落实党的二十大精神的重大举措。党的二十大报告提出加快建设贸易强国，内涵丰富，为我国贸易发展方向提供了明确指引。我们要坚定不移扩大对外开放，坚持真正的多边主义，全方位扩大国际经贸合作，深度参与全球产业分工和合作，维护多元稳定的国际经济格局和经贸关系，为建设贸易强国营造良好的外部环境。习近平总书记指出，人类生活在同一个地球村里，生活在历史和现实交汇的同一个时空里，越来越成为你中有我、我中有你的命运共同体。自古以来，和平发展往往伴随着贸易繁荣，贸易繁荣又促进了世界各民族友好交往，本书的推出正是符合时代潮流。

党的二十大报告思想深邃、内涵丰富、博大精深。本教材重点结合专业实际，切实把党的二十大精神转化为实践指南，认真构思编写内容，坚持为党育人、为国育才，为加快建设教育强国、科技强国、人才强国贡献力量。

习近平新时代中国特色社会主义思想是中华文化和中国精神的时代精华，因此，《商务谈判实训（双语）（第二版）》以习近平新时代中国特色社会主义思想为指导，强化中华优秀文化在高校外语教育中的作用，落实在高校英语教学中融入思想政治教育，是为中华民族的伟大复兴培养全面发展的高素质国际化应用型人才而编写的一本商务谈判教材。这为推动我国对外经济的发展、抓住新的战略机遇和提高核心竞争力具有重要意义。

经济全球化进程加快了中国与世界各国的频繁交往，中外经贸领域的交流与活动进一步促进了我国国际经济与贸易的新繁荣。在对外经贸活动中，商务谈判既是商务活动的重要内容，又是商务活动的必要手段，商务谈判能力已成为现代商务人员必须掌握的一项基本职业技能，因而商务谈判技能在跨文化商务交际中起着越来越重要的不可替代的桥梁和纽带作用。在当今多元文化背景下，与人沟通的专业知识能力，优雅得体的仪态对商务事业的成功起着重要的作用。具备这些综合素质，就容易赢得更多的客户及合作者。我们深知，中华之崛起离不开经济贸易往来，为适应新形势下全球社会经济的发展和广大读者对商务谈判书籍的需要，我们编写了此书。

本书针对社会各界英语爱好者和广大从事国内外经贸业务人员及国际贸易、国际商务、国际金融、国际物流、国际财会、电子商务、市场营销、商务英语、跨文化交际、经济类、管理类、文秘类等专业的学生熟悉商务谈判理论与技巧的需要而编写。本书在编写中注重结合当今跨文化商务谈判中可能遇到的新情况、新问题，突出重点，便于读者学习与了解参与谈判时可能遇到的各种情景及沟通对策，内容紧跟国内外经贸活动最新发展，知识点覆盖面广、实用性强。通过引导进行模拟商务谈判，锻炼学习者的应变能力，基本掌握国际商务谈判的流程，了解谈判各个过程环节的要求与注意点以及风格的体现，以便把所学的知识应用到实际谈判之中。

全书以英文为主，中文为辅，以便让读者更深刻地理解用于沟通的语言，掌握国际商务谈判的基本原则和技巧，并能流利地用英语或中文进行商务沟通、完成商务谈判，有效地提高学习者的实践能力。每一章中的要点、部分短语或词汇等都提供了中文注释，可以满足不同需求和不同英语水平学习者的需要，力求实效，也可弥补所谓全英文太难或全中文讲解又不易掌握英文用法的不足。本书主要特色如下：

1. 本书由十二章构成，每章设置若干任务引领，涵盖了商务谈判流程的方方面面，内容丰富多彩，文字流畅，信息量充足，语言难度适中，对社会各界的使用者和大专院校的学生具有极强的适用性。书中既提供了大量商务谈判的基础理论指导内容，也有应用性很强的商务谈判中的实战技巧内容，谈判过程中的激烈争辩、讨价还价、迂回战术等策略，能在一定程度上锻炼学习者的语言表达能力和应变能力，并能使他们认识到自己的不足之处。让学术性与职业性有机统一，能满足不同层次、不同用途使用者的需要，涉及读者面广。

2. 本书各章节根据商务谈判涉及的相关内容编写，所述内容既有相互照应之处，也能凸显各章特点，汉语注释与说明起到互补作用，对尽快提高学习者的英语水平和熟悉谈判技巧具有积极意义。

3. 本书各章内容融基本谈判知识和实例为一体，注重贯彻“任务引领、项目导向”的指导思想，介绍的知识点力求多方位覆盖具有普遍性的商务谈判技巧，以“任务驱动”为理念，强化教材的任务驱动效应。每个任务都包括案例学习、案例思考、案例解析、理论知识拓展、要点小结、综合实训等内容，以真实谈判情景为主线，突出谈判流程的可操作性，并注意沟通细节和文化差异，理论联系实际，注重实用性，充分体现“基于工作过程系统化的项目导向、任务驱动、教学做”一体化的课程改革理念，以适应经贸领域业务谈判的需要。

4. 本书以综合性、应用性作为编写定位，尽可能结合国际经贸发展业务中对商务谈判的需要，模拟商务谈判的流程设计，针对学习者进行综合性和实践性环节的培养与锻炼。由于目前国内绝大多数的商务谈判书籍均用中文编写而成，因此，本书也有助于大中专院校或社会培训机构进行国家提倡的双语教学，具有独特性、新颖性。

5. 优化理论，突出实践，学以致用。每章均提供不少实战谈判案例，模拟情景丰富，活动形式多样，注重从不同的角度提高学生的实际操作能力，如场景对话、角色扮演、案例分析、会议发言、演讲、模拟谈话以及辩论等活动。此外每单元还提供相关的实践语句，让使用者通过实践或互动环节加深理解和运用，提高商务谈判能力，适合对应用型人才培养的要求。

6. 选材广泛，涉及面大，知识点集中，主题突出，内容翔实，注重培养学生的职业适应能力，突出实践教学的内涵，是主要针对国内读者编写而涉及要点非常全面的商务谈判类书籍。

综上所述，本书突出了理论性、系统性、应用性和实践性，有利于培养学生的跨文化交际能力、思辨与创新能力以及自主学习能力，能满足不同层次、不同水平的社会各行业涉外从业人员、英语爱好者的需要和大专院校国际贸易、国际管理、国际金融、电子商务、市场营销、跨文化交际、经贸英语、涉外文秘等专业学生的需要，也可作为面向全校的素质教育选修课用书。使用者在选用本书时，可根据实际情况，进行适度的取舍或补充，对书中的内容或观点，应带着思考去看。在实践中，应根据实际酌情调整己方的商务谈判策略与技巧，运用和加强谈判所需的组织、策划与管理能力，培养和加强逻辑思维能力及应变能力。只有策略周详，措辞得当，举止得体，才能在当今竞争激烈的商务环境中赢得先机。毕竟国与国之间、地区与地区之间的文化、习俗差异是巨大的，而且商务谈判的过程是动态发展的，沟通成功与否取决于当事人自身的灵活性以及当事人捕捉信息质量和应变的能力。所以，每单元提供的谈判理论技巧与要点仅供参考。当内容上有交叉或看法不一致的情况出现时，读者应注意国情的不同、区域的不同、文化差异、宗教信仰等的不同，学习中不要机械地生搬硬套。另外，为方便教师课堂教学需要，本书特配备了 PPT 课件供参考使用，请到网站 http://www.uibepresources.com 下载。

本书自第一版面世以来，一直受到广大读者的喜爱。其间，国际商务谈判的理论和实践也在不断发展、不断变化。我们实时对全书进行修订，使国际商务谈判实训跟上时代的发展变化，自然显得尤为必要。本书的修订以综合性、应用性和现实性作为编写定位，政治导向正确，无意识形态隐患。修订版以习近平新时代中国特色社会主义思想为指导，贯彻落实党的二十大精神，强化中华优秀文化在高校外语教育中的作用，落实在高校英语教学中融入思想政治教育，内容紧跟国际商务活动对商务谈判的新需要、新要求，更新的内容都与时代同步。具体来说，修订版在案例分析和选择上更加注重思政内容，注重中国元素的融入，有些单元修订了案例，有些单元更换了新材料，部分单元的练习也进行了重新设计，练习形式既考虑方便教师授课指导，又利于学生实践工作坊（workshop）的实训练习，使修订后的内容更加突出实用性和实践性，这不仅有利于学习者提升其在国际商务场合的素养与竞争力，还有助于其掌握地道英语，转而向世界讲好“中国故事”。

本书在编写及出版过程中，得到对外经济贸易大学出版社编辑的大力支持，在此表示诚挚的谢意。

由于编写时间有限，不妥之处在所难免，敬请广大读者和同仁批评指正。

编 者

2023 年 7 月

目　录 Contents

Unit 1　Business Negotiation Thinking, Psychology and Language Arts
商务谈判思维、心理与语言艺术……1

Task 1　Business Negotiation Thinking 商务谈判思维……1
Task 2　Business Negotiation Psychology 商务谈判心理……5
Task 3　Language Arts in Business Negotiations 商务谈判语言艺术……13

Unit 2　Types of Business Negotiations
商务谈判的类型……27

Task 1　Domestic Business Negotiations 国内商务谈判……27
Task 2　International Business Negotiations 国际商务谈判……30
Task 3　Negotiations for Merchandise Trade 商品贸易谈判……36
Task 4　Negotiations for Non-Merchandise Trade 非商品贸易谈判……39
Task 5　Multi-Party and Multi-Phased Negotiations 多方多阶段谈判……43

Unit 3　Preparation and Organization for Business Negotiations
商务谈判准备与组织……51

Task 1　An Introduction to International Business Negotiations 认识国际商务谈判……51
Task 2　Determination of Negotiating Goals 谈判目标的确定……54
Task 3　Information Gathering in Business Negotiation 商务谈判信息收集……58
Task 4　Avoidance of Negotiation Risks 谈判风险规避……61
Task 5　Making a Negotiation Plan 谈判方案的拟定……65
Task 6　Choices of Negotiation Styles 谈判方式的选择……69

Unit 4　Business Negotiation Communication
商务谈判沟通……83

Task 1　Factors and Types of Business Negotiation Communication 商务谈判沟通的要素和分类……83

Task 2 Language in Business Negotiation Communication 商务谈判沟通的语言 ······ 87
Task 3 Language Skills in Business Negotiation Communication 商务谈判沟通的语言技巧 ······ 92
Task 4 Non-Verbal Language in Business Negotiation Communication 商务谈判沟通的行为语言 ······ 97

Unit 5 Strategies and Tactics for Business Negotiations 商务谈判策略与技巧 ······ 111

Task 1 Strategic Considerations 策略思考 ······ 111
Task 2 Five Common Negotiation Strategies 五项基本谈判策略 ······ 115
Task 3 Tactics for Each Negotiation Strategy 谈判策略的技巧 ······ 120

Unit 6 Initiating Business Negotiations 商务谈判开局 ······ 129

Task 1 Creating a Good Atmosphere of Negotiations 营造良好的谈判氛围 ······ 130
Task 2 Strategies in Initiating Negotiations 谈判开局策略 ······ 133
Task 3 Opening Statements 开局陈述 ······ 137

Unit 7 Business Negotiation Consultation 商务谈判磋商 ······ 147

Task 1 Strategies of Offer 报价策略 ······ 147
Task 2 Strategies of Bargaining 议价策略 ······ 151
Task 3 Making Concessions 让步 ······ 155

Unit 8 Deadlock Settlement in Business Negotiation 商务谈判僵局处理 ······ 167

Task 1 The Causes Leading to Deadlocks 僵局产生的原因 ······ 167
Task 2 Strategies of Breaking a Deadlock 突破僵局的策略 ······ 170
Task 3 Making a Deadlock 制造僵局 ······ 175

Unit 9 Business Contracts 商务合同 ······ 185

Task 1 Strategies to Bringing to Sign a Contract 合同签订促成策略 ······ 185
Task 2 Format and Content of a Business Contract 商务合同格式与内容 ······ 190
Task 3 Strategies for Signing a Business Contract 签订商务合同的技巧 ······ 194

Unit 10 Business Negotiations on Settling Disputes
商务谈判纠纷处理 ······ 205

Task 1 The Identification of Business Disputes 商务纠纷事故认定 ······ 205
Task 2 Liability Ascription 责任归属 ······ 208
Task 3 Claim and Settlement 索赔与理赔 ······ 211
Task 4 Mediation and Arbitration 调解与仲裁 ······ 214

Unit 11 Business Negotiation Etiquette
商务谈判礼仪 ······ 221

Task 1 General Requirements of Business Negotiation Etiquette 商务谈判礼仪的一般要求 ······ 221
Task 2 Telephone Communication Etiquette 电话沟通礼仪 ······ 224
Task 3 Meeting Etiquette 会面礼仪 ······ 228
Task 4 Business Welcoming and Seeing-off Etiquette 商务迎送礼仪 ······ 234
Task 5 Business Seating Etiquette 座次安排商务礼仪 ······ 237

Unit 12 Cultures and Taboos in Business Negotiations
商务谈判中的文化与禁忌 ······ 245

Task 1 The Influence of Cultural Differences on Business Negotiation 文化差异对商务谈判的影响 ······ 245
Task 2 The Strategies of Dealing with Cultural Differences in Business Negotiation 商务谈判中应对文化差异的策略 ······ 249
Task 3 Taboos of Different Negotiating Rivals 不同谈判对手的禁忌 ······ 253
Task 4 Cultural Differences and Negotiating Styles 文化差异与谈判风格 ······ 256

References ······ 263

Unit 1 Business Negotiation Thinking, Psychology and Language Arts
商务谈判思维、心理与语言艺术

任务目标

1. Understanding business negotiation thinking
2. Knowing the types of negotiation thinking
3. Mastering the psychology of negotiation
4. Applying language arts in business negotiations

商务谈判既是一门科学，又是一门艺术。商务谈判是在人与人之间进行的，左右商务谈判结果的是人。所以要取得商务谈判的成功，不仅需要研究商务谈判本身，而且要研究参与谈判的人。因此，研究商务谈判思维、心理与语言艺术就显得至关重要。

Task 1 Business Negotiation Thinking
商务谈判思维

人类的任何活动都离不开思维，人类的任何成就都是科学思维的结果，可以说，人类没有了思维，也就没有了一切。商务谈判是一项既紧张激烈又复杂多变的活动。对谈判的双方来讲，在既定的客观条件下，如何正确地分析和判断谈判对手的实力、谈判策略、谈判心理以及在谈判中提出的每一个建议和要求，如何充分地调动每一个人员的积极性，发挥本方的有利因素，争取谈判的优势，这一切都有赖于谈判者科学正确的思维。

案例学习

Case 1

A negotiator walked into the office of a bank manager to promote his products. The female manager was bowing her head in writing some things. From her expressions, the negotiator could see that she was in very bad mood; the ashtray full of cigarette butts and the extent of the mess table suggested that she had been busy for a long time certainly. The negotiator thought: how could I make the woman manager put down her work and pleasantly accept my promotion? After observation, he found that the manager had a glossy black hair. So he flattered: "What pretty long-hair! My wife dreams about it, but her hair is yellow and scarce." At that time, tired eyes of the manager appeared shining and replied: "No pretty than before. Too busy, you see, the mess." The negotiator immediately handed a comb and said: "I just wash it, please use it to hair and you must look more beautiful. You are too tired and should have a rest." At this time the manager recovered and asked: "Are you?" The negotiator indicated his intention at once. The manager was very interested in listening to the introduction and quickly decided to buy his products.

(From *International Business Negotiation*, 2014)

案例思考

1. Did the negotiator directly promote his products to the manager when he walked into the office? Why?
2. What did the negotiator do before he made his promotion?
3. What have you learned from the case?

案例解析

该案例充分说明了商务谈判中思维的重要性。在该案例中，人类的思维艺术得到了充分的展示，谈判代表并未直接向银行经理推销商品，而是对谈判活动中的谈判环境及谈判对手进行仔细观察后，找准话题切入点展开交流活动，争取到对方的好感，从而顺利完成了谈判任务。

Case 2

A substantial electronics firm faced considerable difficulties in one of their **subassemblies**. The root core of the problem revolved around certain types of fittings and pins that were becoming bent and distorted by the operation of the machinery. Units which were being produced were damaged and had to be rejected because of imperfections. These rejected components were put aside and then re-worked later on in the month.

This **duplication** of effort resulted in increased costs as workers had to work overtime to meet their **quotas**. These extra costs for the extra work performed had not been considered in the manufacturing budget. The manager of this subassembly line did not want to be charged with these **overhead expenses** because he felt it was not their responsibility. Likewise, the manager who was the **overseer** of the final assembly department also refused to accept the increased costs to his budget. He argued that the extra costs were a direct result of the poor work of the personnel in the subassembly department as this was where the problem originated.

The subassembly department manager **countered** this argument by claiming that the parts were in good condition before they left his department and that the damage must have occurred in the final assembly manager's department instead. Both parties fell into an **impasse**.

Some time passed before a resolution to the matter was worked out that was agreeable to both parties. What both parties were really seeking was to find a long term solution to this **dilemma**. It was only when they truly understood the nature of the problem were they able to negotiate a reasonable solution that was acceptable to both of them.

It was ascertained that the subassembly workers had some **slack time** available during every working month. The damaged parts were returned in small batches from the final assembly plant so that the subassembly personnel could work on them during these slack periods. Also, when they examined the problem in more **minute** detail, the managers learned that some of the personnel in the final assembly plant may not have been adequately trained and may have also been partially responsible for the damaged **incurred**. These personnel were identified and were sent to the subassembly plant to further their training and to learn more about what **transpired** in that department.

The resulting solution addressed the increased cost concerns of both departments on the one hand. On the other hand, overtime was reduced by allocating the personnel where and when they most needed and finally, because of the enhanced training, the number of damaged parts was considerably reduced.

(From https://www.studymode.com/)

案例思考

1. What reason do you think made both parties fall into an impasse?
2. How did they solve the problem?
3. Is it a successful case for business communication and why?
4. What do you learn from the case?

案例解析

该案例充分展示了双方通过创造性和互利的方式成功地进行谈判。在该案例中，谈判代表遇到的最大的障碍之一是要清楚地了解真正的问题，这是谈判的根源和基础。太多时候，谈判代表不能采取足够的时间清楚地识别问题或需要解决和谈判的问题所在。这是任何谈判的至关重要的第一步。如果谈判过程的第一阶段处理不当，很可能其余的谈判过程无法展开，因为核心问题并非一开始就得到正确的理解。这个案例强调了跳出固定思维，善于甄别问题的必要性。

理论拓展

Three Negative Thoughts Holding You Back from Negotiation Success[1]
阻碍谈判成功的三个消极思维

If you've successfully started your own business, decided to go **freelance**, or work at a **startup**, you're used to rolling up your sleeves, working hard, and doing whatever it takes to get things done.

But when it comes to negotiating, do you still freeze up or freak out?

If you find it hard to approach investors, raise your rates, or talk about money and contracts in any way—you're not alone. Thought traps women have about their perceived inadequacy when it comes to negotiation are pervasive: In surveys, two and a half times more women than men said they feel "a great deal of apprehension" about negotiating.[2]

So how do you become comfortable asking for what you want and deserve?

It starts by shifting some fundamental beliefs you have about yourself and your ability to negotiate. Only from there can you **slough off** what's been blocking you from getting the rates, contracts and deals you want and your business needs.

Which of these common self-limiting beliefs is holding you back from negotiating and limiting your chances of outrageous success?

"I'm not the negotiating type"

Women often attribute their success to luck or the help of others, rather than to their own hard work and strengths. But if you want to succeed, you need to let go of the false thought that negotiating is a skill that you either are or aren't born with. Negotiation is a skill you have to—and can—learn.

Much like a muscle, you have to practice your "ask" in order to bulk up your strength. It's up to you to pump negotiation iron!

"I hate talking about money and numbers"

Many women are uncomfortable with confrontation. We make ourselves sick with concerns that people will think we're self important or pushy if we make or counter an offer. We get scared about what others will think about us. But you can turn those anxious thoughts into an asset by asking yourself: What's really behind the discomfort I have asking for things from other people?

"I won't get what I want, so why bother?"

Women tend to operate from a "playing small" **mindset**, often thinking of our businesses as side hustles, while men think of ventures in terms of enterprises. Coming from this place, women **acquiesce** power, hoping for "just enough", and crossing our fingers that the other person will do us a favor by simply accepting to work with us. This scarcity mindset is both damaging and unrealistic.

(From https://www.linkedin.com/)

Notes

1. 本文主要比较了女性与男性在商务谈判中所体现出来的差异性。

2. In surveys, two and a half times more women than men said they feel "a great deal of apprehension" about negotiating：调查研究表明，对谈判感到"非常不安"的女性是男性的 2.5 倍。

Read the text and answer the questions.

1. Are you afraid of negotiating with others and why?

2. What negative thoughts presented in the article may hold you back from your successful negotiation?

3. What do you learn from the text?

要点小结

谈判思维是谈判者在谈判过程中理性地认识客观事物的行为与过程，是谈判者对谈判活动中的谈判目标、谈判环境、谈判对手及其行为间接的、概括的反应。谈判思维分为散射思维（Scattering Thinking）、超常思维（Supernormal Thinking）、跳跃思维（Jump Thinking）、逆向思维（Reversed Thinking）及快速思维（Speedy Thinking）五大类。谈判中要巧妙运用心理战术去攻破对方的心理防线，迫使对方改变谈判态度，从而达到既定的谈判目标，使谈判得以顺利达成协议。

Task 2　Business Negotiation Psychology
商务谈判心理

不管人们是否愿意，每个人都是一名谈判者。谈判是生活中永远无法避免的事实。比如说，你要求加薪，就要和老板谈判；你买菜也要和小贩讨价还价……事实上，谈判贯穿了我们每个人全部的生活细节，我们所面对的现实世界就是一个巨大的谈判桌。如何在谈判中洞察对手的心理特点，知己知彼，有的放矢，已成为谈判成功与否的关键因素。

案例学习

Case 1

It's at one of the city's best restaurants. Mr. Lin is hosting the dinner. He is to make remarks before the dinner starts.

Mr. Lin: Dear Mr. Ford and my dear colleagues. We are very happy to have Mr. Ford here with us tonight. Confucius once said, "What a joy it is to have friends coming from afar!" Mr. Ford is an old friend of ours, coming from the other side of the earth, so our joy tonight is beyond expression.

Mr. Ford is a pioneer in the US trade with China. He was one of the first American businessmen who came to China right after the **implementation** of our policy of opening to the outside world in the late 70's of the last century. Since then, we've signed 16 contracts with IBM. Though there have been ups and downs in the trade volume, we've developed a mutually beneficial and therefore very solid relationship. And we are very proud of this. As our present contract is expiring next month, we're very pleased to have you here to work with us on a new contract. I firmly believe that through our mutual efforts, the new contract will further strengthen the ties between our two companies and benefit both sides.

Our negotiation will begin the day after tomorrow. I'd like to take this opportunity to propose a toast to the success of the negotiation, and to the further cooperation between our two companies. Bottoms up! (All the guests stand up.)

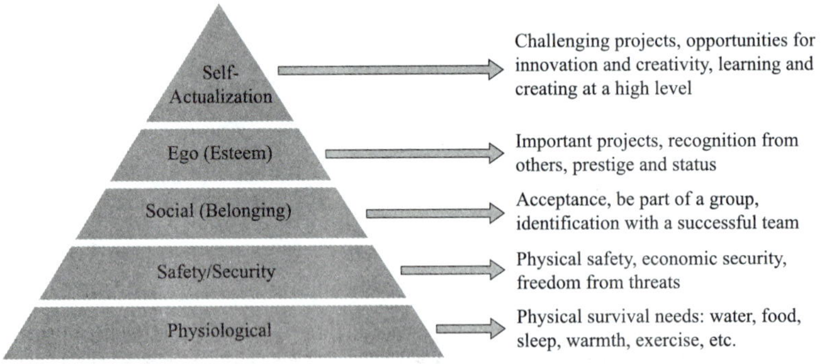

Maslow's Hierarchy of Needs is shown above. The pyramid illustrates the five levels of human needs. The most basic are physiological and safety/security, shown at the base of the pyramid. As one moves to higher levels of the pyramid, the needs become more complex.

(From *International Business Negotiation*, 2014)

案例思考

1. Which level of *The Need Theory of Maslow* is presented in this case?

2. Does esteem presented in the case refer to the esteem to the other party, or to own party, or to both, or to even more?

案例解析

该案例反映了心理需求理论与商务谈判之间的密切关系。该案例体现的是尊重需求。一个人的尊重需求可以通过物质的东西和尊敬得到满足。在该案例中，Mr. Lin 的讲话首先表达了他对 Mr. Ford 及 Mr. Ford 所代表的公司的尊敬，其次表达了自己对所代表公司的自豪感，并且还体现了自己对来自同事、对方及成功达成协议后能够获得的物质及带来的尊重的需求感。

首先，商务沟通时了解对方背景，表现出对对方的尊重是起码的职业素养；其次，商务沟通，特别是国际商务沟通时，一定要表现出道路自信、理论自信、制度自信、文化自信，做到不卑不亢，树立大国形象意识。

Case 2

A **distributive negotiation** will focus on the division of a set amount of resources, largely determined by the aspiration price (the maximum that Party A would like to get, and which is also the least amount that Party B would like to pay), and the reservation price (the least amount that Party A would accept, and the maximum that Party B would prepare to pay). Well over 90% of all civil lawsuits in the America are settled out of court, and most are largely resolved through the application of a distributive negotiation.

On a dreary, rainy night in October of 1968, a young woman was driving behind a lorry truck in the U.S. Perhaps impatient with the speed of the transport in front of her, the young woman by the name of Ms. Anderson steered her vehicle to peer around the lorry driver's side to see if the way was clear. Before she could react, she was struck head on from an oncoming vehicle from the opposite direction. Ms. Anderson sustained permanent and debilitating injuries as a result of this horrific crash. Just recently, she had retrieved her vehicle from Sorensen **Chevrolet** which she had been having some repairs completed. **Unbeknownst** to her, Ms. Anderson did not notice that her front driver's side **headlight** was **malfunctioning**. The oncoming driver who had struck her had not seen her on that dark misty night when the accident occurred.

Mr. Miller, lawyer representing Ms. Anderson, held Sorenson Chevrolet as **being liable for** the accident and subsequently filed a $1,633,000.00 law suite against Sorensen. Sorensen had a faulty repair policy with an insurance company (which shall be called ABC Insurance).

The policy had a ceiling of $500,000.00. Sorensen made it very clear to ABC Insurance that they would readily **sue** ABC if they settled for anything over the half million limit of the policy, urging them to settle out of court.

Miller, the **plaintiff's** lawyer countered that he would not accept an out of court settlement for anything less than the maximum half million allowed under Sorensen's insurance policy. ABC went to court and won a summary judgment where the decision rendered entailed that the plaintiff had no legal basis for a trial. ABC made a **tentative** offer of $25,000.00. Miller countered this with a demand for $400,000.00 and had **in the interim**, appealed the court's decision not to **hear** the case.

ABC upped their offer to settle at $50,000.00. In December of 1973, the appeal was heard. The Appellate Court reversed the decision and the summary judgment was overturned. The case could now be heard before a jury which turned the game around. Miller, once again demanded the full half a million. It was not until February of 1973 that ABC upped their offer to $200,000.00 which was rejected, and then upped their offer to $250,000.00. Miller lowered his demand to $400,000.00, as a counter offer. This was rejected by ABC, and he then lowered it again to $350,000.00. The time factor was beginning to play on the plaintiff, and Ms. Anderson was becoming risk averse to the whole negotiation process.

In January of 1975, Miller told ABC that the "bottom line" settlement that he would accept would be $325,000.00. ABC said they would go to trial over the difference. It was virtually on the court steps that ABC discovered that Miller had been replaced as Ms. Anderson's **counsel**. Her new **attorney** offered ABC another "bottom settlement" of $300,000.00. ABC agreed to the settlement.

(From https://www.negotiations.com/)

案例思考

1. Is it a case for successful business communication, why or why not?

2. How many rounds of negotiation take place in this case and how do both parties make an agreement?

3. In this case, what do you think are the elements of a successful business negotiation?

案例解析

该案例是一个分配性谈判的例子。在分配问题的讨价还价中，各方的利益是具有直接冲突性的。一个人对“谈判协议最佳备选方案”（**BATNA**[1]）和利益方面的评价界定了谈判的结构，谈判人员就是在这种心理状态下试图达成彼此都认同的结果。但是，如果谈判人员认为谈判从开始时就必然存在自身利益与对方利益的直接冲突，抱着“非赢即输”的偏见，再加上“强硬的”谈判策略，必将加剧谈判中的竞争态势，进而阻碍问题的圆满解决。

商务谈判要有前瞻意识、全局意识，设定最佳底线。有计划有目标的准备工作可以事半功倍。

Note

BATNA (Best Alternative to a negotiated agreement)：谈判协议最佳备选方案。常用在采购谈判过程中，采购方为了供需双方的平衡而选择的最佳的代替方案。此方案并非采购方最想获得的价格、服务、运输、付款期等条件的最佳方案，而是退而求其次的选择，被设定为谈判的最佳底线。

理论拓展

Seven Psychological Strategies for Mastering Sales Negotiations
掌握销售谈判的七条心理策略

Preparing for a negotiation when a lot is on the line can elicit a tremendous amount of fear and negative thinking.

This kind of thinking can mean the negotiation is lost before the salesperson has even started to prepare for it. The first war to be won is the battle inside the salesperson against defeatist thoughts. By becoming clear on desired outcomes, he or she has the greatest chance at negotiation success and making a sale.

1. Eliminate anxiety.

The brain loves options. A salesperson should always have more than one significant opportunity in the pipeline. This leads to increased confidence and less anxiety when negotiating.

Thus the salesperson doesn't feel desperate and can more confidently acquire new business by directing negotiations to the point where the potential customer ends up selling the salesperson on why they should do business together.

2. Score a small yes or two.[1]

Negotiate for what's easy first and never assume a potential customer will say yes to everything. Sometimes, the prospect may offer to take a smaller order before going for bigger, more **lucrative** orders or contracts.

For the salesperson, getting a foot in the door can be the start of longer-term, more profitable partnership opportunities in the future. A smaller win can help prove the worth of the services being sold. It gives the salesperson evidence of prior successful work to use in negotiations for bigger projects.

3. Take full advantage of listening.

Salespeople have two ears and one mouth for a reason. People love to be listened to. Taking the time to listen can set the sales professional apart from competitors who push too hard.

Even sharks become calm amid calm waters. So when negotiating, a salesperson should listen twice as much as she speaks and repeat back to the customer what the client said and ask for agreement.

When a sales professional has the self-control to listen, she learns to speak the language of the customer and this enables her to use this language in a way to outsmart the competition.

4. Choose a "partner" approach.

In a negotiation, the seller needs to view a potential customer as a partner rather than an opponent. Psychologically this puts each party on the same team, bringing more confidence in the sales professional's negotiation.

It changes the whole mindset and creates a communication space based more on agreement than desperate acts of getting.

If the potential customer is not willing to come to agreement, then the sales professional can shock the customer by removing the offer. Often what happens then is the potential customer rethinks a **stance** and returns to negotiate with a higher level of respect for the salesperson's offer. A lack of fear of rejection is respectable and compelling.

5. Think existentially.

When the salesperson tries to put herself in the shoes of the customer and can see the big picture, a positive psychological environment for negotiation is reached. She gains clarity about the potential customer's demands, strengths and weaknesses and it's easier to move through the negotiation.

The potential customer feels connected to the negotiations because his viewpoint has been considered, which goes a long way toward making a favorable impression and building trust.

6. Put people first, numbers second.

If a salesperson bullies her way into a deal, a customer will feel defensive, which blocks effective negotiation. Defensiveness means a lack of openness to new information. A salesperson should **refrain** from criticizing the needs, demands, motives or behaviors of the potential customer.

She should listen and be smart, rational and calm. Strategically the sales professional must keep the focus off the offer and create an arena of fairness in mediating discussions about the numbers in a mutually beneficial fashion—one where she does not settle for less than what is desired.

7. Mimic the emotional environment.

Negotiation always involves manipulation. A useful strategy is to **feign** indifference once the negotiation has reached a sticking point. If a potential customer senses desperation or neediness in a pitch, the salesperson becomes prey to being taken advantage of.

If the sales professional can limit her sense of urgency about closing a sale and reflect indifference to the customer by seeming relaxed or asking for a delay in the negotiations, she creates psychological tension in the other party. This can result in an agreement.

Negotiation is purely a psychological strategy. Psychologically, a sales professional must be the master of his or her own mind and emotions. She needs to enter the negotiation prepared, knowing the needs of the potential customer through research, listening, spending time and paying attention.

When a sales professional goes into a negotiation well-informed, she can keep her expectations under control. The most effective working relationships, which can then evolve into long-standing partnerships, are always based in trust between partners. In this way negotiation is not about winning but rather about mediating for the best outcome for all involved.

(From https://www.entrepreneur.com/)

Note

Score a small yes or two：能够取得一两个小的订单也是一种胜利。

Read the text and answer the questions.

1. Among the seven psychological strategies for mastering sales negotiations presented in the article, which one do you think is the most important and why?
2. What's your understanding of "score a small yes or two"?
3. Why is listening in negotiation very important?
4. To what extent does "thinking existentially" help smooth negotiation?

要点小结

美国犹太裔人本主义心理学家亚伯拉罕·马斯洛于 1943 年在《人类激励理论》一书中提出的需要层次论，将人类需求像阶梯一样从低到高按层次分为五种，需要层次论被广泛运用于商务谈判中。

为了达成双方同意的协议，谈判者可采用两种方式：分配性谈判和整合性谈判。

分配性谈判是对于一份固定利益应分得多少进行的协商，其中双方都追求利益最大化并希望对方损失最大，又被称为赢输情境或零和情境。整合性谈判是一种旨要激励谈判双方获得双赢前景的谈判过程，也就是通常我们所说的双赢情境。

一、商务谈判的心理

1. 需要层次论与商务谈判的关系

2. 成功谈判的出发点

二、商务谈判的心理技巧

1. 消除焦虑：保持正常心态，坚守正确的世界观、人生观和价值观。

2. 避免谈判误区：仔细观察、实事求是。

3. 善于倾听：换位思考，尊重他人的观念和意见。

4. 友好合作的心态：树立正确的职业态度与职业素养，强化社会主义核心价值观。

5. 知己知彼：进一步了解国际形势，他国人文背景，做到知己知彼，进一步增强爱国主义情怀。

6. 以人为本的原则：换位思考，尊重他人的观念和意见。

7. 善于情绪的调控：保持初心、平和心态、坚持善良。

三、马斯洛的五种需求层次理论（Maslow's Hierarchy of Needs，依次由最低需求至最高需求）

1. 生理需求层次（Physiological Needs），指空气、水、食物、睡眠等基础的需求。马斯洛认为，只有这些最基本的需要满足到维持生存所必需的程度后，其他的需要才能成为新的激励因素。

2. 安全需求层次（Safety Needs），指人身安全、财产安全、健康保障、工作职位保障、家庭安全等需求。

3. 社交需求层次（Social Belonging），指爱的需求、交往的需求、有所作为的需求、家庭需求等。

4. 尊重需求层次（Esteem），它可分为内部尊重和外部尊重。内部尊重是指一个人希望在各种不同情境中有实力、能胜任、充满信心、能独立自主，即人的自尊。外部尊重是指一个人希望有地位、有威信，受到别人的尊重、信赖和高度评价，使自己充满信心，对社会满腔热情，体验到自己的价值。

5. 自我实现需求层次（Self-Actualization），指实现个人理想、抱负，发挥个人的能力到最大程度，达到自我实现境界的人，接受自己也接受他人，解决问题能力增强，自觉性提高，善于独立处事，要求不受打扰地独处，完成与自己的能力相称的一切事情的需要。也就是说，人必须干称职的工作，这样才会使他们感到最大的快乐。马斯洛提出，为满足自我实现需要所采取的途径是因人而异的。自我实现的需要是在努力实现自己的潜力，使自己越来越成为自己所期望的人物。

Task 3 Language Arts in Business Negotiations
商务谈判语言艺术

美国企业管理学家哈里·西蒙说过：“成功的人都是出色的语言表达者。”语言艺术是为了人与人之间的沟通，在商务谈判中使用语言艺术能够和谐谈判双方的人际关系，使谈判在活跃的气氛中进行，促进双方的理解、信任和支持，提高谈判的成功率。

案例学习

Case 1 Your Price Is Really High

Black: Now, Mr. Li, I've compared your **quotation** with the prevailing market prices and with that of other origins, and I find your price is really high.

Li: But this is the best quotation we can make. We consider it a **rock-bottom price** indeed.

Black: I'm sorry to hear that. But we still find no way to accept your quotation.

Li: Mr. Black, I think you will agree that our products are of the best quality compared with similar products in the world. What's more, they are brightly colored and beautifully designed.

Black: I agree. But you know, no material, however attractive, will sell well if it's too expensive. We must always bear in mind the fact that all of us are operating in a highly competitive world market.

Li: Well then, what is the price you would pay?

Black: The best we can accept is US $280 per **bale**, **CIF** Sydney.

Li: Did you say 280?

Black: Exactly.

Li: But, the best we can do is to reduce our price by $10 and I should think we could strike a deal at $310.

Black: I do appreciate the effort you're making towards reaching an agreement, but frankly speaking, the gap between your price and mine is still enormous. I really don't see how we can go above $290.

Li: Sorry, we may not be able to sell anything near that price.

Black: That would be a pity, indeed.

Li: One thing I want to make clear is whether the quantity you ordered can be bigger.

Black: If that is the question, then the answer is yes. I would order 300 bales more.

Li: Then, the price will be US $295 per bale, CIF Sydney.

Black: Is it possible $290?

Li: I couldn't have said it any more.

Black: I'm in a difficult position. It's beyond my capability to decide it.

Li: In that case, let me think it over. Now I have to say that my rock-bottom price is US $292 per bale, CIF Sydney. Anything lower than this is impossible.

Black: All right. Considering our newly-established business relationship and the good quality of your product, I accept your lowered price of $292 per bale CIF Sydney to bc delivered in July this year.

Li: Then with this settled, I hope we will have no difficulty in reaching an agreement concerning terms of payment.

Black: I hope so.

(From *International Business Negotiation*, 2014)

案例思考

1. Do you think it is a successful negotiation and why?
2. What language features of negotiation do you find in this bargaining?

案例解析

大多数的谈判是以长期合作为目标。因此，无论是在处理家庭、朋友，还是商业合作伙伴的谈判事务时，都应持友好的态度，尽量双赢。表现在语言上要谦和，不要过于强势，给对方带来不舒适；此外，在讨价还价的商业谈判中，当对方提出你不能接受的较低或较高的价格时，学会用语言表现你的惊讶，这就暗示对方，他（她）的价格简直不能接受，这样随后他（她）会考虑一个更加合情合理的价格来谈判；价格是一步一步谈下来的，谈判时要保持良好的心态，这次的一小步，会带来将来的一大步，能够取得一两个小的订单也是一种胜利，总比没签协议、空手而归强。不能抱着你不同意我的提议，就不谈了的态度，语言上要留有可商讨的余地，比如采用疑问句等。

Case 2 Negotiating with Wal-Mart Buyers

Wal-Mart, the world's largest retailer, sold $315 billion worth of goods in 2006. With its single-minded focus on "EDLP" (everyday low prices) and the power to make or break; suppliers, a partnership with Wal-Mart is either the **Holy Grail** or the kiss of death, depending on one's perspective.

There are numerous media accounts of the corporate monolith riding its suppliers into the ground. But what about those who manage to survive, and thrive, while dealing with the classic hardball negotiator?

In "Sarah Talley and Frey Farms Produce: Negotiating with Wal-Mart" and "Tom Muccio: Negotiating the P&G Relationship with Wal-Mart," HBS professor Jim Sebenius and Research Associate Ellen Knebel show two very different organizations doing just that. The cases are part of a series that involve hard bargaining situations.

"The concept of win-win bargaining is a good and powerful message," Sebenius says, "but a lot of our students and executives face counterparts who aren't interested in playing by those rules. So what happens when you encounter someone with a great deal of power, like Wal-Mart, who is also the ultimate non-negotiable partner?"

The case details how P&G executive Tom Muccio pioneers a new supplier-retailer partnership between P&G and Wal-Mart. Built on proximity (Muccio relocated to Wal-Mart's turf in Arkansas) and growing trust (both sides eventually eliminated elaborate legal contracts in favor of **Letters of Intent**), the new relationship focused on establishing a joint vision and problem-solving process, information sharing, and generally moving away from the "lowest common denominator" pricing issues that had defined their interactions previously. From 1987, when Muccio initiated the changes, to 2003, shortly before his retirement, P&G's sales to Wal-Mart grew from $350 million to $7.8 billion.

"There are obvious differences between P&G and a much smaller entity like Frey Farms," Sebenius notes. "Wal-Mart could clearly live without Frey Farms, but it's pretty hard to live without Tide and Pampers."

Sarah Meets Goliath

Sarah Talley was 19 in 1997, when she first began negotiating with Wal-Mart's buyers for her family farm's pumpkins and watermelons. Like Muccio, Talley confronted some of the same hardball price challenges, and like Muccio, she acquired a deep understanding of the Wal-Mart culture while finding "new money" in the supply chain through innovative tactics.

For example, Frey Farms used school buses ($1,500 each) instead of tractors ($12,000 each) as a cheaper and faster way to transport melons to the warehouse.

Talley also was skillful at negotiating a coveted co-management supplier agreement with Wal-Mart, showing how Frey Farms could share the responsibility of managing inventory levels and sales and ultimately save customers money while improving their own margins.

"Two sides in this sort of negotiation will always differ on price," Sebenius observes. "However, if that conflict is the centerpiece of their interaction, then it's a bad situation. If they're trying to develop the customer, the relationship, and sales, the price piece will be one of many points, most of which they're aligned on."

Research Associate Knebel points out that while Tom Muccio's approach to Wal-Mart was pioneering for its time, many other companies have since followed P&G's lead and enjoyed their own versions of success with the **mega-retailer**. Getting a ground-level view of how two companies achieved those positive outcomes illustrates the story-within-a-story of implementing corporate change.

"Achieving that is where macro concepts, micro imperatives, and managerial skill really come together," says Sebenius. And the payoffs—as Muccio and Talley discover—are well worth the effort.

Sarah Talley's Key Negotiation Principles

When you have a problem, when there's something you engage in with Wal-Mart that requires agreement so that it becomes a negotiation, the first advice is to think in partnership terms, really focus on a common goal, for example of getting costs out, and ask questions. Don't make demands or statements. Rather ask if you can do this better. If the relationship with Wal-Mart is truly a partnership, negotiating to resolve differences should focus on long term mutual partnership gains.

Don't spend time griping. Be problem solvers instead. Approach Wal-Mart by saying, "Let's work together and drive costs down and produce it so much cheaper you don't have to replace me, because if you work with me I could do it better."

Learn from and **lobby** with people and their partners who have credibility, and with people having problems in the field.

Don't ignore small issues or let things fester.

Try not to let Wal-Mart become more than 20% of your company's business.

It's hard to negotiate with buyers who know that their company could put your company out of business.

Never go into a meeting without a clear agenda. Make good use of the buyers' face time. Leave with answers. Don't make small talk. Get to the point; their time is valuable. Bring underlying issues to the surface. Attack them head on and find resolution face to face.

Trying to **bluff** Wal-Mart buyers is never a good idea. There is always someone willing to do it cheaper to gain the business. You have to treat the relationship as a marriage. Communication and compromise is key.

Don't take for granted that just because the buyer is young they don't know what they are talking about or that it will be an easy sell. Most young buyers are very ambitious to move up within the company and can be some of the toughest, most educated buyers you will encounter. Know your product all the way from the production standpoint to the end use. Chances are your buyer does, and will expect you to be even more knowledgeable.

(From https://www.negotiations.com/)

案例思考

Could you sum up Sarah Talley's key negotiation principles?

案例解析

该案例分析了当谈判对象是一个比你强大的谈判对手时应该注意的一些语言艺术：（1）友好合作；（2）解决问题；（3）关注细节；（4）保证自己可谈判的立场与地位；（5）切入主题；（6）实事求是。

理论拓展

How to Avoid a Bad Bargain: Don't Threaten
如何避免失败的讨价还价：不要做出威胁

An award-winning social psychology experiment reveals why we often fail to bargain effectively with each other.

Bargaining is one of those activities we often engage in without quite realizing it. It doesn't just happen in the boardroom, or when we ask our boss for a raise or down at the market, it happens every time we want to reach an agreement with someone. This agreement could be as simple as choosing a restaurant with a friend, or deciding which TV channel to watch. At the other end of the scale, bargaining can affect the fate of nations.

Big-scale or small-scale, bargaining is a central part of our lives. Understanding the psychological processes involved in bargaining can provide us with huge benefits in our everyday lives. In a classic, award-winning series of studies, Morgan Deutsch and Robert Krauss investigated two central factors in bargaining: how we communicate with each other and how we use threats (Deutsch & Krauss, 1962).

To do this, they used a game which forces two people to bargain with each other. Although Deutsch and Krauss used a series of different conditions—nine in fact—once you understand the basic game, all the conditions are only slight variations.

So, imagine you were a clerical worker at the Bell Telephone Laboratories in the late 1950s and you've been asked to take part in a psychology study. Every psychology study has a story, and this one revolves around two trucking companies…

Experiment 1: Keep on trucking

Before the experiment proper starts, the researcher explains that you'll be playing a game against another participant. In the game you will run a trucking company. The object of the game is the same as a real trucking company: to make as much money as possible.

Like the real-life trucking company you have to deliver as many of your goods as possible to their destination in the shortest possible time. But in this game you only have one starting point, one destination and one competitor. It looks like a pretty simple game.

● Here's the catch.

The road map your one truck has to travel across presents you with a dilemma. You are the "Acme" trucking company and your fellow participant is the "Bolt" trucking company, although both of you have an identical problem. Have a look below.

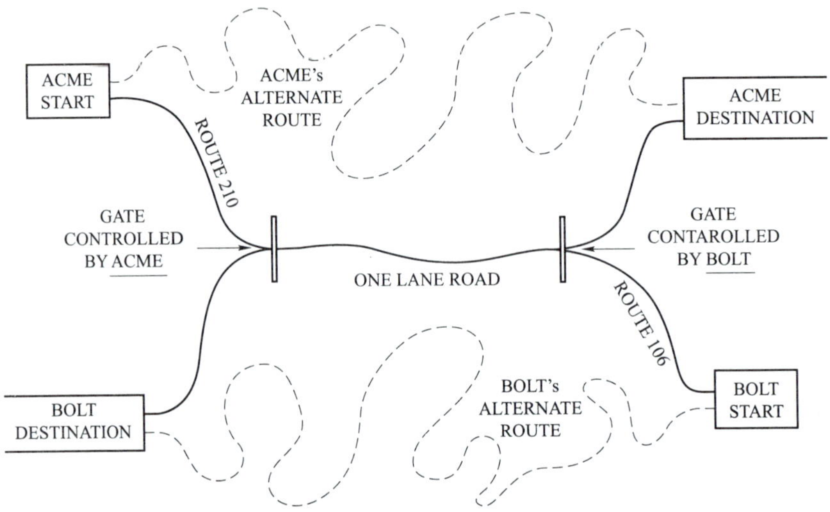

Deutsch & Krauss, 1962, p. 55

As you'll see there are two possible routes you can take from the start to your destination: the short and the long. Remember, time is money, so the longer it takes you to get to your destination, the less profit you make, which is the aim of the game. Unfortunately the short route has a major shortcoming: it is one-way. Only one of you can travel down it at a time towards your destination.

It seems you'll be forced to work out some agreement with your unknown rival to share this one-way route so that you can both make money. How you'll do this is another mystery, though, as there is going to be no communication between the two of you during the experiment. You are to be seated in a cubicle from where you'll only be able to see the control box for your "truck" and the experimenter.

● Threatening gates

You are to be given one method of communication with your rival, albeit indirect communication. Each of you controls a gate at your own end of the one-way road. Your gate can be opened or closed whenever you pass through it. This will be your threat. It is reinforced by the experimenter that you are out to make as much money as you can for yourself—the other person's profit is not a concern.

Once the experimenter sets you off, it soon becomes clear you're not going to make much money at all. In the first of 20 trials, both you and your rival shut your gates, forcing both trucks onto the alternative route. This is 50% longer and means you make a loss on the trip as a whole. In the second trial your trucks meet head-on travelling up the one-way road. You both have to reverse, costing you time and money.

The rest of the trials aren't much better. Occasionally you make a profit on a trip but more often than not it's a bust. You spend more time on the long route or reversing than you do chugging happily along the main route making money.

At the end of the experiment, the researcher announces how much profit you made. None. In fact you made a crippling loss.[1] Perhaps trucking companies aren't so easy to run.

- Comparing threats

You find out later that you were in one of three experimental conditions. The only differences in the other two conditions were that in one there were no gates at either end of the one-way road. In the other there was only one active gate controlled by one player.

Before I tell you the results of the other two conditions, try to guess. One condition, which you've taken part in, contained **bilateral** threat—you could both threaten each other. One condition had **unilateral** threat—only one could threaten the other. And the final condition had no threat at all. What was the order of profit?

In fact it turns out that your condition, of bilateral threat, made the least profit when both participant's scores were added up. The next most profitable was the unilateral threat condition, while the most profitable overall was the no-threat condition.

Here's the first rather curious result. While the person who had the threat—control of the gate—in the unilateral condition did better than the person who didn't, they were still better off, individually and collectively, than if they both had threats. What this experiment is showing is that the availability of threats leads to worse outcomes to the extent that unilateral threat is preferable to bilateral threat to both parties.

Experiment 2: Lines of communication

But surely a little communication goes a long way? You weren't allowed to talk to the other participant in this experiment, so your trucks had to do the talking for you. Bargaining is all about reaching a compromise through negotiation—surely this should help?

To test the effect of communication Deutsch and Krauss (1962) set up a second experiment which was identical in all respects to the first except participants were given headphones to talk to each other.

Here's the next curious result: allowing the two participants to communicate with each other made no significant difference to the amount of money each trucking company made. In fact the experimenters found no relationship between words spoken and money made. In other words those who communicated more did not manage to reach a better understanding with each other.

Like the experimenters themselves, I find this result surprising. Surely allowing people to communicate can let them work out a way for them both to make money? And yet this isn't what happened in the experiment at all. Instead it seems that people's competitive orientation was stronger than their motivation to communicate.[2] On the other hand, perhaps something specific to the situation in this experiment is stopping people talking?

Participants in the second study reported that it was difficult to start talking to the other person, who was effectively a stranger. As a result they were considerably less talkative than normal. Could it be that it was this situational constraint that meant little talking, and therefore little bargaining was going on?

Experiment 3: Forced communication

Deutsch and Krauss decided to test the effect of forced communication in their third experiment. Again the procedure is the same as last time but now participants are instructed that on each of the 20 trials they have to say something. If they don't talk on one of the trials they are gently reminded by the experimenter to do so. They are told they can talk about whatever they like, as long as they say something.

The results finally showed some success for communication. Performance in the one-gate (unilateral threat) condition came close to that achieved in the "no-threat" condition (remember the no-threat condition has the best outcomes). Forced communication didn't have much effect on the "no-threat" condition when compared with no communication, and neither did it improve the bilateral threat condition much. It still seems that people are so competitive when they both have threats it's very difficult to avoid both sides losing out.

- Threat causes resentment

The most surprising finding of this study is how badly people do under conditions of bilateral threat. In this experiment not even forcing communication can overcome people's competitive streaks. Deutsch and Krauss provide a fascinating explanation for this.

Imagine your neighbour asks you to water their plants while they're on holiday. Socially, it looks good for you if you agree to do it. On the other hand, if they ask you to water their plants otherwise they'll set their TV on full blast while they're on holiday, it immediately gets your hackles up[3]. Suddenly you resent them. Giving in when there is no threat is seen by other people as pro-social. Duress, however, seems to make people dig in their heels.

- Applying the brakes

Before drawing some general conclusions from these studies, we should acknowledge the particular circumstances of this research. Deutsch and Krauss's experiment covers a situation in which bargaining is carried out under time pressure. Recall that the longer participants take to negotiate, the less money they make. In real life, time isn't always of the essence.

The present game also has a relatively simple solution: participants make the most profit if they share the one-way road. In reality, solutions are rarely that clear-cut. Finally, our participants were not professional negotiators, they were clerical and supervisory workers without special training.

- Real-life implications

Despite these problems the trucking game has the advantage of being what game theorists call a non-zero-sum game[4]. In other words if you win, it doesn't automatically mean the other person loses. When you total the final results, as you sometimes can in a financial sense, they don't add to zero. In real life many of the situations in which we find ourselves are of this nature. Cooperation can open the way to more profit, in financial or other form, for both parties.

As a result the trucking game has clear implications for real life:

Cooperative relationships are likely to be much more beneficial overall than competitive relationships. Before you go "duh!", remember that increasing proportions of the world's societies are capitalist. Deutsch and Krauss's experiment clearly shows the friction caused by competitive relationships, such as those encouraged by capitalism. I'm not saying capitalism is bad, I'm just saying competition isn't always good. This simple fact is often forgotten.

Just because people can communicate, doesn't mean they will—even if it is to their advantage.

Forcing parties to communicate, even if they already have the means to communicate, encourages mutually beneficial outcomes.

In competitive relationships, communication should be aimed at increasing cooperation. Other methods will probably create more heat than light.

Threats are dangerous, not only to other's interests, but also to our own.

Remember all these the next time you are bargaining with your partner over a night out, about to shout a threat at a motorist blocking your path on a one-way road, or even involved in high-level political negotiations between warring factions with nuclear capabilities. It could save you, and the other side, a lot of trouble.

(From https://www.spring.org.uk/2007/)

Notes

1. In fact you made a crippling loss. 事实上你的损失严重了。

2. Instead it seems that people's competitive orientation was stronger than their motivation to communicate. 相反，似乎人们的竞争的目标要强于他们交流的动机。

3. gets your hackles up：竖起毛来，形容马上变得好斗起来。

4. non-zero-sum game：非零和博弈，有多个赢家或多个输家。zero-sum game 是指参赛者利益相反，一方得到的利益，必定是另一方损失的利益。

Read the text and answer the questions.

1. What central factors in bargaining are investigated in the study of Morgan Deutsch and Robert Krauss?

2. What truth do the three experiments respectively prove?
3. What do you learn from the psychological experiments?

要点小结

商务谈判的语言艺术：
1. 友好合作，避免威胁；
2. 解决问题；
3. 关注细节，多用赞赏的语言；
4. 保证自己可谈判的立场与地位：既坚定又委婉；
5. 切入主题；
6. 实事求是；
7. 注意文化差异。

综合实训

Task 1

1. Directions: Read the following case and then answer the questions.

A manager of a store burned a hole in an expensive wool skirt by mistake, which made the price of the skirt fall down a lot. If taking darning measure, he is cheating customers. However, the manager got an inspiration and dug several small holes around that hole and decorated them exquisitely. The skirt was named "Phoenix-tail skirt". All of a sudden, the market for "Phoenix-tail skirt" was open and the fashion shop also became famous.

Questions:

1) Which type of negotiation thinking is used in the case and how?
2) Could you think about other examples of such type of negotiation thinking?

2. Negotiation Scenario: Asking for a raise of income

You're sure you deserve a raise of income, but this is a tricky thing to ask for given that you don't want to rock the boat with your boss. How do you negotiate with your boss cooperatively and achieve win-win?

Task 2

1. Directions: Read the following case and then answer the questions.

1986 年，日本的一个客户与东北某省外贸公司洽谈毛皮生意，条件优惠却久拖不决。转眼过去了两个多月，原来一直兴旺的国际毛皮市场货满为患，价格暴跌，这时日商再以很低的价格收购，使我方吃了大亏。

据记载，一个美国代表被派往日本谈判。日方在接待的时候得知对方需于两个星期之后返回。日本人没有急着开始谈判，而是花了一个多星期的时间陪他在国内旅游，每天晚上还安排宴会。谈判终于在第12天开始，但每天都早早结束，为的是客人能够去打高尔夫球。终于在第14天谈到重点，但这时候美国人该回去了，已经没有时间和对方周旋，只好答应对方的条件，签订了协议。

Questions:

1）阅读此案例后谈谈你对商务谈判心理的感受。

2）一个成功的商务谈判者应注重收集哪些信息?

2. Directions: Read the following case and then answer the questions.

You represent a shoe manufacturer. Your latest product is the so-called "self-heating" boots. The boots themselves control the temperature inside automatically through friction and rubbing of your feet against the inner side of the boots, and your feet will never feel cold. Your sale price is FOB Shanghai, $58 a pair. Now an American businessman wants to place an order for your shoes, but the price he counter-offers is only $48 a pair. So, you need to bargain.

Questions:

1) What should you learn before you begin to bargain with the American buyer's team?

2) Do you really believe $48 a pair is his minimum level?

3) Present the scenario with your classmates.

Task 3

1. Directions: Read the following case and then answer the question.

广东玻璃厂厂长率团与美国欧文斯公司就引进先进的玻璃生产线一事进行谈判。从我方来说，美方就是顾客。双方在部分引进还是全部引进的问题上陷入了僵局，我方的部分引进方案美方无法接受，我方遭到拒绝。

这时，我方首席代表虽然心急如焚，但还是冷静分析形势，如果我们一个劲儿说下去，就可能会越说越僵。于是他聪明地改变了说话的战术，由直接讨论变成迂回说服。"全世界都知道，欧文斯公司的技术是一流的，设备是一流的，产品是一流的。"我方代表转换了话题，从微笑中开始谈天说地，先来一个第一流的诚恳而又切实的赞叹，使欧文斯公司由于谈判陷入僵局而产生的抵触情绪得以很大程度的消除。"如果欧文斯公司能够帮助我们广东玻璃厂跃居全中国一流，那么全中国人民很感谢你们。"这里刚离开的话题，很快又转了回来，但由于前面说的那些话，消除了对方心理上的对抗，所以，对方听了这话，似乎也顺耳多了。

"美国方面当然知道，现在，意大利、荷兰等几个国家的代表团，正在我国北方省份的玻璃厂谈判引进生产线事宜。如果我们这次的谈判因为一点点的小事而失败，那么不但是我们广东玻璃厂，而且更重要的是欧文斯公司方面将蒙受重大的损失。"这损失当然不仅是生意，而说话中只是用"一点点小事"来轻描淡写，目的是引起对方对分歧的关注。同时，指出谈判万一破裂将给美国方面带来巨大的损失，完全为对方着想，这一点对方不容拒绝。

“目前，我们的确有资金方面的困难，不能全部引进，这点务必请美国同事们理解和原谅，而且我们希望在我们困难的时候，你们能伸出友谊之手，为我们将来的合作奠定一个良好的基础。”这段话说到对方心里去了，既通情，又达理，不是在做生意，而是朋友间的互相帮助，因此迅速就签订了协议，打破了僵局，问题迎刃而解，为国家节约了大量外汇。

Question:

What do you learn from the case?

2. Directions: You are asked to make a business negotiation with your partner according to the information given below. Pay attention to the language arts when negotiating.

1) **Situation:** Mr./Mrs. Li and Mr./Mrs. Rose are talking about the damage of consignment.

You are Mr./Mrs. Li, purchasing manager of Hyde Company.

A. Tell about the damage on the cotton goods.

B. File a claim: damage 20%, during loading.

C. Ask for discount for 20%, finally discount at 15%.

2) **Situation:** Mr./Mrs. Li and Mr./Mrs. Rose are talking about the damage of consignment.

You are Mr./Mrs. Rose, a sales representative from a company.

A. Ascribe the damage to improper handling.

B. Ask for the extent to the damaged goods.

C. Insist on a 15% reduction in price on the shipment.

D. Finally discount at 15%.

实践语句

在商务谈判中，特别是讨价还价时，常用的一些语句:

1. But this is the best quotation we can make.
   但是这是我们最好的报价。
2. I'm sorry to hear that.
   我很抱歉听到这个消息。
3. I agree. But you know, ...
   我赞同，但是你知道，……
4. Did you say...
   你说的是……
5. I do appreciate the effort you're making towards reaching an agreement, but frankly speaking, the gap between your price and mine is still enormous.
   我感谢你为达成协议做出的努力，但坦率地说，你的价格和我的价格之间的差距仍然是巨大的。

6. Sorry, we may not be able to sell anything near that price.
   对不起，我们可能无法以这个价格出售。
7. Is it possible…
   ……可能吗？
8. It would be very difficult for us to push any sales if we buy it at this price.
   如果按这种价格买进，我方实在难以推销。
9. Well, if you take quality into consideration, you won't think our price is too high.
   如果你考虑一下质量，你就不会觉得我们的价格太高了。
10. How about granting us a 10 discount on the final price?
    在最后的价格上给我们打个九折怎么样？

核心词汇

acquiesce	*v.* 默认，默许
attorney	*n.* 代理人，律师
bale	*n.* 包，捆
bilateral	*adj.* 双边的
bluff	*v.* 欺骗，虚张声势
Chevrolet	（美国）雪佛兰牌汽车
CIF	*abbr.* Cost, Insurance, and Freight 到岸价格
counsel	*n.* 法律顾问，辩护人
counter	*v.* 反驳，回答，还击
dilemma	*n.* 窘境，困境，进退两难
duplication	*n.* 复制，重复
feign	*v.* 假装
freelance	*n.* 自由作家，自由记者，自由职业者
headlight	*n.*（汽车等的）前灯，照明灯
hear	*v.* 审理，听审
impasse	*n.* 绝境，僵局
implementation	*n.* 贯彻，执行
incur	*v.* 招致，引起，遭受
lobby	*v.* 游说
lucrative	*adj.* 获利多的，赚钱的，合算的
malfunction	*v.* 失灵，发生故障
mega-retailer	*n.* 大型零售商
mindset	*n.* 观念模式，思维倾向，心态
minute	*adj.* 极小的，微不足道的

overseer	*n.* 监工，监督者
plaintiff	*n.*〈律〉原告
quotas	*n.* 定量，定额，配额
quotation	*n.* 估价单
refrain	*v.* 忍住，制止，克制
stance	*n.* 态度，立场
startup	*n.* 新开张的企业，新兴公司
subassembly	*n.* 部件，组件
sue	*v.* 起诉，控告
tentative	*adj.* 试探性的，不确定的
transpire	*v.* 蒸发，泄露
unbeknownst	*adj.* 未知的，不为人知的
unilateral	*adj.* 单边的

be liable for	对……应负责任
distributive negotiation	分配性谈判
holy grail	〈宗〉圣杯，圣盘
in the interim	在此期间，与此同时
letters of intent	意向书
overhead expenses	间接费用，管理费用
rock-bottom price	最低价（格）
slack time	富裕时间，松弛时间
slough off	抛弃，除掉

Unit 2 Types of Business Negotiations
商务谈判的类型

任务目标

1. Knowing the types of business negotiations
2. Mastering the features of different types of business negotiations
3. Knowing the types of non-commodity trade negotiations

商务谈判在客观上存在着不同的类型，认识其不同类型，目的在于根据其不同特性和要求更好地参与谈判和采取有效的谈判策略。可以说，对商务谈判类型的把握，是商务谈判成功的起点。

Task 1 Domestic Business Negotiations
国内商务谈判

国内商务谈判是国内各种经济组织及个人之间所进行的商务谈判。它包括国内的商品购销谈判、商品运输谈判、仓储保管谈判、联营谈判、经营承包谈判、借款谈判和财产保险谈判等。

案例学习

A foreign trade enterprise in Hangzhou does business with its client on **cotton-polyester fabric**. Both parties hold tightly on the price, which made the negotiation fall into an impasse. Afterwards, the salesman of the enterprise knows that the client just welcomed his newly-born baby and he prepares a big present for him. The client is so pleased that he expresses his willing to cooperate then and there.

(From https://wenku.baidu.com/)

案例思考

What features of Chinese business negotiation are presented in this case?

案例解析

从该案例中可以得知，中国式商务谈判不是简简单单的商业往来，或许掺杂着人情世故、家庭生活等。中国人谈生意，开场的时候，不会立刻进行谈判，而多是相互寒暄一下，询问一下对方是哪里人，在哪里居住，有什么经历等等。往往是在人情世故上找共同点，拉近双方之间的距离，特别是老乡、亲属、校友、战友这几个关系，是最能影响到双方心理距离的因素。我们经常会听到某些人讲：对方的王总与我很熟的，我们都是广西桂林人等等，其实这正是西方谈判学理论中的谈判优势。

理论拓展

Chinese Negotiation
中国人的谈判

Cross-cultural negotiation requires very detailed preparation on cultural differences. The history of business negotiation shows that many negotiations failed not because of lack of common ground but rather because of ignorance of cultural differences.

Many western academics have commented that China sees herself as Chung-Kuo—the middle kingdom, the centre of the universe. This view states that the Chinese feel superior in the area of moral and spiritual values and their sense of moral righteousness makes them critical of western societies. Superior Chinese values are: modesty, patience, respect for hierarchy, pride (no losing face), loyalty and tradition. All these show that in negotiation, there is something more important than the purely substantive matters for the Chinese—the relationship. As a result, decisions have a longer term focus.

Negotiations in China are important social events used to foster relationships. The Chinese generally negotiate in an unhurried manner. They usually open proceedings with a discussion of general principles of mutual interests. They do not like the western eagerness to sign a contract and this typically means that you will be dealing with people who place values and principles above money and **expediency**.

There are two distinct phases of negotiating business deals in China—the technical and the commercial phase[1]. There are usually two negotiating teams. The technical phase comes first and is very detailed. This is a stage where you need to send someone representative and competent in technical issues. Of course you can send the same team to negotiate at both stages but you will risk ending up with a **suboptimal** solution. Generally speaking, you need to prove your competency in substantial issues so that the Chinese see the reason for a relationship. If your company will be represented by two teams, it will probably be several days before your commercial team sees any action, but both teams should join the technical stage of negotiation in order not to miss any aspect during the commercial stage. To the Chinese, a contract is a commercial agreement, not a legal document and should be based on friendship and goodwill. In this context, a lawyer would not be the most appropriate resource to conduct the negotiation. In China, whenever unexpected circumstances arise, they are typically sorted out through the strong relationship bonds that exist. During negotiation, a team of negotiators is welcomed but the Chinese will look for the leader with authority to make decisions.

It is definitely advisable to bring your technical experts to the negotiation table. Like in any negotiation, you need to be sure that both substantial and relationship issues are considered in terms of negotiation goals. While composing your negotiation team, choose delegates who are competent in building relationships, creating and claiming value. Briefly speaking, if you can create a team that will naturally fit to the negotiation context and relationship style, you are more likely to achieve an optimal outcome[2].

(From http://www.negotiationtraining.com.au/)

Notes

1. the technical and the commercial phase：技术阶段与商业阶段
2. achieve an optimal outcome：达到最佳的结果

Read the text and answer the questions.

1. This article points out a phenomenon that usually occurs in Chinese business negotiation: building relationships. What do you think of this phenomenon? Is it good or not, and why?
2. What do you think about the author's point of view? Do you agree or not, and why?

要点小结

一、国内商务谈判的特点：

1. 职位对等；
2. 人情世故；
3. 酒场即商场（目前这种现象有所改变和缓解）。

二、国内商务谈判与国际商务谈判的区别：

1. 地域。国际商务谈判涉及两个国家及以上，国内商务谈判只在一国内进行。
2. 支付。国内贸易的支付不出国境，而且使用本国货币。国际贸易的支付可用外币。
3. 适用的法律。国内贸易只受本国法律的管辖。
4. 参与者。国内贸易的参与者一般为国人，而国际贸易的参与者至少涉及多个国家的人。
5. 行政干预。国内贸易有时受行政干预多。
6. 随意性较小。商务谈判的多样性促使偶然因素的出现，这就带来更多的随意性。在国际商务谈判中，多样性越多，随意性就越大；而国内商务谈判的多样性相对较小，因而随意性也较小。

三、中国传统文化对商务谈判的影响：

中国强调儒商，重在培养儒魂商才。儒家教义归为五项普遍法则：仁、义、礼、智、信。

1. 仁：强调与人友善，谈判双方建立和谐的关系。
2. 义：体现儒商的基本义利观。商务谈判中把握好度，不得损害国家利益和集体利益，不能见利忘义。
3. 礼：中国是传统的礼仪之邦，崇尚礼尚往来。
4. 智：同“知”，是人必备的重要品德。“智（知）者不惑”，不单纯指掌握科学知识，更重要的是指在道德领域，具有明辨是非的能力。
5. 信：讲究“言而有信”“一诺千金”，诚信是经商的基本准则。

Task 2　International Business Negotiations
国际商务谈判

国际商务谈判是指在国际商务活动中，处于不同国家或地区的商务活动当事人为了达成某笔交易，彼此通过信息交流，就交易的各项要件进行协商的行为过程。国际商务谈判是国内商务谈判的延伸和发展。

案例学习

Pfizer, the pharmaceutical industry **behemoth**, was growing increasingly uneasy in early 2008. It had few **blockbuster** drugs in the pipeline, and several of its major revenue-generating drugs were about to lose **patent** protection. Pfizer had made several major acquisitions earlier in the decade and now looked to acquire another drug company to **offset** potential revenue losses. CEO Jeffrey Kindler placed a call to Wyeth Pharmaceutical's chief executive that spring.

Talks heated up in the summer months but appeared to collapse when the global banking system went into a **meltdown** that September. Each in a series of what appeared to be restarts over the next several months faltered on Wyeth's concerns that Pfizer could not finance the deal. Only in late January 2009, when a **consortium** of banks signed a loan commitment, was an agreement reached.

Pfizer, like many firms that have engaged in **mergers** and **acquisitions** (M&As) over the years, followed a pattern: management determined that an acquisition was the best way to implement the firm's business strategy; a target was selected to fit with the strategy; and a **preliminary** financial analysis yielded satisfactory results. It was time to approach the target and initiate negotiations. A process that generally begins with the buyer establishing what it believes to be a reasonable initial offer price range based on preliminary information. Although a potential buyer may wish to avoid being too specific at first contact, it may be unavoidable. The seller may demand some indication of price before proceeding to release any additional information to the buyer. A wise buyer intent upon proceeding will provide a **tentative purchase** price or indication of value for the target firm subject to performing adequate due diligence.

In Tel Aviv, a Palestinian and an Israeli college student are trying to establish a dialogue for peace in the region. In the U.S., the CEO of a biotech company is weighing a buyout offer. An auto union in Detroit is voting whether to go on strike. Two parents in Beijing are discussing where to sent their child to school.

(From *International Business Negotiation,* 2013)

案例思考

1. What features of negotiation does this case present?
2. What characteristics do these people have in common?

案例解析

该案例反映了国际商务谈判具有一般贸易谈判的共性：以经济利益为谈判的目的；以经济利益作为谈判的主要评价指标；以价格作为谈判的核心。

该案例中，谈判中的人们都面临着需要深思熟虑的问题：他们尽力去协商出一种解决办法，或者是建立一种新的关系，或者是对对方需求的全新理解。

理论拓展

Chinese Water-Selling Negotiation
中国水销售谈判

Overview

Acqua International (AQ[1]) is a Europe-based multinational company that has interests in water and other environment-related businesses.

In China, the company has joint ventures with medium-size and large municipalities to produce and sell potable water. To increase its investments in China, the AQ Group arranged, through its local subsidiary Pacific Acqua International (PAQ[2]), to enter into a strategic alliance with Tak Foy and Co.[3], a Chinese conglomerate with strong roots in China in the service industry (mainly leisure-related). The venture is called Haoyu China Limited (HCL).

The Scene

These negotiations concerned an urban water supply system providing potable water to around one million people. Through an agent in the province, the China subsidiary PAQ had secured a sales negotiation contract to construct a water treatment plant for the system. In negotiation training on selling skills in China, we share how having Chinese team members and a local agent can make the difference in securing a sales contract.

Some time after the completion and commissioning of the plant, PAQ learned from the same agent that the municipality was short of funds for some urgent development projects. One of its options was selling off or privatize the **municipality**'s water supply facilities.

The selling price value of the facilities was set by the municipality, and bidders were sought from within its **jurisdiction**; there would be no recourse to the central government for selling approval.

HCL, located in the municipality, submitted a purchasing proposal to buy the facilities, to set up a joint venture with the municipality's water company on a 3:1 ratio, and to operate the facilities on a twenty-five-year contract.

The unresolved issues when bids were called for were:

Initial water charges. The only things that had been agreed on up to this date were how much would be invested in the facilities and spent on improvements.

The demand for water. To make the business financially viable, a take-or-pay selling mechanism[4] would have to be introduced, and local wells would have to be closed.

The formula to calculate annual water selling **tariff** revisions. Devaluation of the yuan would affect foreign exchange sales-based investment.

The new company's structure. Who would be the shareholders, board members, and those responsible for its day-to-day management?

Selling Negotiations Begin

At the request of the Chinese, a memorandum was signed by HCL and the municipality to record the negotiation selling issues still outstanding.

It was only then that PAQ—and through it HCL—was informed by the local PAQ agent (who was supposedly very close to high levels in the municipality) that other international competitors had also visited the municipality in connection with the same selling project.

After meeting high-ranking officials in the city, the PAQ team was advised to lower its starting price for water supply if it wished to remain the preferred partner.

In a bid not to lose the municipality's interest, PAQ organized visits to PAQ operations in other provinces for a group of municipal officials, whose reaction was positive. Then, believing it a good time to start selling negotiations, PAQ submitted a revised proposal, which was followed up by visits requesting negotiation selling discussions.

The mayor's office arranged a selling negotiation session to be attended by representatives of all the municipal departments concerned, at which PAQ and HCL were represented by four people: John King, Hans Christian, Cheng Peng Li, and Xu Jing.

For several weeks the unresolved selling issues and other negotiation matters were discussed, and every evening the municipality hosted a formal banquet, which lent ambiance to the talks. Cheng and Xu were the representatives on these social occasions, while King and Christian remained in the background.

Strategy Applied

PAQ did not begin negotiating using the water rates as the deciding factor in the belief that, were its selling ideas not well accepted, the entire selling project might be placed on hold. Instead, it picked secondary selling issues with noncritical impact to give both parties some wins to balance the losses.

Discussions started with water demand. Municipalities are generally optimistic about development and, therefore, ready to accept or propose relatively high demand levels where the take-or-pay selling mechanism is applied. Moreover, PAQ believed the municipality would not be in the joint venture if it were not ready to enforce the selling laws concerning wells. So **consensus** on water demand was reached quite quickly in their selling negotiation agreement.

Next in the selling agreement to be negotiated was the tariff adjustment formula. Both parties agreed to an inflation-adjusted tariff, while the provincial government representative insisted that foreign exchange should represent less than five percent of investment and be used for no more than ten years.

Due to PAQ's favorable reputation, post agreements on the post selling shareholding structure and management were reached without too much difficulty.

Last came the water rate negotiations. PAQ impressed on the municipality that, as an old friend, it was right for the project, being technically and financially sound with a good track record in China. PAQ's sincerity was demonstrated by the number of Chinese staff on its team—a point clients learn more about on sales negotiation courses.

Coup de Face[5]

A Selling Agreement was reached in two weeks, with the mayor himself voicing his support. Wishing to give face to their lead negotiator, and aware of Chinese sensitivity to pricing of the sale, PAQ then offered to reduce the starting water rate. In return, to give face to PAQ, the municipality offered preferential tax treatment over a five-year period.

In Retrospect

Later, PAQ managers described some of the problems commonly faced by foreigners in selling negotiation situations, and how they might be resolved.

Most foreigners without Chinese sales training and new to China do not know how the Chinese perceive them, nor does it bother them.

Some Chinese see foreigners as cheats, motivated only by the desire for profit.

The Chinese point to history: relationships with foreigners are short term, the foreigners leaving after attaining their short-term sales negotiation goals.

China has a high-context society. Who you and your associates are is more important to success than the mere excellence of your product or your competitive selling price.

The Chinese may renegotiate a selling contract even after it is signed. They believe in people—not legal packages.

China has a haggling culture; there are no ethics where sales price is concerned, and they will stop at nothing to get you to lower your selling price.

Time is not money in China, although this is starting to change.

The Chinese will not sign on the dotted line until they feel intuitively that the time is right, even if all points have been clarified.

Chinese negotiators are not decision makers; the CEO or the government is the ultimate boss.

Language is a big barrier in Chinese-foreign business sales negotiations.

Solutions

Be patient. In China's family-centered society it takes time to build trust with non-family members.

Local Chinese employees can help establish trusting selling relationships.

Once the Chinese trust you, negotiations are less troublesome.

Identify the negotiators. They may be top leaders at central and local levels.

It is important to be honest and sincere with the Chinese.

Commentary

As a supplier of potable water facilities in many Chinese municipalities and cities, PAQ had a good performance record that brought with it and reinforced personal relationships, friendships, and trust.

The idea of leaving discussion of the water rates until after the easy to agree on selling issues had been tackled proved a good negotiation move. The principal sign that negotiations were in PAQ's favor was the number and high level of officials invited to the negotiation meeting arranged by the mayor's office. That it still took some weeks to craft a final selling agreement is not, however, surprising, since there would have been numerous selling issues outstanding.

Most important of all, when the final agreement was reached, a gesture was made to give the Chinese face within their community.

(From https://www.negotiations.com/)

Notes

1. AQ：Acqua International Company 的简称，是欧洲一家主要经营饮用水的国际公司。
2. PAQ：Pacific Acqua International 的简称，太平洋饮用水国际公司。
3. Tak Foy and Co.：公司名，是一家以休闲娱乐服务业为主的中国联合大企业。
4. take-or-pay selling mechanism：照付不议的销售机制，是指在市场变化的情况下，付费不得变更，用户实际使用未达到此量，仍须按此量付款。
5. Coup de Face：为了面子做出的出乎意料的改变。

Read the text and answer the question.

What have you learned from this article?

要点小结

国际商务谈判既具有一般贸易谈判的共性，又具有国际商务谈判的特性。

一、共性：

1. 以经济利益为谈判的目的；
2. 以经济利益作为谈判的主要评价指标；
3. 以价格作为谈判的核心。

二、特殊性：

1. 较强的政策性；

2. 应按国际惯例办事；
3. 国际商务谈判涉及面很广；
4. 影响谈判的因素复杂多样；
5. 谈判的内容广泛复杂。

Task 3 Negotiations for Merchandise Trade 商品贸易谈判

根据商务谈判内容的不同，商务谈判可分为商品贸易谈判和非商品贸易谈判。

商品贸易谈判是指商品买卖双方就商品的买卖条件所进行的谈判。商品贸易谈判的内容是以商品为中心的，它主要包括商品的品质、数量、包装、运输、价格、货款结算支付方式、保险、商品检验及索赔、仲裁和不可抗力等条款。

案例学习

On arbitration

A: Everything has been talked over and agreed upon. Shall we sign the contract right now?

B: Just a moment please. This **transaction** is quite different from the usual. Besides the large quantity, the medical instruments we have ordered are very valuable. In case disputes arise, we should include an arbitration clause in the contract.

A: Well, we are old friends. If disputes arise, I believe, they can be settled through an **amicable** negotiation.

B: That sounds fine. But the **provision** of arbitration is really very important and a matter of serious concern to both of us. It's generally the last resort.

A: OK, we have no objections. But where are we to hold arbitration?

B: Is it agreeable to you to adopt our usual practice that arbitration is conducted in China?

A: We'd better not fix the location for arbitration and the arbitral organization now. We can discuss setting up a temporary arbitration body when needed. As for the place of arbitration, maybe we'll have it in a third country in order to seek a fair and equitable solution to the problems.

B: It sounds reasonable. The clause should be like this: "Any disputes arising from the execution of this contract shall be settled in a friendly way. If no settlement can be reached through consultation and conciliation, the disputes shall be submitted for arbitration by a mutually-nominated arbitrator. The arbitrator's decision on the disputes is final and binding."

A: Fine. Only one thing is not mentioned. How is the cost of the arbitration to be divided?

B: Generally speaking, all the fees for arbitration shall be borne by the losing party.

A: It's acceptable.

(From *Business Negotiation*, 2005)

案例思考

1. Do you think it is necessary to add an arbitration clause to the contract?
2. What are the specific elements that need to be negotiated in this clause?
3. What are the other resorts to solve disputes? What are the advantages of arbitration over other solutions?

案例解析

The sales contract provides legal basis for determining the rights and obligations of seller and buyer. **Breach of contract** arises where any party does not abide by the **stipulations** of the contract. Since a sales contract is legally binding on the contracting parties, any party who has violated the contract shall be legally held responsible for the breach, and the injured party can exercise its right to claim damages against the other party.

In settling disputes, it is necessary to resort to arbitration when conciliation does not work. More flexible, less expensive and much quicker in handling cases than litigation, arbitration has become the most popular method in settling disputes. Arbitration is a means of settling a dispute between two parties through the medium of a third party whose decision on the dispute is final and binding.

理论拓展

Once at an Export Trade Fair (Fall) held in Guangzhou, a Chinese food import and export corporation and a Kuwaiti client closed a deal on a batch of Beijing ducks. The following are the major contents of their contract:

Name of the commodity: Frozen Beijing Duck

Specifications: first grade, at least 2 kilo per duck, with head, wings, webbed feet, without feathers

Packing: 700 cases, total weight of 10 tons

Total price: £2,415,000.00 CIF C2%[1] Kuwait

Date of shipment: August, September, 20xx

Place of shipment: Tianjin Port

Terms of payment: By 100% **Irrevocable** Sight Letter of Credit[2]

Insurance: To be effected by the seller for 110% of the CIF invoice value covering all risks and war risks.

Claim: Any claim by the buyer concerning the goods shall be filed within 30 days after the arrival of the goods at the port of destination and supported by a survey report issued by a surveyor approved by the seller.

Force Majeure[3]: The seller shall not be held liable for non-delivery or delay in delivery of the goods hereunder by reason of natural disasters, war or other causes of Force Majeure.

Arbitration: All disputes arising out of the performance of this contract, shall be settled through negotiation. In case no settlement can be reached through the negotiation, the case shall then be submitted to the China International Economic and Trade Arbitration Commission. The arbitration shall take place in Beijing. The arbitral award is final and binding upon the parties.

Note: A certificate must be issued by the Chinese Islamic Association to certify that this batch of frozen ducks is butchered in the Moslem way under the Islamic rites by knife.

(From *International Business Negotiation*, 2013)

Notes

1. CIF C2%：CIF 是 Cost, Insurance and Freight 的缩写，指到岸价格；C2 中的 C 是 Commission 的缩写，2%是指 CIF 价格中保函 2%的佣金。
2. Sight Letter of Credit：即期信用证
3. Force Majeure：不可抗力

Read the text and answer the question.

What are the main contents of Negotiations for Merchandise Trade?

要点小结

一、商品买卖谈判有以下特点：

1. 难度相对简单。商品买卖谈判的难度相对简单，一是大多数货物均有通行的技术标准；二是大多数交易均属重复性交易；三是谈判内容大多围绕与实物商品有关的权利和义务。但绝不能因此而轻视，特别对初次合作、大宗交易、国际货物买卖更是如此。

2. 条款比较全面。货物买卖是商品交易的基本形式，商品买卖谈判也是商务谈判的基本形态。

二、在商品买卖的谈判中，通常要包括：

1. 货物部分的谈判：如标的、品质、数量、包装、检验等；
2. 商务部分的谈判：如价格、交货、支付、索赔等；
3. 法律部分的谈判：如不可抗力、仲裁与法律适用等。

在这些内容中，习惯上将货物部分和商务部分的条款列为主要条款，它们属于交易的个别性条款；而将其他条款列为一般条款，它们是适用于每一笔交易的共同性条款。

Task 4 Negotiations for Non-Merchandise Trade 非商品贸易谈判

非商品贸易谈判包括知识产权谈判（Negotiations for Intellectual Property Right）、技术转让谈判（Negotiations for Technology Transfer）、合资合作谈判（Negotiations for Joint Ventures）、商务代理服务谈判（Negotiations on Agency）以及招投标谈判（Negotiations on Inviting Tender and Bidding）等。

案例学习

The Technology Would Soon Be Out of Date

Wendt represents a French Textile company and Jiang represents a Chinese Textile Import and Export company.

J: Yesterday we talked about the general idea of the documents of our joint venture. It is high time for us to discuss the detail of technology transfer thoroughly.

W: Oh, yes, I'm just coming to that point. If you want to produce the competitive products which successfully meet the need of the international markets, you have to acquire advanced technology.

J: You are extremely right. The technology you are going to introduce to our new project should be advanced and appropriate to China's needs.

W: We promise that we transfer the advanced technology—what we are adopting in our production at the present. As a result, you'll pay for it in the form of royalties, except for a certain initial down payment, am I right concerning that?

J: You are partly right and partly wrong.

W: Why?

J: Of course, we will pay for the imported technology. But you can't expect to labor for something that holds good for all time. If you transfer only the existing know-how, this company's technology would soon be out of date.

W: Then what kind of solution to this question can you think of?

J: My solution is simple. That is during the 20 years of our cooperation we hope you keep on renewing your know-how. In other words, you continue offering us your improved technological expertise. I suppose we should not be requested to pay extra money for that.

W: Oh, no, that is too much. We can't promise that. You certainly understand that technology has a price tag. Your proposal is as different as chalk from cheese from ours. Such an unreasonable clause would drive our business to dead end.

J: Well, Mr. Wendt, we consider you as the partner of our company. Your share is 46% of the registered capital of the company, that means you will get almost half of the profit.

W: I should say what you've mentioned just now is correct, but I still want to make it clear that technology itself can produce new value. It makes sense that we ask for payment in some way for our technology.

J: No, no, Mr. Wendt, as you know, there is a famous saying "You can't eat your cake and have it too." If I were you, I would introduce the up-to-date technology to our project without considering charging any extra dollars.

W: OK, let's hold back our discussion for the moment. We agree that will share developments and costs fairly.

J: Super! Thank you so much.

(From *International Business Negotiation*, 2014)

案例思考

1. What are they negotiating about?
2. What have you learned from the case?

案例解析

国际技术贸易是国际技术转让的主要形式之一，采用的主要方式有许可贸易、技术服务与咨询、特许专营、合作生产以及含有知识产权和专有技术许可的设备买卖等。

在该案例中，谈判双方就技术转让的几个细节进行了商讨。首先谈论了技术出让方必须确保所出让技术的先进性，其次对技术更新是否支付额外的费用进行了谈判，最后谈判结果为技术接收方不必为技术更新付出额外款项。

理论拓展

Seven Suggestions for Investment
投资的七条建议

Attorney Yitzhak Rosenbaum, manager of the hi-tech department at Zysman, Aharoni, Gayer[1], provides seven valuable suggestions for you so that you raise the money you need to make your dream a reality.

1. Sign **confidentiality** agreements before the meeting.

Try to have your investor sign—before the meeting—a confidentiality agreement not to disclose or compete with your technology. You have to protect your technology, yet be able to go forward with your potential investor. The worst thing is to go to a meeting, open up your briefcase, stick a document under the nose of your potential investor, and demand it be signed. Keep in mind that the investor may refuse to sign the confidentiality agreement and if so you may not want to meet with him. Also, keep in mind that most **venture capitalists** do not sign confidentiality agreements.

2. Learn who will be attending the meeting.

After the potential investors have signed the confidential agreement, ask them who are going to be in the room for the meeting and what is on the agenda. Ask them if there were any questions, they would like to be answered before the meeting, by telephone or in writing.

3. Don't go alone.

Negotiation is both an art and a science. The art is the persuasion and the science is remembering who said what, when and in response to what in the meeting. Someone should be taking notes all the time. Further, you should come with your **mentor** or maybe a partner who has a good business head. Do you need your lawyer with you in the meeting? No, assuming that you feel you can handle any preliminary investment issues and that the potential investor will not have their lawyer in the room either.

4. Only one chance for a good first impression.

The initial presentation must be the best you can do. The first impression is everything. Practice numerous times before the meeting. Use the latest methods for making business presentations and have your mentor walk you through the steps. After you finish the presentation, you should tell them how much money you need, when you need the money, why you need it and how you see the valuation of your company.

5. Take control.

The potential investor first looks you in the eye then at your lips. Remember never let them see you sweat.

6. Don't **shop around**.

You did it. Tomorrow they will sit with you. Tomorrow you will not let the analyst leave until he is satisfied, one way or the other, and tomorrow you will call some other investors. Wrong! No more investors until you finish with this one tomorrow. Remember, bad news travels fast, and good news is worth the money. If the analyst walks out of your place tomorrow, satisfied you have something, this investor will back you all the way. So will others.

7. Use your lawyer.

Believe it or not, your lawyer can save your time and money, and bring home the investment. Within days, you will sign this term sheet and within months this signed term sheet will be replaced with many more documents. This is your lawyer's world. Your lawyer must have the proven experience, maturity and the drafting skills to fight the war of the written and spoken word.

(From *Business Negotiation*, 2005)

Note

Zysman, Aharoni, Gayer：缩写为 ZAG-S&W，是以色列与美国的一家国际合资企业，主要从事法律服务。

Read the text and summarize the 7 suggestions with your own words.

要点小结

一、知识产权谈判

简单地说，就是指双方就专利、商标、版权等知识产权进行磋商谈判的行为。随着知识产权创造、运用、保护和管理力度的加大，知识产权谈判也越来越活跃。

二、技术转让谈判

技术转让谈判是指当事人就专利权转让、专利申请权转让、技术秘密转让、专利实施许可问题确定各自权利与义务而进行的谈判。技术转让就是当事人通过科技谈判将现实拥有的特定技术成果的权利进行有偿转让。在技术转让谈判中，转让技术成果的一方称为转让方（或让与方），接受技术成果并支付价款的一方称为受让方，受让方支付的价款叫作使用费。

三、合作谈判

合作谈判是指在经济谈判中谈判双方因为合作生产或经营而进行的谈判。具体来说，经济活动中的合作各方以人力、智力（管理或技术）、财力及物力共同协作完成某一共同制定的目标，并按各自承担的协作分量对经济利益进行分配。这种生产经营合作具体包括合资经营、合作生产、来料加工、来图加工、采样加工、补偿贸易等形式。

四、商务代理服务谈判

有些商务谈判是一种代理或委托活动，代理人充当卖方或买方的发言人，在买卖双方中起中介作用，在这种情况下代理人也成为商务谈判的当事人。

Task 5 Multi-Party and Multi-Phased Negotiations 多方多阶段谈判

有时，谈判同时会包含多方在内。比如，仲裁就是多方谈判的一种形式；一个重要投资方案的获得需要供应商提供不同的产品与技术，与一个供应商的谈判可能取决于与其他供应商谈判的结果。多方多阶段谈判要比多方谈判更为复杂，因为多方谈判的协议必须一步一步地完成，因此谈判的进程将会更慢。

案例学习

Two corporate presidents know it is in the best interests of both their companies to merge. In fact, they know that if they continue on the present course, they will both eventually be leading unprofitable companies. The problem is that they have met twice before to negotiate a merger. Since each of them had different ideas on the size of King Kong (金刚，这里指合并后的公司), they have left the table without a deal each time, and their relationship has ended up even more strained. A vendor who sells machinery to both companies and is well liked by both presidents enters the picture. This vendor starts to talk with each president separately about merging the companies and eventually brings the two presidents face-to-face to create a win-win outcome.

(From *International Business Negotiation*, 2012)

案例思考

Study the case carefully and identify the key to the solution in it.

案例解析

在该案例中，当谈判陷入僵局时，第三方的介入使得谈判顺利进行，最终实现双赢的结局。有时候，在谈判进行中，双方都力求自身利益时，各自都不愿让步，谈判陷入了僵局，不能顺利进行下一步，而中立的第三方，对于整个谈判有着重要的作用。之所以能化解矛盾，就是因为第三方能本着双方共同的利益，提出符合实际并能为大家接受的解决办法，并从不同的角度刺激和启发双方，促使得到相对满意且公平的结果。那如何选择第三方呢？可以是个人也可以是组织，可以是与双方没有直接利益关系的第三方，也可以是与双方都有贸易往来的共同商业伙伴（如案例）。谈判中，我们一定要改变一种狭隘的观念，谈判的本质不一定是你争我夺，你多我少，恰恰相反，谈判最好的状态，往往是一种合作，能达成共赢，这就是最好的结局。

理论拓展

Multi-Party and Multi-Phased Negotiations
多方多阶段谈判

Multi-party negotiations are usually only necessary for large projects (as a rough guide a large project may be anything over about $30 million USD), but smaller projects with special considerations may also be the subject of multi-party negotiations. Large projects or projects with special considerations such as complexity, novel processes, security or health considerations will usually entail a call for tenders. Many governments have a regulation that any project where the government is the buyer shall only be awarded after all potential suppliers have had an equal chance to submit a bid, this equality requirement is usually met by a call for tenders.

A tender is a document which gives details of a project, and asks suppliers to bid on supplying the goods or services called for. In exceptionally large projects, such as a major construction project, a tender call may be split into parts. An example of this might be a tender call for the design and construction of a particular building where one call would be for the design following which, the successful design would be put out for tenders to build the building. Many of the Olympic projects were the subject of tender calls.

Large projects will rarely be undertaken by a single company simply because few companies possess in house all the expertise[1] that is necessary to complete the project. Usually, tender bids will be submitted by one company, called the main contractor or simply the contractor, which leads a consortium of other companies, each of which will have negotiated a deal with the lead company even before the lead or main contractor submits a tender bid. For instance, in a large building project, the lead company (usually called the contractor) will have agreement with other companies such as structural steel, concrete, electrical and mechanical firms (called the subcontractors) to complete the contract if the bid is successful.

The buyer will usually (but not always) negotiate with the contractor and leave to the contractor any negotiations with the subcontractors. The buyer will, however, have undertaken the financial institution to ensure bridge financing; that is, the financing of the project during construction. Once the construction is complete, the buyer will then negotiate a mortgage with the bank, which mortgage will carry an interest rate lower than the bridge financing rate. When the building is complete and fully operating, the mortgage will be paid by the occupants in the form of rents.

Multi-party and phased negotiations are more complex in that multi-party agreements must be obtained at each step, so the sequence of negotiations will be slower. Progress over the contract may require an iterative process while each party in sequence agrees to articles[2] before negotiations continue to the next article. That having been said, some of the contracts between the buyer and individual parties may be signed without reference to other parties if the contracts can be served into discreet elements without interdependence. Standard supply contracts, for instance, can be signed with sub-contractors, whereby the sub-contractor's obligations are only dependent on delivery scheduling terms to be coordinated with other sub-contractors.

As may be guessed, not all agreements are negotiated at the table. Private discussions, often called "back-room" discussions, can produce agreements which are subsequently formalized at the negotiating table. Back-room agreements are usually not welcome since they are informal discussions to which not all parties are invited; however, they can be very effective and are a feature of negotiations.

(From *International Business Negotiation*, 2012)

Notes

1. possess in house all the expertise：相当于 possess all the expertise in house，原文将 all the expertise 置于后面是因为接有 that 从句修饰该短语。

2. articles：条款

Read the text and answer the question.

What do you learn about multi-party and multi-phased negotiations after reading the article?

要点小结

多方多阶段谈判通常出现在较大项目的谈判中。谈判的原则与两方谈判一致，一般包括谈判准备阶段、实际谈判阶段以及促成协议阶段等。

综合实训

Task 1

Role-play

1. Divide a group of four into two teams.

2. Team 1 represents a soft drink manufacturer. Team 2 represents the local sports stadium concession vendors who would like to sell soft drinks during sports matches in the stadium.

3. Team 1 would like to sell 10,000-15,000 bottles of water at Chinese RMB0.90 to be delivered each week. Team 2 would like to buy 8,000-12,000 bottles of water at Chinese RMB0.80 to be delivered each week.

4. Have a 10-minute-negotiation to try to reach an agreement over the terms of the contract.

Task 2

Group Work

The following table lists negotiation focuses during Sino-US talks on China's accession into WTO. Each group chooses one and practices it.

Sectors	US Offer	China's Counter Offer
Telecom	Remove all limitations on neighborhood tele service and import of mobile phones, open market of fixed line service in 6 years after joining WTO; allow foreign capital to go into all telecom fields, holding up to 49% of tele company shares and 51% of value-added and neighborhood phone service.	In the main area of telecom service ceiling of foreign shares is 25% and 30% for value-added service; forbid foreign capital in China's internet business.
Banking	Allow foreign banks to do RMB business two years after China's accession and manage financial retail business in five years.	Foreign banks doing RMB business already allowed in Shanghai and Shenzhen and will be extended gradually; not yet the proper time to open financial retail market.
Security	Allow foreign capital into stock and bond market.	Never promise to open stock and bond market to foreign capital.
Insurance	Allow foreign business people to have 51% of shares of insurance company; set up sole foreign capital company in two years.	Have allowed foreign capital to have 50% of shares.
High-tech	Reduce current import tariffs on high-tech products from 13.3% to 0; before 20xx remove tariff on computers, telecom products and technological products.	Have committed to reduction of industrial tariffs; the present obstacles are US limitation on export of high-tech products.
Textile	By 20xx, keep quota limitation on China's exporting of textile products into US.	Immediate removing of discriminate clause after China's accession.

Task 3

1. Dialogue interpretation.

A: We're glad that you have developed new products and hope to conclude the business with you.

B: 谢谢。听您这么一说，我们真是太高兴了。您看中了哪种型号？

A: We're interested in BW1218.

B: 好的，这是询价单。所需品种、规格、数量均在上面。希望能报 CIF 多伦多最低价。

A: Thanks for your inquiry. USD689.00, this is our lowest FOB quotation, which is subject to our final confirmation. How about commission? We usually can get 3% commission from other suppliers.

B: 如果订单大，我们可以考虑给佣金。从价目单上看，我们的价格已经够优惠的了。但不管怎样，我们还可以谈。

A: Are the prices your firm offers?

B: 是的。我们愿意以此价格向你们报实盘。我们认为这些价格很有竞争力。

A: How long will this firm offer be valid?

B: 这个盘一个星期有效。

A: Ok. How long will it take you to make the delivery?

B: 通常是收到信用证后 3 个月内交货。

A: Ok. We will study your offer and inform you of the result as soon as possible.

B: 我们期待尽快收到你们的首次订单。

2. Directions: Role play the scenario and answer the question: What are the major issues identified and bargained in this negotiation?

Price negotiation

The seller: Mr. Wang, the Export Manager of a Zhejiang-based Company producing plastic products.

The buyer: Mr. Welsh, the Import Manager of a large chain store company in the US.

The setting: After a factory tour, Mr. Welsh picks up several products and starts to negotiate prices with Mr. Wang.

Task 4

Directions: You are asked to make a business negotiation with your partner according to the information given below.

Situation: Mr./Ms. Wood and Mr./Ms. Qing are negotiating to establish the joint venture in Shenzhen.

You are—Mr./Ms. Wood, the general manager of American Philly Ltd.

1. Express your happiness for the good news.
2. Hope to establish a microwave stove joint venture of moderate scale.
3. Ask about the registered capital.

4. Suggest investing 7 million and raise the loans.
5. Ask about the lower limit for the foreign party.
6. Show the means of investment.
7. Ask about the termination of joint venture.
8. Show your agreement.

Task 5

Role-play

Directions: Form five teams of two people each as follows, then negotiate a contract that is satisfactory to all parties concerned.

Team A: A buyer wishing to buy a large cruise liner to take 5,000 passengers on week long luxury voyages

Team B: A shipbuilder qualified and capable of building the ship as specified

Team C: A financial institution

Team D: A labor organization representing the ship's crews

Team E: A resort hotel owner and travel agent

Situation:

The buyer has issued a tender call to which the shipyard has successfully replied. The successful tender price is US$100 million. The financial institution has agreed to finance 80% of the project through debt to be paid over 10 years at 5% annually. The resort owner has indicated the upper limit that passengers would pay for a one-week cruise which, after deducting the costs of operating the ship and caring for the passengers, leaves the owner with 40% of revenues to service the debt (15% of revenues), pay taxes (25% of profits after debt and taxes) and take home a profit. The resort owner has also agreed to offer a reduced cost package for any traveler that comes to his resort for a week if the traveler comes on the cruise ship. The deal is ready to go ahead and all conducts are ready for signing.

The representative of the ship's crews notes that profits are so high that the ship's crews should get at least a 20% pay increase or they will not agree to the deal. The cost of labor accounts for 60% of the operating costs for every day that the ship is at sea and 70% of costs when the ship is in harbor. The shipbuilder reports that every week's delay in starting construction will increase the cost by 25%. The financial institution says that it will not finance the deal unless there are signed contracts with all parties. If the contract is not signed, the financial institution may withdraw and put its funds to another project. The resort owner says that he will withdraw his offer for a reduced travel package if the project is not underway within three months.

Time is of the essence, but the ship's crew's representatives have privately indicated they are ready to negotiate for as long as it takes.

实践语句

在商务谈判中，商务谈判的双方需要介绍或了解谈判中涉及的产品。

卖方：

1. Perhaps you've heard our product's name. Would you like to know more about it?
   你也许听说过我们产品的名称，你想了解更多吗？
2. We'd like to recommend our new model.
   我们很乐意向你推荐我们的新型号。
3. The product gives us an edge over our competitors.
   这种产品可以使我们胜过竞争对手。
4. No one can match us as far as quality is concerned.
   就质量而言，没有任何厂家能和我们相比。
5. Our product is competitive in the international market.
   我们的产品在国际市场上具有竞争力。
6. They've met with great favor home and abroad.
   这些产品在国内外很受欢迎。
7. Our service, so far, has been very well-received by our customers.
   到目前为止，顾客对我们的服务质量评价甚高。
8. Our market analysis tells us our prime user will be between the age of 19 and 35.
   我们的市场分析告诉我们，我们产品的主要使用者年龄将在 19 岁到 35 岁之间。

买方：

1. Could you give me some information?
   你能给我提供一些信息吗？
2. What can you tell me about this product?
   你能向我介绍一下这个产品吗？
3. Could we see the specifications for the new model?
   我们能看一下新型号的详细规格吗？
4. Would it be possible for me to have a closer look at your samples?
   可以让我参观一下你们的产品陈列室吗？
5. Has your company done any research in this field?
   请问贵公司对此范畴做了任何研究吗?
6. Would you care to answer my question on the warranty?
   你可以回答我有关保修的问题吗?
7. We really need more specific information about your technology.
   我们确实需要贵公司提供关于技术的详细信息。
8. Could you tell me some more about your market analysis?
   请你多告诉我一些你们的市场分析好吗?

核心词汇

acquisition	*n.* 收购
amicable	*adj.* 和睦的，友好的
arbitration	*n.* 仲裁
behemoth	*n.* 巨兽，庞然大物
blockbuster	*n.* 重磅炸弹，了不起的人或事，风靡一时的事物
confidentiality	*n.* 保密，机密性
consensus	*n.* 一致同意
consortium	*n.* 财团
expediency	*n.* 适宜，方便
irrevocable	*adj.* 不可改变的，不可取消的
jurisdiction	*n.* 司法权，权限
meltdown	*n.* 彻底垮台
merger	*n.* 合并
municipality	*n.* 自治市，市政当局
offset	*v.* 抵消，补偿
patent	*n.* 专利
preliminary	*adj.* 初步的
provision	*n.* 条项，条款
stipulations	*n.* 规定，条文
suboptimal	*adj.* 未达最佳标准的，非最理想的
tariff	*n.* 关税
transaction	*n.* 交易，业务
mentor	*n.* 导师，顾问
breach of contract	*n.* 违约
cotton-polyester fabric	*n.* 棉涤纶布
tentative purchase	试购
venture capitalist	风险资本的股东
shop around	货比三家而后买，比较选购

Unit 3

Preparation and Organization for Business Negotiations

商务谈判准备与组织

任务目标

1. Understanding international business negotiations
2. Mastering the factors concerning of preparation for business negotiations
3. Mastering the factors concerning of organization for business negotiations

国际商务谈判是有计划、有目标、有组织的经济活动，是一个企业市场营销策略的重要组成部分。谈判前做好准备与组织工作，如谈判目标的确定、市场的调研、谈判对手的背景及实力评估、谈判方案的拟定及方式的选择等对谈判的成功起着至关重要的作用。

Task 1 An Introduction to International Business Negotiations

认识国际商务谈判

国际商务谈判是指在对外经济贸易活动中，买卖双方为了达成某笔交易而就交易的各项条件进行协商的过程。国际商务谈判既具有一般贸易谈判的共性，又具有国际商务谈判的特性。在谈判中应遵循一些基本原则：合作式谈判的原则、利益分配的原则、信任的原则、两分法谈判的原则、双赢谈判和复杂谈判的原则。

案例学习

In one negotiation in the early 1980s, a Chinese manufacturer was locked in a dispute with an American importer over how many models of the bicycles his company would produce. The American importer wanted four different models to give its customers greater selection. The Chinese company wanted to produce only two models, to keep tooling, **inventory**, and other manufacturing costs down. The position of the Chinese company was that it would produce only two models, while the underlying interest was to keep manufacturing costs down. The position of the American importer was that it wanted four models, while its underlying interest was to increase its profits by selling more bicycles. As long as the negotiators focused on these positions, the dispute could be resolved only through concessions by one or both sides. But an interest-oriented examination of the dispute leads to the question: how can the higher cost of manufacturing four models be **allocated** between the American importer and the Chinese manufacturer? In this example, the parties were able to devise a formula that increased the unit cost of the different models to reflect the Chinese manufacturer's increased manufacturing cost. The interests of the Chinese manufacturer were achieved by the solution—profit per unit remained constant. The interests of the American importer were also met—it sold more units at higher prices, which more than offset the increased manufacturing costs.

(From *Business Negotiation*, 2005)

案例思考

1. What type of negotiation approach was applied to the negotiation?

2. What principle was used to solve the conflict between the Chinese manufacture and the American importer?

案例解析

1. 有原则的谈判（principled negotiation）：

The tips of principled negotiation:

1) Separate the people from the problem. It is possible to be soft on the people but still hard on the problem even if you perceive the people as the reason for the problem.

2) Focus on interests not positions. Sometimes people take positions that don't reflect their real interests. Focus on the reasons why people want what they are asking for. Positions

are changeable.

3) Invent options for mutual gain. In any given scenario, there is more than one solution. Make sure you're brainstorming to think of every possible solution that could get you to a resolution.

4) Use objective criteria: concentrate on using a standard agreed-upon measure of success that everyone can work toward rather than making negotiations a contest of will. When several people or organizations are involved in a negotiation, it becomes a complex interaction that requires serious consideration.

2. 关注利益而非立场的原则：The "Focus on interests, not positions" principle. (详见有原则的谈判中的第 2 条。)

理论拓展

Rules Should Be Abided by in Negotiation
谈判中应该遵循的准则

International business negotiation is a process that is complicated, but of course interesting in international business activities. In order to achieve a favorable outcome from negotiations, the negotiators of both parties should abide by some rules as follows:

- Assume that everything is negotiable.
- Have high aspirations.
- Never accept the first offer.
- Deal from strength if you can, but create the appearance of strength, regardless.[1]
- Put what you have agreed on in writing.
- Recognize that the other party is probably holding back valuable information.
- **Flinch** to create doubt in the counterpart's mind and to add value to a concession.
- Find out what your counterpart wants. Don't assume that their wants are the same as yours.
- Concede slowly and call a concession a concession.
- Keep your counterpart in the dark about your strategy and your stake in the deal.
- Try to get your counterpart to lower his/her level of aspiration.
- Ask questions if you do not understand what is going on. Do not let your counterpart deliberately confuse you.
- Answer a question with a question to avoid giving away information needlessly.
- Invoke[2] the higher authority to buy more time.
- Information is power—get as much as possible.
- Verify anything you are told that you do not know to be fact.

- Be cooperative and friendly. Avoid abrasiveness[3], which often breaks down negotiations.
- Use the power of competition. Remember the power can be real or imaginary.

(From *Business Negotiation*, 2015)

Notes

1. Deal from strength if you can, but create the appearance of strength, regardless. 如果可能的话，处理问题要有力度，不管怎样，至少要表现出这种力量。

2. invoke：借助

3. abrasiveness：磨耗

Read the text and explain each rule abided by in the negotiation.

要点小结

我国国际商务谈判的基本原则：

1. 平等互利的原则；
2. 灵活机动的原则；
3. 友好协商的原则；
4. 依法办事的原则；
5. 原则和策略相结合的原则。

Task 2 Determination of Negotiating Goals
谈判目标的确定

谈判目标是指在谈判过程中要解决的实质性问题，它既是谈判的出发点，也是谈判的归结点，所有的谈判努力都是为了实现这一目标。因此，确定一个合理的谈判目标对于制定谈判计划、选择谈判策略、指导谈判活动具有非常重要的作用。

案例学习

Wang: In my opinion, overly strict regulations are just another way of restricting imports.

Fox: Ah, there's something in what you're saying. According to the present **FDA** regulations, the Ma Ling labels cannot be used if the **lichee** is to be offered for import into the United States.

Wang: Why not? Our canned lichee and other **canned provisions** have already been widely sold in various markets abroad, and Ma Ling label has now been accepted by most overseas customers and importers. Is it impossible for you to use the Ma Ling labels as they are?

Fox: I'd be quite willing to if I could, but we must comply with the label requirements according to our law, or we can't **clear the consignment** of lichee through the Customs.

Wang: In that case, what can we do to help you?

Fox: Would you consider quoting us for the order with neutral cans on a **CIF** basis for delivery in Hong Kong? Our associated company there will have the labels printed to comply with the FDA regulations.

Wang: Do you think that's the only way out? You know we usually do the labeling ourselves as we are responsible for the **brand labels** of our products.

Fox: Well, the present label won't do. Is it possible for you to **get round** the Ma Ling Factory to print different labels for us?

Wang: Yes, I think they might consider it as long as your requirements are reasonable.

Fox: This is great. I could wish for nothing better.

Wang: Well, let's hear what idea you have in mind.

Fox: The FDA insists that only two languages be used on the labels. Since there are two principal display panels on the label, one can be in English and the other in Chinese. The important point is to have information on one of the panels in English only.

Wang: The German or Dutch description on the current labels is to be deleted then, isn't it?

Fox: Yes, that's what we want.

Wang: Any other changes?

Fox: Yes, just one more thing. The **net weight** must be indicated in a type of required size, that is, one-eighth of an inch minimum, and placed in the lower 30% of the panel.

Wang: I see. We shall give it our immediate attention.

Fox: Thanks for your help.

(From *International Business Negotiation*, 2014)

案例思考

What are the negotiating goals in this negotiation?

案例解析

在本案例中，Fox 代表美方公司提出，中方出口到美国的 Ma Ling 牌荔枝的商标需要符合美国联邦食品医药管理局目前的规定。Fox 尽量说服中方配合并更改。

理论拓展

Clarifying Objectives
明确目标

Generally speaking, it is rare to have one goal for a negotiation. Take, as one example, a deal to purchase a computer. The buyer wants 50 computers, each of which should meet his quality requirements, be delivered by a certain date, and payment should take place by documents against payment. Therefore buying computers is not his sole goal, payment terms, time of shipment, and quality requirements are also involved.

So before negotiation starts, one has to list all the goals one hopes to achieve, arrange them in the order of priority, identifying the major goals and the minor ones that can be discarded. Thus, when it comes to compromises, one will know for sure how to trade comfortably and confidently something minor for something major.

In prioritizing one's goals[1], one has to keep in mind three points: which target is most important and which is of minor importance; whether the issues are related or not; if they are, the settlement on one will be linked to the other, and making concessions on one will inevitably be tied to making concessions on the other; which issues are open to compromise and which are not.

Goals can be classified into three levels, i.e. ideal goal, realistic goal, and minimum goal.

Ideal goal

Ideal goal, also called desirable goal, is the best goal one hopes to pursue, and are also the highest points the opponent can tolerate. In reality, ideal goal is seldom realized, for negotiations are a process of redistribution of interests between the parties since no one would like to give up all obtainable benefits to the other side. Yet setting an ideal goal is still useful in a sense that it will set the starting point for the negotiations, that there is a goal for the negotiator to strive for, and that there is enough room for maneuvering.

Realistic goal

The realistic goal is also termed the acceptable goal, or medium goal. It is a flexible goal instead of a fixed one. After bargaining back and forth[2], finally a medium value between the ideal and bottom goals will be met, namely the acceptable goal. Although this level of goal is not a fixed one, it plays a very important role in negotiations. The acceptable goal is a strong driving force for negotiators, for within this zone, agreement is likely to be reached. At any point within this zone the agreement reached is beneficial to both parties.

Minimum goal

Minimum goal, also called bottom goal, or reservation price[3], or walk-away price, which refers to the lowest price or terms one can accept. To a negotiator, this is the minimum goal which he tries to defend or safeguard and fulfill so that one feels that the negotiation is not a failure. In other words, the negotiator would be willing to risk walking away from the negotiating table rather than give up his lowest goal. When that point is reached, further concessions are impossible.

(From *International Business Negotiation*, 2012)

Notes

1. prioritizing one's goals：按照目标重要性优先处理
2. back and forth：来来回回地
3. reservation price：保留价格

Read the text and answer the questions.

1. What are one's different levels of goals?
2. What concessions will one make and prioritize them?

要点小结

谈判的具体目标可分为四个层次：

一、最高目标

最高目标也叫最优期望目标。它是己方在商务谈判中所要追求的最高目标，也往往是对方所能忍受的最大程度。如果超过这个目标，往往要冒谈判破裂的危险。

二、实际需求目标

实际需求目标是谈判各方根据主客观因素，考虑到各方面情况，经过科学论证、预测和核算后，纳入谈判计划的谈判目标。

三、可接受目标

可接受目标是指在谈判中努力争取或做出让步的范围。它能满足谈判一方的部分需求，实现部分经济利益。

四、最低目标

最低目标是商务谈判必须实现的目标，是谈判的最低要求，若不能实现，宁愿谈判破裂也没有讨价还价、妥协让步的可能。

Task 3　Information Gathering in Business Negotiation
商务谈判信息收集

谈判信息是指那些与谈判活动有密切联系的条件、情况及其属性的一种客观描述，是一种特殊的人工信息，包括背景分析（政治背景及制度背景、经济文化背景、谈判对手的背景等）、市场调研（如相关信息的收集、整理、分析等）及谈判双方实力评估（如商务谈判人员的业务素质、公司经济实力等）。

案例学习

Case 1

Huang: Do you want to visit our workshop/plant?

Wood: Yes, of course.

Huang: This is our brochure. It's a brief introduction to our plant.

Wood: Thank you, I will read it.

Huang: Well, our plant floor area is about 3,000 square meters.

Wood: Great, so what's the white building over there?

Huang: The white one is the Technique Department, the blue one beside it is the storehouse and the red one far away is our refinery workshop.

Wood: Is your productive capacity up to our demands?

Huang: I think so. We have a large productive capacity.

Wood: That's good.

Huang: Now we are in the control room. From the screen and computers here, you can learn the situation of this plant… Do you want to have a rest?

Wood: That's fine. It looks good and efficient.

Huang: What do you think of our plant?

Wood: It's good. I have reasons to believe that we can definitely make a deal.

(From *International Business Negotiation*, 2014)

案例思考

What is the advantage of visiting other part's plant before negotiation?

Case 2

A Chinese Electronics Company once held negotiations with a Korean company on a joint venture. After several rounds of negotiations, the major conditions were agreed, and only the contract remained unsigned. Both sides were satisfied with the results. To give best wishes to their future cooperation in advance, they had a dinner together. At the dinner table, the Chinese liked to fill other people's cups when they were half full, indicating a warm welcome. After the dinner, the representative from the Republic of Korea left for home and the contract was not signed. It turned out that in the Republic of Korea, a cup can only be filled when empty. Filling one's cup while it is half empty indicates the person is not welcome.

(From *International Business Negotiation*, 2012)

案例思考

What is the cause for the Chinese failure to sign the contract?

Case 3

Once a foreign fur dealer came to China to contact a Chinese fur company. He promised to give a big order at a relatively higher price level. But then he turned to sell his stock of goods at a low price level. Later on when the Chinese company wanted to sell their goods, they could not be sold at all. It is clear that the dealer's real intention is to know the price of Chinese goods and to make highly priced Chinese goods difficult to sell.

(From *International Business Negotiation*, 2012)

案例思考

What do you learn from this case?

案例解析

对于案例 1，谈判前参观谈判对方的公司或工厂以尽可能多地了解对方公司的情况，收集相关信息，这对谈判己方来说是非常必要的，既有利于了解对方的实力，又有利于制定自己的谈判计划，决定自己的谈判策略等；

对于案例 2，中方之所以未能成功签约在于事先没有对谈判对手做充分的了解，缺乏对方的文化知识；

对于案例 3，中方缺乏对谈判对手背景的了解，泄露了己方的商业秘密。相应地，该外方公司是在做市场调研，抢占了市场先机。

理论拓展

Preparation for Negotiation
谈判准备

A Chinese engineering company in Gabon[1] dismissed quite a number of local workers after it had completed the framework of a construction, which gave rise to a strike lasting for 40 days. The company had to hold a tough negotiation with the local workers, who demanded a large sum of **subsidies** in line with the labor law of the country. Only by this time was the company aware of their ignorance of the local law and heavy losses thus happened. The company was informed that, according to Gabon's labor law, a casual laborer automatically turns into a permanent laborer if he keeps the job for a week without being fired. As a permanent laborer, he is entitled to family subsidies (enough for two wives and three kids), transportation fee and unemployment subsidies. An unskilled laborer working continually for a month will naturally become a skilled laborer and be promoted to a technical worker after three months. Their salaries will increase along with their upgrading. The Chinese managers, understanding of casual and permanent labors, unskilled and skilled workers, and technical workers is apparently quite different from that of Gabonese. The result of the negotiation was obvious: the company had to pay a large sum of subsidies, which was as much as the salaries the company had already paid to the workers, and which was not included in the budget of the project.

A lesson learned from the case is that all the concepts and practices suitable for domestic business activities may not fit foreign situations. This crucial point is often neglected because most negotiators are used to the environment of their domestic operations and are not conscious of the **constraints** and changes of the business activities in foreign countries.

Far too many business negotiations fail because of inadequate preparation on one side or the other. So it is important for the participants to make a good job of preparation before the negotiation begins. Preparation is necessary to achieve the highest level of success in business negotiation.

(From *International Business Negotiation*, 2013)

Note

Gabon：（国名）加蓬（位于非洲中西部，首都利伯维尔）

Read the text and answer the question.

What preparation should one make before negotiation?

要点小结

国际商务谈判前的信息准备：

一、市场信息：国内外市场分布的信息、消费需求方面的信息、产品销售方面的信息、产品竞争方面的信息、产品分销情况等。

二、有关谈判对手的资料：对谈判对手资信情况的审查、对谈判双方谈判实力的判定、摸清谈判对手的最后谈判期限、摸清对方对己方的信任程度等。

三、科技信息：与企业产品的研制、设计、生产、包装等有关的科学技术信息。

四、有关的政策法规：有关国家和地区的政治状况、有关谈判内容的法律规定、有关国家和地区的各种关税政策、有关国家和地区的外汇管制政策等。

五、金融方面的信息：收集国际金融市场的信息、收集进出口地主要银行的营运情况、收集进出口地政府对进出口外汇管制的措施或法令等。

Task 4 Avoidance of Negotiation Risks
谈判风险规避

在国际商务合作过程中，风险可谓无处不在、无时不有。商务谈判中需要研究的风险，既包括国际商务活动进行过程中存在的风险，也包括由谈判活动所带来的风险。对此，必须搞清楚在国际商务谈判中所可能造成的直接和间接经济损失的原因与程度，以及在谈判中采取怎样的对策，以避免和减少这种损失。

案例学习

Back in the 1980s a small US company signed a long term agreement with a Japanese manufacturer to purchase a brand of **adhesive** that was much cheaper than could be obtained in the US. The Japanese negotiating team was **adamant** that they were to be obtained in Japanese yen. The American company, eager to lock in this cheap supply of this particular adhesive, agreed. This meant that the US company would now assume any risk in **currency fluctuation** for the Japanese yen.

At the time the agreement was signed the value ratio between the yen and the US **greenback** was 185 yen to $1.00 US dollar. For a while the US company prospered even more as the exchange rate fell from 250 yen to $1.00 US. It was looking like a really good bargain. Unfortunately, the tide shifted the other way and by 1988, the yen was valued at 140 yen to $1.00 US, much to the dismay of the US company.

(From *International Business Negotiation*, 2013)

案例思考

In this case, what kind of risk did the US company take? How did the risk happen and how to avoid it?

案例解析

在该案例中，美国的这家小公司面临着美元对日元的币值波动风险。这是市场风险中的汇率风险。汇率风险是指在较长付款期内，由于汇率变动而造成结汇损失的风险；或指一个组织、经济实体或个人的以外币计价的资产与负债，由于汇率变化而引起的价值上涨或下降的可能。

在国际货物买卖中，计价及支付货币选择是非常重要的。计价货币通常与支付货币为同一种货币，这些货币可以是出口国货币或进口国货币，也可以是第三国的货币，由买卖双方协商确定。在当前国际金融市场普遍实行浮动汇率制的情况下，买卖双方都将承担一定的汇率变化风险。因此，作为交易的双方当事人，在选择使用何种货币时，就不得不考虑货币汇价的风险。首先，应考虑所选用的货币是不是可自由兑换的货币；其次，对可自由兑换的货币要考虑其稳定性。特别是在远期交货的大宗货物买卖中，选用汇率稳定的货币作为支付货币，是国际货物买卖合同洽商的基本原则，也是买卖双方都易于接受的条件。

在本案例中，合同期限较长，美方急于签约，未选用较为稳定的美元作为支付货币，接受以日元为支付货币的交易条件，这就给合同留下了汇率风险损失的隐患。

理论拓展

Negotiation Risks
谈 判 风 险

Like any other business, international business also involves risks. However, there are different types of risks involved in them. A lot of companies had been crippled down as its lack of in depth consideration of the business risks in international negotiation.

Many risks in business have to be considered so that entrepreneurs could prolong their lives in the business arena. Factors such as national laws, political situations, international treaties as well as globalization should be taken in consideration since they could directly affect international business **transactions** in one way or another. Some of the common risks involved in international business, which should be dealt with in the negotiation phase are:

Exchange rates[1]

This is a common problem that needs a keen observation for international business especially those who are in import and export business. Take for example a company in the United States that imports products from China. There is a risk that profits would decline if the US economy is stable since the prices would be cheaper if customers would buy directly from China.

Therefore, the company should plan ahead of time so as not to be affected much by currency fluctuations[2]. They should consider buying out **in bulk** in economic situations that would favor more profit to them. They should develop a strategic plan in backing up the supplies during currency fluctuations so that the increase in net profit would be at hand.

Existing national laws

Putting up business in other countries could greatly be affected by existing laws of the country. The company should therefore make the most of the "free trade system" so as not to suffer much from **tariffs**, **quota** regulations and other business taxes that may be required of them.

Shipment

There is a risk for products to be damaged while it is being shipped to the customers. This is a common scenario especially for plastic, glass, house wares and other utility products.

Agreement implement

Obviously, no one can predict the future in this constantly changing business and international climate. Any single thing can change what might challenge the terms of the agreement, ranging from labor disruptions, civil strife, interest rates, supply and demand, just to name a few. All of these things have the potential to upset the apple-cart and may require that the agreement be re-negotiated, to adapt to these new challenges.

Country risks

There is also a risk of interference in the business by the government of the foreign country, which increases where the enterprise has a branch of subsidiary in the foreign country. The government may decide to discriminate against foreign companies by imposing unfair health and safety regulations, fines, punitive taxes or even nationalizing the business or parts of it.

There are some other risks involved in international business. They may emerge at any time during the business activity. However, these risks are not here to discourage people from doing business international. There are here to remind us that there are several risks, which are involved, and that it is our responsibility to avoid these risks.

(From *International Business Negotiation*, 2013)

Notes

1. exchange rates：（货币）兑换率
2. currency fluctuation：币值波动

Read the text and answer the questions.

1. What risks in business have to be considered before negotiation?
2. Explain each risk mentioned in this article in your own words.

要点小结

商务谈判中的风险防范、商务谈判中常见的风险类型、商务谈判风险的规避、商务谈判风险的转移等。

一、谈判中的风险类型

1. 政治风险：指由于政治局势的变化或国际冲突给有关商务谈判活动的参与者带来的可能的危害和损失。

2. 市场性风险：汇率风险、利率风险、价格风险。

3. 谈判人员风险：素质性风险（谈判人员的内在素质缺陷带来的风险、缺乏必要的知识、缺乏充分的调查、研究、求教等带来的隐患）、技术性风险（技术上过分奢求引起的风险、合作伙伴选择不当引起的风险、强迫性要求引起的风险）。

二、风险的预见与控制

1. 纯粹风险和投机风险共存：

1）纯粹风险是指那些只有损失机会而无获利可能的风险。纯粹风险的发生，对当事人而言必有损失形成。例如，火灾、沉船等事故发生；投机风险是指那些既有损失可能也有获利机会的风险。例如，市场行情的变化，对此企业造成损失。

2）纯粹风险的风险事故及其损失，一般可以通过大量的统计资料进行科学测量，而投机风险则难以做到，因为投机风险在很大程度上受到政治环境、市场变化和道德因素等的制约。

3）纯粹风险与投机风险有时相互交织，这时进行风险分析，就必须根据风险因素的形成和风险事故的发生过程进行逻辑分析和判断，以准确认定风险的性质。

2. 对风险的预测与控制：人员风险的预测与控制、保险转移自然风险、风险损失的控制与转移。

三、规避风险的手段

1. 提高谈判人员的素质；
2. 请教专家，主动征询；
3. 审时度势，当机立断；
4. 规避风险的技术手段：财务手段、期货期权交易；
5. 利用保险和信贷担保工具；
6. 公平负担。

Task 5 Making a Negotiation Plan
谈判方案的拟定

商务谈判方案的拟定包括确定谈判主题、目标、谈判人员或组建商务谈判团队人员的分工、谈判地点的选择及协商谈判议程、谈判的程序和模式等。

案例学习

In the 1970's, Canada's economic health rose and fell like the **proverbial** yo-yo. It was too resource-based and needed to add some meat to its manufacturing industry to stabilize the economy. A Royal Commission concluded that Canada's only means to achieve this stability was to engage in an open free trade partnership with the United States.

The problem was that the United States wasn't especially interested in such a free trade partnership agreement. The U.S. was in addition also becoming increasingly protectionist during this same time period. The result was that Canada was facing a whole host of penalties and **countervailing** actions against Canadian goods. Canada clearly needed a plan.

The first step that Canada took was in the form of preparation by developing a **succinct** plan. A chief negotiator, Simon Reisman, was appointed by the Canadian Prime Minister himself. He established an ad hoc organization called the trade negotiations office (TNO) which reported directly to the Canadian Government Cabinet and had access to highest levels of bureaucracy. It established in no uncertain terms their negotiation goals and objectives which included a strong dispute resolution mechanism that the Canadians felt were vitally important to their success.

In contrast, the United States did not consider the FTA (Free Trade Agreement) to be especially important and let Canada do all the initial work. The only reason why the U.S. Congress even considered the FTA proposal was that they liked the idea of a bilateral approach to trade and were tired of the previous mechanism that failed to settle a host of trade dispute irritants between the two countries known as **GATT**. It would also allow freer access to other segments of the Canadian economy. President Ronald Reagan decided to fast track the negotiations and appointed Peter Murphy to represent their interests. The U.S. was also concerned about the growing **hegemony** of the European economy.

Strong differences in interest and approach dogged the negotiations. The Canadians used every advantage available including the use of Summit meetings between the leaders of both countries to emphasize their concerns at every opportunity. Yet, the political powers in the U.S. dragged their feet to such an extent that the Canadian negotiators walked away from the talks to express their displeasure. This put some heat on the U.S. administrators to the extent that U.S. Treasury Secretary Baker took over the negotiations.

As a consequence, the talks between the two countries were successfully concluded. Several concessions were made by both countries. The U.S. opened up a larger investment segment in the Canadian economy and removed some of the more time-consuming trade irritants. The Canadians achieved their goals of getting freer access to the U.S. economy, while implementing a strong trade dispute resolution method.

The Free Trade Agreement between the two countries created the largest bilateral trade relationship in the world.

(From *International Business Negotiation*, 2013)

案例思考

What do you learn from the case?

案例解析

该案例充分说明了拟定商务谈判前商务谈判方案的重要性。尽管谈判双方（美国与加拿大）在权利上不对等，但是加拿大方做了详细的谈判方案，充分了解了对方的利益所在，从而也实现了自己的谈判目标。

理论拓展

Negotiation Planning
谈 判 方 案

Identifying Targets

Effective negotiating involves knowing exactly what you want to achieve, and what you are willing to accept if things don't turn out as planned. This is done by setting your objectives, and then using those objectives, or goals, to guide you as you negotiate with another person. Targets of an international business negotiation can be generally divided into three categories:

1. The highest target or the maximum expectation or target
2. Acceptable target or expected target
3. The lowest target or limited target, basic target or must-be-realized target

BATNA[1]—BEST Alternative

Finally, you need to have your **BATNA—Best Alternative to a Negotiated Agreement**. "Don't put all your eggs in one basket." It' s an old saying which has stood the test of time. To a negotiator, this wise old proverb illustrates that if you bring only a single proposal to the table, you may likely end up with a rotten deal, or no deal at all. You need to have an alternative plan waiting in the wings.

1. Determining your BATNA

How do you determine your best alternatives to a negotiated agreement? In order to develop a BATNA, negotiator should brainstorm a list of alternatives that could be considered if the negotiation failed to deliver a favorable agreement. First, you have to **dissect** both your position and your interests. Then, look at the sum of these parts relative to all the alternative options available. Select the most promising alternatives, develop them into practical and attainable alternatives, and identify the most beneficial alternative to be kept in reserve as a fall-back during the negotiation. Finally, do the reverse from your counterpart's perspective. A well prepared negotiator looks at the whole picture.

Some of the most crucial factors which should be considered include:

1) The cost—Ask yourself how much it will cost to make the deal relative to the cost of your best alternative. Cost estimation may entail both the short term and the long term. It boils down to figuring out which of your options is the most affordable.

2) **Feasibility**—Which option is the most feasible? Which one can you realistically apply over all the rest of your available options?

3) Impact—Which of your options will have the most immediate positive influence on your current state of affairs?

4) Consequences—What do you think or estimate will happen as you consider each option as a possible solution?

2. Positive thinking

BATNA is your back-up plan to prevent you from accepting an agreement that is too unfavorable or not in its best interests. Not knowing your BATNA can significantly weaken your negotiation position.

If you want to achieve your objectives, you need to maintain a positive thinking, consider your **tradeoffs** and throwaways, and organize what you need for negotiation.

As to the positive thinking, you need to think positively by defining realistic, optimistic, and pessimistic outcomes.

Tradeoff is something that you consider is not important so that you are willing to give it up to gain another thing. Throwaway is a valuable thing you hold, which is inconsequential to you while desired by the other party. You should decide which items you can abandon and use as **leverage** to get what you really want with respect to the most important issues.

Meanwhile, in order to identify your objectives, you need to organize your team and resources, and to find the link between what the two parties need.

Setting an Agenda

Setting an agenda is crucial to meeting negotiation objectives. A well-written agenda let both parties come prepared and everyone in the negotiating meeting feel at ease.

1. Scheduling of the negotiation.
2. Negotiation site.
3. Negotiation issues.
4. Open agenda and restricted agenda.
5. Key points that need attention when making the agenda for one's own side.

1) Make good use of the factors of climate, favorable geographical conditions and the support from people under the prerequisite of not baffling the partner.

2) Design negotiation strategies to go along with the process of the negotiation.

3) Avoid showing all the cards in one's hand.

(From *International Business Negotiation*, 2013)

Note

BATNA：Best Alternative to a Negotiated Agreement 的缩写，指达成谈判协议的最佳选择方案

Read the text and answer the questions.

1. Why is negotiation planning important?
2. What aspects should an agenda before negotiation include?

要点小结

一、制订谈判方案的基本要求：

1. 谈判方案要简明扼要；
2. 谈判方案要具体；
3. 谈判方案要灵活。

二、谈判方案的主要内容：

1. 确定谈判目标；
2. 规定谈判期限；
3. 拟定谈判议程；
4. 安排谈判人员；
5. 选择谈判地点。

Task 6 Choices of Negotiation Styles
谈判方式的选择

商务谈判的方式多样，恰当的选择对谈判的成功至关重要。

案例学习

Chinese side: Shanghai Chike Company Ltd., the top level of its kind in Shanghai, whose products account for 70% nationally.

German side: Baier Company, the 3rd largest company in Germany, with an annual sales revenues of 60 billion Marks, having more than 100 branches all over the world.

Project: establishing a joint venture

Before the negotiation started, the Chinese company sent a group of 4 persons to the German company on a visit. Based on their first-hand information, they worked out a feasible report. Later another two persons including an advisor and a lawyer were added to their negotiation team. During the preparation period, the German company also researched the Chinese market, and their potential partner. They formed a negotiation team led by the CEO and a lawyer from the company.

From September 1985 to December 1987, they held 10 rounds of negotiations in all, ending with a satisfactory agreement to mutual benefits.

In the opening phase, the German side laid much emphasis on the their advantages. While the Chinese side stressed that since the joint venture would be built in China, it must be subject to the Chinese government and Chinese laws. Finally they reached an agreement on this point.

Then the negotiation entered into a bargaining stage, which was the most complicated period, and during which, the first problem they met was the name of the joint venture. First the German side suggested Baier Chike China Company Ltd., which met with serious objections from the Chinese side, who cited a law **stipulating** that the name of a country cannot be put in the name of an enterprise. Instead the Chinese side suggested Shanghai Baier Chike Corporation. But the German side advised that Baier should before Shanghai, since it held more shares than the Chinese side. Taking that into consideration, the Chinese side agreed on Baier-Shanghai Chike Corporation, Ltd., which was satisfactory to both sides.

During the final phase, the Chinese side met with a problem when the opponent asked for exclusive export rights. Within the feasibility report there were two items: that the foreign side was responsible for exports up to 25% of its total products, while the remaining 75% would be sold in China, and that the export channels of the joint venture included Baier, the joint venture, and a Chinese foreign trading company. **Divergences** arose from the interpretation of the **clauses**. The German side understood that the maximum export quota of the products made with German technology was 25%, while the other two entities were left with the sale of the other products of the joint venture. However, the Chinese side understood that 25% of the products made with German technology could be exported by the German side, the remaining 75%, could be exported by the other two entities. The dispute lay in whether the Chinese side and the joint venture have the right to export. The German side worried that any increase in export quantity and in export channels would break its price system, edge out its international market share and therefore opposed strongly any suggestion of Chinese and joint venture export. The negotiations got stalled. That was the last day of the 3rd round of negotiations. The German side asked for a debate over the issue, but no breakthrough was made, since no one would make any concessions. Then the German side declared a stop to the negotiations. Several days later, the German side sent a telex stating again their reasons: 1) they had already taken a lot of risks in terms of selling 25% of the products made with imported technology; 2) if the rest of 75% was destined for export, it meant they invested in fostering rivals; 3) if the joint venture did export, it would destroy its price system; and 4) if the rest of 75% was exported, it would exceed Chinese targets of obtaining technology and profits, and Baier couldn't realize its goals of sharing the market and earning profits. The Chinese side thought there were some valid reasons here, but they did not want to make concessions.

Later another person who had introduced the German company was invited. They started another round of negotiation. The Chinese side insisted on the right to export based on three reasons: 1) the joint venture was an independent legal entity, enjoying independent right of operation; 2) the international market was huge, both the joint venture and Baier could compete with the rival; 3) if the joint venture increased exports, it was helpful in surviving in the long run. Then the newly invited person from upper authorities asked the German side to indicate their areas of the international market. The fact is that they could not cover the whole world. Right after that the Chinese side asked if the joint venture received orders from abroad, what would they do? After further bargaining, both parties made concessions, and reached agreement that under the precondition that the joint venture did not demolish Baier's international price system, the contract could be enacted with certain conditions: 1) that within 14 working days of receiving the order, if Baier or a third party appointed by Baier did not take the order in written form, the joint venture had the right to execute the order; 2) that if the orders were secured through the joint venture but filled by Baier, the latter should pay 1% **commission** to the joint venture, and that if Baier transferred the order to the joint venture, the joint venture would pay Baier the same percentage of commission.

When they approached the end of the negotiations, the German side **demurred** at the dismissal clause, instead they insisted on adding the clause that whenever there were new regulations, and when the German side deemed that they were not in favor of foreign businesses, they could apply for termination. The Chinese side, of course, could not accept it. Later the German side agreed to replace it with: After approval by certain authorities, even if there were some related regulations from Chinese law, the contract should be carried out according to its original terms. This means that the new law has no **jurisdiction** over the joint venture. Once again the talks broke down. Later the Chinese side made a compromise. The lawyer explained that 1) normally China's open door policy would open even wider; 2) the 40th clause from Economic Contract Law **stipulated** that for any approved contract, even if there are new laws, they can still be carried out as contracted. The essential concession pushed the negotiation to successful.

(From *International Business Negotiation*, 2012)

案例思考

1. Why did both the German and the Chinese sides emphasize their advantages?
2. Why did the Chinese side oppose the name of the joint venture given by the German side?
3. On the whole, in what spirit or with what principle did the negotiations come to a successful agreement to mutual benefits?
4. What are the experiences reflected through the negotiations?

案例解析

国际商务谈判既是一种商务交易的谈判，也是一项国际交往活动，具有较强的政策性。由于谈判双方的商务关系是两国或两个地区之间整体经济关系的一部分，常常涉及两国之间的政治关系和外交关系，因此在谈判中两国或地区的政府常常会干预和影响商务谈判。因此，国际商务谈判必须贯彻执行国家的有关方针政策和外交政策，同时，还应注意国别政策，以及执行对外经济贸易的一系列法律和规章制度。在国际商务谈判中，要坚持平等互利的原则，既不强加于人，也不接受不平等条件。我国是社会主义发展中国家，平等互利是我国对外政策的一项重要原则。由于国际商务谈判的谈判者代表了不同国家和地区的利益，有着不同的社会文化和经济政治背景，人们的价值观、思维方式、行为方式、语言及风俗习惯各不相同，从而使影响谈判的因素更加复杂，谈判的难度更加大。

在该案例中，德方与中方都强调己方的利益，因为他们各自代表自己的公司的利益在谈判，并且还代表了各自国家的利益。由此，中方反对德方提出的合资公司名称（Baier Chike China Company Ltd.），因为公司名称不得置于国家之前。利益焦点谈判法与原则谈判法在该谈判中都得以运用。双方都很有谈判经验，当谈判陷入僵局时，引入了第三方；且在坚持某些原则的基础上，以双方利益为焦点进行谈判，使谈判得以成功。

理论拓展

Understanding the Five Negotiation Styles
了解五种谈判方式

People often ask "which is the best negotiation style?" As with much management theory there is no single "best" or "right" approach. All five profiles of dealing with conflict are useful in different situations. Although we're capable of using all five, most of us tend to have one or two preferred negotiation conflict styles that we use unconsciously in most conflict situations. Why? Either because our preferred styles have worked for us in the past, or because of our temperament (nature) or because of our upbringing (nurture).

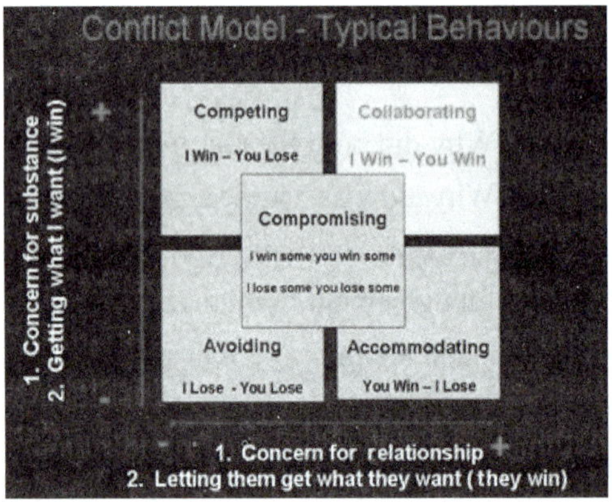

So if you're involved in business negotiations, which negotiation styles are likely to reward you with the biggest profit prizes? This question will be answered later in this article. First let's visit each of these important conflict profile styles.

Compete (I win—You lose)

Competitive style negotiators pursue their own needs-yes, even when this means others suffer. They usually don't want to cause others to suffer and lose, they are just so narrowly focused on their shorter term gains that they **plunder** obliviously through negotiations like a pirate. They often use whatever power and tactics they can muster, including their personality, position, economic threats, brand strength or size or market share. At its extreme negotiators call their behaviour aggressive or psychotic.

When to use?

When you need to act or get results quickly. Competition is critical when you are certain that something is not negotiable and immediate compliance is required.

Competition can be an effective defense or counter balance to use against negotiators with a competitive conflict profile. We would recommend that you use a blended approach though, as both negotiation parties locking horns in a competitive battle can result in a spiraling deadlock.

When you're buying or selling something as a once off (e.g. selling your own home or car to a stranger), then your negotiation will likely be more competitive than say if you were selling to a close friend or family member, or if you were in a business to business negotiation.

If you're buying or selling a commodity product or service, and you have strong competition—look out, as you'd best get used to competing.

What's the danger?

The difficulty with people who are high compete (which a large percentage of buyers are) is that competitive styles overuse competition. This means that the other party knows exactly what behaviour to expect and can prepare more easily. In a negotiation of roughly equal power, high compete behaviour is very likely to lead to deadlock—which will get you nowhere. They may also be more interested in "winning" rather than reaching an agreement. If you're recruiting a negotiator, a very low compete profile score would be something to be careful of. Some negotiators combine high compete with high avoid. These negotiators will compete first, and if they don't claim an easy scalp, they walk away from the negotiation table.

Accommodate (I Lose—You Win)

The opposite of competing. For accommodating style negotiators, the relationship is everything. Accommodating profiles think that the route to winning people over is to give them what they want. They don't just give products and services, they are generous with information too. Accommodators are usually very well liked by their colleagues and opposite party negotiators.

When to use?

When you or your company are at fault, repairing the relationship is critical, and if you have nothing else that would benefit the other party, i.e. an olive branch[1] or gift to rebuild bridges.

If you are in a very weak position then sometimes your best option is to give in gracefully. Think about it: if they can crush you, and they know it, what is likely to be the outcome if you resist? Yes, bring your own bandages. It may be worth (humbly) reminding them that you will both stand to lose if they put you out of business, and ask if they really want to push you out of that market. If you both intend to work together in the longer term, then refocus the negotiations on the longer term, thereby reminding the other negotiation party that their taking advantage of you now may hurt them in the future.

What's the danger?

It is almost always a bad idea to accommodate when negotiating against high compete styles. With high compete negotiators your generosity will be seen as a sign of weakness to be taken advantage of.

To some negotiators, an accommodating style appears to promote harmonious relationships. What these accommodating profiles miss is the myriad of other options that create strong enduring relationships. Giving away the farm usually just creates one happy negotiator, and that's not you.

Avoid (I Lose—You Lose)

This is most often referred to as "passive aggressive". People who habitually use this style really dislike conflict. Rather than talk directly with you about the issue, avoiders may instead try to take revenge without you knowing about it. The avoid style can be a typical reaction to high compete negotiators. Sellers will frequently call less often on high compete buyers (i.e. avoiding competitive buyers)—and may choose to invest marketing money and share their best ideas and prized promotions with buyers who make themselves available (those who are not avoiding the sales person).

When to use?

When the value of investing time to resolve the conflict outweighs the benefit; or if the issue under negotiation is trivial (trivial to both parties).

Sometimes there is just not enough at stake to risk a difficult conflict situation. If there is a lot of emotion in a negotiation, it's pointless pushing through and hammering it out. Better to allow people to calm down first, let the testosterone hormone leave everyone's system first so that reason and rationality can reappear. At that point an avoid style is likely the most pragmatic alternative—suggest a timeout of 15-20 minutes.

What to do when you're dragged into a negotiation unprepared? Under these circumstances, avoidance is probably the most sensible strategy. Either avoid the meeting, or avoid discussing the issues upon which you need to prepare.

What's the danger?

Whoever has the greater urgency will usually end up with the short end of the avoidance stick. Stalling is a common sales tactics[2], when sales/the vendor knows that procurement needs their product or service yesterday.

Conversely a buyer may hold out until the last day of a quarter or month, knowing that the sales person needs to meet his or her target. So be careful about what information you reveal about the urgency of your need.

Compromise (I Lose/Win Some—You Lose/Win Some)

Too many people confuse the word "compromise" with "negotiation". In reality compromising is usually little more than haggling and splitting the difference, with no deep understanding or value creation having taken place. Compromising often involves one or both negotiators settling for less than they want or need, usually resulting in an end position of roughly half way between both party's opening positions. In the absence of a good rationale or properly exchanged trades, half way between the two positions seems "fair". What compromising ignores however, is that the people that take the most extreme positions tend to get more of what is on offer, and the path they're treading with blinkers on doesn't allow the pie to be expanded.

When to use?

When you are pushed for time and you are dealing with someone who you trust.

They also need to be clear that it would not be in their best interest for them to "win" a cheap victory. Both parties win and lose—but make sure you win the right things and lose the right things.

Meeting half way reduces strain on the relationship, but usually leaves precious gold on the table (and with the central banking cartel's gold suppression scheme losing its grip right now, every ounce of gold counts).

When you have nothing left to offer, and this is the only way to seal the deal. i.e. a **lousy** situation.

What's the danger?

When you use compromising as an excuse for not preparing properly. Without quality negotiation training, most negotiators wing it, and end up compromising. If the outcome of the negotiation is critical, then you should not compromise on things that you absolutely must have.

One of the problems with compromising is: if you make concessions within your position with no strong rationale, the other party may assume that you are going to continue to make more concessions, and appeal to you using weak rationale.

Whichever negotiator starts with the more ambitious opening position wins the compromise. So calculate early on who stands to gain if it comes down to compromises.

If you get known for being a compromise styled negotiator, look out! Your trading partners will wise up to your negotiation style and they will start to make more and more extreme opening positions. Bigger opening positions result in greater chances of deadlocks. Compromises cheat both sides out of innovative solutions.

Collaborate (I Win—You Win)

Most people confuse "Win/Win" or the collaboration style with the compromising style. This is most definitely not the case. "Win/Win" is about making sure both parties have their needs or goals met, while creating as much mutual value as time and resources allow. "Win/Win" negotiators usually evolve through the other profiles, growing into collaborative negotiators. This means collaborative profile negotiators can revert to one or two of the other styles when pushed or when the situation calls for it. Collaborative profile negotiators are adamant that their needs must be met—and they acknowledge that the other party has needs that must be met too.

Tragically, too many account managers are overly accommodating and compromising. Resulting in competitive style buyers claiming more than their fair share. When these same competitive style buyers come up against skilled collaborative style negotiators, the competitive styles blunt coercion methods don't get rewarded with concessions. Too many buyers are stretched and under tremendous time pressure, so temptation to compromise rather than invest time in collaborating wins out.

Often referred to as "expanding the pie"[3], collaborative negotiators are willing to invest more time and energy in finding innovative solutions, feeling secure in the fact that there will be more value to share out later on. The **mantra** of collaborative negotiators is: "it's not enough that I win, I will not be happy until you have won too."

When to use?

Under most circumstances collaboration is the primary style you should use for most goals in business to business negotiations.

As mentioned briefly in the compete section: if a relationship is important to you, and if your market reputation is important, if the other party needs to perform and not just exchange a standard product for cash, high risk (e.g. new market or new product or both), if there is a large amount of money at stake, then you are best advised to think about all the ways in which you can build a more trusting collaborative working relationship.

If you need to understand the feelings and deeper interests or motivations of all negotiators, then collaboration is your best path.

What's the danger?

Be careful not to collaborate with competitive style negotiators—unless they agree to and live up to your agreed (written or unwritten) rules of collaboration. Die hard competitive negotiators[4] can be treated in **transactional** trading manner—e.g. "I'll only give you this if you give me that."

When we share information we need to make sure that we share information at the same level of detail.

Collaboration requires more time and needs to be at the right level. So if you're a vendor and your buyer doesn't have the authority or knowledge or won't invest the time, save your effort. Best to talk with them about your style of negotiation or build a relationship at another level of their organization. Same advice goes for buyers in reverse.

Remember

Before you negotiate, stop and ask yourself:

What is my preferred style of negotiation? The generalist TKI profile is a reasonable conflict profile. Once you know your style, you've taken the first step to gaining flexibility in your negotiations. There is much you can do as a member of a negotiation team, if you know your fellow team members' profiles.

Which of these five styles best describes your business client or vendor negotiation relationship? You may find it useful to **allocate** a percentage score to each style, and then ask yourself whether you're happy with the current styles balance. If not happy, then make a plan to migrate to your preferred styles.

Don't blindly apply one negotiation style to your negotiation. Work through your list of goals in your trading plan, and decide which issues are best to: collaborate, compete, compromise, avoid, accommodate.

Finally, there's very seldom an escape from having to use a competitive style. At some point, you're going to need to do some claiming or sharing out the value you've created. So think carefully about which point in the negotiation you need to switch to competing. So if the other party compete too early, be prepared to pause the negotiation and have words ready to revert to another style.

(Form https://www.negotiations.com/)

Notes

1. an olive branch：橄榄枝，以示和解
2. stalling is a common sales tactics：暂缓是一种常用的销售策略
3. expanding the pie：扩大利益
4. die hard competitive negotiators：顽固的竞争型的谈判者

Read the text and then summarize the five negotiation styles in your own words.

要点小结

在理论拓展部分，我们了解了谈判中的五种方式：竞争型方式（Competing）、迁就型方式（Accommodating）、回避型方式（Avoiding）、折中型方式（Compromising）和合作型方式（Collaborating）。文章中的图表及分析告诉我们其中最可取的一种就是合作型方式。该方式在物质需求上、维持关系上以及满足双方的利益上都达到了最高值，是一种可实现双赢的方式。

那么，为了达到双赢，商务谈判中主要有以下三种谈判方法：

隔离谈判法：在谈判过程中从对方角度看问题，善用感情，理智地对待感情，区分人和事，在追求经济利益的同时，注意保持与谈判对方的长期友好关系。

利益焦点谈判法：针对利益而非立场进行谈判；利益决定问题；寻求对立立场背后的利益。当谈判因立场相左而陷入僵局时，绕开问题本身，向对方征询之所以坚持立场的原因。

原则谈判法：在双方利益难以调和的情况下，要想说服对方必须使用某些客观、公平的标准，使对方接受这个条件不会感到吃亏或屈尊，从而使协商得到公平的解决方案。

综合实训

Task 1

1. Translate the following English sentences into Chinese and Chinese sentences into English.

1) The unique characteristic of international versus domestic business negotiations is that international negotiations are influenced by a wide diversity of environments.

2) As a result, negotiators' personal feeling is mingled with interests and events to be discussed.

3) Trust is particularly delusive in high stress, high-stakes conditions, as when you are negotiating with strangers, facing deadlines coping with differences in power and status, or hammering out unenforceable contracts.

4) Comparatively speaking, personal interests can be easily brought into line with that of organizations since realization of one's personal value, social status and his reputation in others' expectation are linked closely with his performance and achievements done for the organizations.

5) Win-win approach has proved to be successful and effective in many tough negotiations because it takes into full consideration of both sides' interests, which contributes greatly to the mutual understanding of negotiating parties.

6) 在当代商务中，平等互利是最根本的原则。

7) 这个原则的核心是通过强调利益和价值，而不是以讨价还价的方式来达成一项对双方都有利的解决方案。

8) 一旦获得个人利益的欲望占上风，谈判的结果将是可预见的，如，为了满足个人的小私利而损失组织的大的利益。

9) 双赢的做法是一个合作的过程。

10) 我很高兴你来续签今年进口我们冻禽的订单。

2. Simulation drills

You are asked to make a business negotiation with your partner according to the information given in the cue cards.

Cue Card A

Situation: Mr./Mrs. Cole and Mr./Mrs. Tang are negotiating about the quality and pattern of hand-embroidered silk products (手工绣丝制品).

You are Mr./Mrs. Cole, the American businessman.

1) Discuss quality, quantity and other particulars of the goods with Mr./Mrs. Tang.

2) Speak out your own views: like silk scarf, but not like handkerchiefs.

3) Tell the reason why you don't like silk handkerchief.

4) Indicate your love for the latest designs.

5) Place the order.

Cue Card B

Situation: Mr./Mrs. Cole and Mr./Mrs. Tang are negotiating about the quality and pattern of hand-embroidered silk products (手工绣丝制品).

You are Mr./Mrs. Tang, the Chinese dealer of silk products.

1) Ask about the response to samples and pattern book.

2) Doubt the opposite's view and prove it.

3) Offer the latest design for choosing.

4) Express thanks.

Task 2

Directions: If you are in the process of applying for a new job, how should you prepare for the negotiation on the package?

When you start a new job, you have a unique opportunity to position yourself as a valuable asset in the organization and to set our level of **remuneration** accordingly. To achieve this you need to establish an appropriate asking price. On one hand, you don't want to oversell yourself and price yourself out of the market. On the other hand, you need to avoid selling yourself short, for it is extremely difficult to change your position significantly once you're placed in a complex pay structure.

Task 3

Situation: Mr./Mrs. Evan and Mr./Mrs. Hong are negotiating about the details in **arbitration** clause.

You are Mr./Mrs. Evan, the French medical equipment exporter.

1) Point out good quality of equipment.
2) Explain that there is an arbitration clause in the contract.
3) Ask about arbitration in details: the place, fee and enforcement in another country.
4) Hope to resolve the dispute through friendly negotiations.

Task 4

Role-play

Divide a group of four into two teams. Team A represents a buying company; Team B represents a selling company.

The buyer has delayed closing but the seller has already incurred costs. The buyer has verbally indicated that he is now considering an alternate supplier and is not sure that he will close the deal with the seller. Identify the options open to both sides and the risks that are attached to the options. Negotiate a successful deal.

Task 5

1. Decide on whether the following statements are true or false.

1) ______ The objective at the opening phase may be described as exploration with commitment.

2) ______ The negotiators are forced to make concessions during the opening stage in order to push forward the negotiation.

3) ______ At the opening stage, each party reads signals from what the other says and does and forms its own attitudes. The negotiating team should seek to establish the resistance points for each major issue based on their original plan and what they have learned from the opening stage.

2. Scenario

A **logistics** manager has to fly to a supplier in Atlanta next week for material delivery problems. His company has established a good relationship with an Atlanta supplier over the past two years. The Atlanta supplier has always had good faith but this time, unfortunately, no warning has been given about the supply problems. The issue is that his factory in Manila has had to stop productions because of material shortages. Since his company and the Atlanta factory have a contract that includes a penalty cause for non-delivery or late delivery, the president wants him to negotiate a **down-time** payment for $6,500 per day or go to court.

Discuss the question below in small groups and afterwards select a person from each group who will then present the group's view.

Question: What would be the logistics manager's best plan in this situation?

Task 6

Role-play

Scenario: A company advertises for a project engineer urgently. Among the applicants there is one meeting the requirements, but he asks for a yearly salary of RMB120,000. The company can only pay him RMB100,000 a year. If they stick to each position, there would be no agreement.

Two students are to work together. One represents an applicant for a job, another represents the HR head responsible for new project recruitment. The two parties negotiate an agreement with mutual benefits with the methods proposed in this task.

实践语句

1. We know you are leading exporters of umbrellas in Hangzhou. Would you please send us your latest samples and best prices?

我们知道你们是杭州伞业的主要出口商，能给我们最新的样品和最好的价格吗？

2. If your quality is good and price is suitable for our market, we would consider placing a big order and signing a long term contract with you.

如果你们产品质量好，价格适合我国市场，我们将考虑大量订货并与你方签订长期合同。

3. Could you give us CIF price instead of FOB?

能给我们报 CIF（成本加保险费加运费）价格吗？不要 FOB（装运港船上交货）价。

4. You know, the price of materials has gone up sharply. But the prices of our products haven't changed much.

你知道，材料的价格已经急剧上涨。但是我们产品的价格变化不大。

5. Please quote us your best price for articles named.

请对所述产品向我们报最低价。

6. Please do not hesitate to contact me.

请随时与我联系。

7. Through the courtesy of your commercial counselor, we get to know your company name and address.

承蒙贵国商务参赞告知，我们得悉贵公司名称和地址。

8. Can you give me more background on the company's financial position?

你能向我多提供有关该公司财务状况的资料吗？

9. For our credit situation, please refer to the Bank of China, Shanghai Branch.

有关我们的资信情况，请向中国银行上海分行查询。

10. We note with pleasure the items of your demand just fall within the scope of our business line.

我们很高兴地了解到您需要的产品正好属于我们的业务范围。

核心词汇

adamant	*adj.* 坚硬无比的；牢不可破的；坚定不移的；坚决的
adhesive	*n.* 黏合剂，黏着剂
allocate	*v.* 分配，分派
arbitration	*n.* 仲裁，公断
CIF	*abbr.* Cost, Insurance, and Freight 到岸价
clause	*n.* 条款，款项
commission	*n.*〈商〉佣金，手续费
constraint	*n.* 强制；限制；约束
countervail	*vt.* 补偿，弥补
demur	*vi.* 表示异议，反对
dissect	*vt.* 解剖；仔细分析
divergence	*n.* 分叉；分歧
down-time	*n.* 停机［停歇，故障，中断运转］时间；窝工
FDA	*abbr.* Food and Drug Administration 联邦食品医药管理局
feasibility	*n.* 可行性；可能性；现实性
flinch	*v.* 退缩
GATT	*abbr.* General Agreement on Tariffs and Trade 关贸总协定
greenback	*n.*〈美，非正〉美钞
hegemony	*n.* 霸权；霸权主义；领导权；盟主权
inventory	*n.* 存货
jurisdiction	*n.* 司法权；管辖权；管辖范围；权限
leverage	*n.* 杠杆作用；优势，力量；影响力；举债经营
lichee	*n.* 荔枝
logistics	*n.* 物流
lousy	*adj.* 讨厌的
mantra	*n.* 准则
plunder	*v.* 掠夺；偷；私吞
proverbial	*adj.* 谚语的；众所周知的，出名的；已成话柄的
quota	*n.*（正式限定的）定量，定额；配额；指标
remuneration	*n.* 薪酬
tariff	*n.* 关税制度；关税
tradeoff	*n.* （公平）交易，折中，权衡
transaction	*n.* 处理；事务；（一笔）交易
stipulate	*vt.* （尤指在协议或建议中）规定，约定，讲明（条件等）
succinct	*adj.* 简明的，简洁的，简练的

subsidy	*n.* 补贴；津贴；助学金；奖金
transactional	*adj.* 相互作用的
brand label	品牌标签
canned provisions	罐装食品
clear the consignment	为货物结关
currency fluctuation	币值波动
get round	说服
in bulk	大量；整批，不加包装；成堆；成块
net weight	净重

Unit 4 Business Negotiation Communication

商务谈判沟通

任务目标

1. Understanding factors and types of business negotiation communication
2. Knowing the importance of language in business negotiation communication
3. Practicing the language skills of business negotiation communication
4. Applying the non-verbal language in business negotiation communication

在商务交往中，双方为了达成最终的共同协议，需要把各自的信息、思想和情感相互进行传递，这个过程称之为商务沟通，其中包括语言沟通和非言语沟通，但不论哪种沟通方式，都要将信息准确地传递出去，即有效的沟通。

Task 1 Factors and Types of Business Negotiation Communication

商务谈判沟通的要素和分类

商务活动的关键在于信息交流，只有参与的双方或多方明白了对方的意图，才能做出正确的判断和反应，有效的沟通是商务谈判成功的前提。

案例学习

This case occurred between one particular U.S. company and their Japanese partner. The agreement that they signed stipulated that the Japanese company would supply the manufacturing, management, and marketing components of the deal, while the American company would supply the technology.

The American representative, who was based in Hong Kong, met with their Japanese counterparts only once every three months where all aspects of the operation would be discussed.

In between these quarterly visits, the two parties exchanged communications through written correspondence and infrequent phone calls. To the Japanese partner, this periodic but infrequent contact signaled that the American partner was not overly committed to the relationship. Needless to say, the Japanese commitment to the partnership began to dwindle as well. As time progressed, the U.S. company's strategy altered as they began to concentrate on a smaller product line. The American company never bothered to advise their Japanese partner of the change in their strategy. Also, due to this smaller line, there was the additional fiasco in that the Japanese company was not going to be receiving the technology it had negotiated with the American firm.

The Japanese took a dim view of what they now perceived as an agreement that was signed in "bad faith". The Japanese became bitter as the relationship soured and ended in arbitration. What was the result of arbitration? The partnership was dissolved.

(From https://www.negotiations.com/case/business-relationship/)

案例思考

1. Is it a successful case for business communication? Why and why not?

2. How many types of business communication does this case present?

3. Can you name other types of business communication and explain the advantages and disadvantages of each of them?

4. What do you think are the elements of a successful business negotiation communication?

案例解析

该案例充分说明了交流的重要性。在该案例中出现了电话谈判和函电谈判两种谈判类别，这两种谈判形式双方代表不见面，就无法通过观察对方的语态、表情、情绪以及习惯动作等来判断对方的心理活动，从而导致美国公司没有观察出日本公司的不满情绪，也未对其商业伙伴的策略改变进行评价；日本的公司也未将其不满及时表达出来，导致这种情绪继续深化。

沟通主要包括三大要素：要有明确的目标，要能达成共同的协议，使信息、思想与情感能传递并得到反馈。双方没有将各自的想法和意见进行沟通，最终导致了合作关系的破裂。因此，绝不能忽视有效交流沟通对商业关系的影响。

理论拓展

Effective Communication & Negotiation
有效沟通与谈判

Regardless of the type of small business an owner may be involved in, there are always negotiations that take place on a daily basis. These may be as simple as choosing a meeting time and place, or they could be much more important to the overall business structure, such as working out the details of a big contract. Business people need to be skilled in negotiation tactics and understand how to effectively communicate during the negotiation process.

Non-Verbal

In every type of communication scenario, including during negotiations, non-verbal communication is sometimes more important than what is actually being said. You should pay attention to the non-verbal cues of the opposing negotiator as well as to any non-verbal cues he may be portraying[1]. For instance, if someone suddenly crosses his arms across his chest during the discussion, it can indicate that he is disagreeing with what is being said. Paying attention to non-verbal cues can help you to change your strategy.

Verbal

What is verbally being stated with the negotiation is also important. Negotiators should aim to follow some simple rules during a negotiation, such as never raising voices, not interrupting the other person when he is speaking and avoiding using **jargon** that may not be easily understood by the other. A negotiator can easily assess the effectiveness of her verbal communication by asking the listener to paraphrase his understanding of the exchange.

Preparation

Before a negotiation begins, you should prepare for the exchange. This includes identifying the goal of the negotiation, brainstorming multiple solutions and determining what the main negotiation **tactic** may be. In addition, you should create an outline of the main points that you will make during the verbal exchange of the negotiation. You should also take some time to determine which elements of the project you are willing to give up or compromise on in order to reach a successful agreement.

Open-Ended Communication

While questions that can be answered with one word such as "yes" or "no" have their place in effective communication and negotiations, open-ended questions can reveal much more information. For instance, asking the person what you would have to do to negotiate this deal today and **walk away with** a signed contract can reveal his objections to the deal. This tells you exactly what you need to focus on and overcome within your presentation. After asking an open-ended question, sit quietly and wait for an answer from the other person. Do not try to fill the silence with further communication.

Considerations

There are certain power plays that can be used in negotiation strategies and which can impact effective communication during the exchange. For instance, sitting behind a big desk while the other person is effectively exposed in just a chair is a power play that gives power to the person behind the desk. While this may be effective in a psychological manner, it does not facilitate effective communication. Focus on creating a win-win deal with honest and open communication rather than tricks that can possibly provide an upper hand through **intimidation**[2].

(From https://smallbusiness.chron.com/effective-communication)

Notes

1. You should pay attention to the non-verbal cues of the opposing negotiator as well as to any non-verbal cues he may be portraying. pay attention to 后接两个宾语：the non-verbal cues of the opposing negotiator 和 any non-verbal cues he may be portraying，这两个宾语用 as well as 连接。

2. ...tricks that can possibly provide an upper hand through intimidation. that 从句中的 "provide an upper hand through intimidation" 表示"通过恐吓占上风"。

Read the text and answer the questions.

1. What types of business negotiation does it present?
2. What kind of non-verbal cues indicate that one is disagreeing with what is being said?
3. What rules should be followed during a negotiation?
4. What should you prepare for the exchange before a negotiation?
5. What information can open-ended question reveal?
6. What do you think is an effective communication in negotiation?

要点小结

一、商务谈判沟通的要素

沟通主要包括三大要素：要有明确的目标，要能达成共同的协议，使信息、思想与情感能传递并得到反馈。

二、商务谈判沟通的类别

1. 按沟通手段划分，可分为面对面谈判、电话谈判、函电谈判和网上谈判等。
2. 按沟通形式划分，可分为言语交流和非言语交流。

Task 2 Language in Business Negotiation Communication

商务谈判沟通的语言

商务谈判者的思想都是通过语言来表达的，一方面，通过语言准确地表达各自的要求和目的；另一方面，通过对方的语言探寻对方的要求和目的。因此，语言水平直接决定了谈判的最终结果，必须十分重视商务谈判中的语言。

案例学习

Rod Zemanek, the principal negotiator, designer and project manager of an Australian chemical engineering consultancy, (Predict Pty Ltd) has been successful in China and is responsible for the design of many of China's modern breweries.

When Rod Zemanek first arrived in China, he discovered that the Chinese were also talking to German, French, and Belgian companies, and that the Chinese company's plans for the brewery were not as well defined as had initially appeared. The Chinese arranged the accommodation for the tendering companies. Each foreign team—the French, Germans, Belgians, and Australians—was lodged by the Guangdong government at the same hotel. "We would go and have a meeting with the Chinese. When we got back to the hotel, the other businesses would always be waiting in the lobby to be picked up for their meetings. It was made pretty clear that we were competing against each other," Rod Zemanek said.

The negotiations took place over several weeks, during which each of the foreign companies met with the Chinese team almost daily. To ensure he was not misunderstanding the negotiations, which were being conducted through an interpreter with the Chinese team, Rod Zemanek had brought from Australia two of his China-born staff—a chemical engineer and an accountant.

"I decided to use my two Chinese team members as my interpreters, because the Chinese language is often not explicit: The meaning of what they were saying was often only implied. It was the best decision I made, because I got the chance to log onto real feedback."

Rod Zemanek also began to see the language barrier as an advantage. "Not knowing the language gave me **carte blanche** to completely change my mind on things I already had said, because I could use the excuse that I had not properly understood. They kept changing the negotiations on me, so it gave me the chance to do the same back and get away with it."

After several weeks, the French, Germans, Belgian businesses pulled out, frustrated at the drawn-out negotiating process. They had not realized it is the language that matters.

(From https://www.negotiations.com/case/giving-face/)

案例思考

1. Why did Rod Zemanek choose the interpreters of his own team instead of the one with Chinese team?
2. Why did Rod Zemanek see the Chinese feature as an advantage instead of a barrier?
3. Why do you think Rod Zemanek can succeed in this competitive negotiation?

案例解析

该案例充分说明了语言在商务谈判中的重要性。在该案例中，Rod Zemanek 用自己团队中两个华裔同事代替了中方的翻译，这一小小的举动帮他赢得了这场谈判的胜利。案例中 Rod Zemanek 说了这么一句话"…the Chinese language is often not explicit: The meaning of what they were saying was often only implied."，模糊性是汉语的语言特点之一，Zemanek 起初把这个作为谈判的阻碍，但是很快意识到汉语的模糊性在谈判中是一种优势而不是阻碍；另外，他用的翻译是自己的同事，而没有去请专门的翻译人员，这是因为商务谈判对语言的专业性要求极高，将专业的术语准确地翻译出来实属不易。案例中 Rod Zemanek 取胜的关键还在于他将语言障碍转化成为一种优势，这说明在谈判过程中，谈判者需具有灵活的语言应变能力，做到随机应变。

理论拓展

Business Negotiation Metaphors
商务谈判中的隐喻

"A good metaphor is something even the police should keep an eye on."

—Georg Christoph Lichtenberg[1]

Words can have a powerful impact. The manner in which words are applied in a business negotiation can make or break the deal. This is especially clear if our dialogue is phrased poorly, misinterpreted or misunderstood. Words can evoke visceral reactions or emotional responses such as **boiling rage** or **howls** of laughter.

The language we use also provides some clues and insight about the individuals on our own negotiation team. **Unraveling** these clues can tell us a lot about our counterpart in a negotiation, and can even lend some introspection into our own psyche along the way.

The particular area of dialogue we are going to examine in our business negotiation examples is the use of metaphors; how they apply to a negotiator or might impact our negotiations. Webster's Dictionary defines a "metaphor" as a "*figure of speech in which a name or quality is attributed to something which it is not literally applicable, e.g. 'an icy glance', or 'nerves of steel'*[2]". A metaphor is often used in framing a dispute or situation, or the means by which we address or approach a negotiation problem. Often, the metaphors used in business are at the core of how a person perceives the situation and suggests how they might react or respond.

Metaphors as an Emotional Mirror

In business negotiations, whether we're sitting on the opposite side of the negotiation table or in the middle as a third party mediator, the metaphors used can help orientate us to how people think or identify the event as the negotiation unfolds. Metaphors mirror our emotional perspectives; the conscious perspective and more importantly, the unconscious perspective. Additionally, the use of metaphors provides a means to discern not just what they said, but also what they *intended to say*!

These two points are especially important in the more collaborative negotiation process that has emerged in recent times. The parties to a negotiation who adopt positions in a negotiation are in fact fuelled by underlying interests such as security and self esteem. In other words, we must unravel what the negotiation is "*really*" about. Unless a negotiator can unlock these underlying interests, the negotiation may stumble along like a stuttering auto **in fits and starts**. How we view our counterpart's real interests is dependent on our ability to get them to reveal their understanding of the issues or conflicts. It's all about dialogue management.

We can use the other person's use of metaphors to "hear" what they are really saying, as well as to understand their true thoughts or feelings. This will guide us in how we should respond, react, or when necessary, to intervene in conflict management.

What does this mean in practical application? Let's explore and use examples to illustrate.

How Metaphors Reflect a Negotiation Relationship

Let's take one glaring example to illustrate the point and the underlying psychological component that lies beneath the surface. If one negotiating party is using a "*combat*" **connotation** as a metaphor in their dialogue, this could be very telling about their makeup and attitudes. They may see the negotiation process in terms of either "*win or lose.*" This might present an attitude of an "*all's fair in love and war*" type mentality where they are suspicious of our motives.

A combative approach may also influence them to apply unethical tactics against us. Our negotiating counterpart might withhold vital information or use a negotiation approach that is designed to conceal their real intent. As a negotiator or mediator, we might need to use a combat metaphor to change the mood of the dispute by suggesting something along the lines of "*making a truce or ceasefire.*"

Another means to address combative business metaphors is to change the metaphor into something else to alter the direction of the negotiation. The idea is to prompt the opponents into a different mindset and engage in negotiation conflict resolution. For example, if one party says "*we've been fighting over this for weeks,*" you might change the combative context to something more benign by replying that the dispute does indeed appear to be "*well choreographed.*" This subtle change in metaphor usage suggests a collaborative mentality instead of an "*us versus them*" attitude.

How Metaphors Affect the Negotiation Process

The use of metaphors in business can provide a clue about the negotiation style being employed by one or both parties and how they can result in negotiation conflicts. Let's examine some of the most common positive and negative metaphors employed by negotiators and see what their meaning might convey.

Negative Metaphors

War metaphors: Could mean "anything goes". Any such references suggest a combative approach or business negotiation style. Such an attitude should prompt a negotiator to approach the negotiation with considerable caution.

Poker metaphors: Poker and related **terminology** could suggest that the other party will resort to the use of "bluffing" in their repertoire of tactics, so we have to be **vigilant** about of the possibility of this tactic being employed against us.

Games or sports metaphors: There are both positive and negative references here. Some negotiators view a negotiation like a chess game. The idea is to outsmart your opponent by strategizing with the plan of mating the opponent's king. Chess players don't play for a draw if they can avoid it—they want to win! When we play games or sports, we always play to beat our opponent. Negotiators might be inclined to vigorously defend the positions they adopt in making proposals or in responding to offers.

Sports metaphors can sometimes be ambiguous. If reference is made to a "*level playing field,*" it may mean they are talking about the negotiation strengths of either side. On the other hand, this expression may show their desire to take a more collaborative approach.

Mountain climbing metaphors: This one is not good at all. It suggests an uphill struggle all the way, especially if one of the parties makes reference to heading towards a "*precipice.*" There won't be much "*smooth sailing*" here, if you'll please pardon the pun.

Positive Metaphors

There are also positive metaphors that can provide vital clues to the negotiator's style or the type of negotiation you might be encountering. Positive phrases that suggest a collaborative approach might include such phrases as:

- "mending fences"
- "building bridges"
- "hammering out our differences"
- "working through our problem"

Metaphors as a Self-Reflection

More importantly, we should ask ourselves what metaphors **we** like to use. The language we use during the business negotiation, even a casual, *off the cuff* remark, could have **reverberations** down the road. Metaphors can be used to telegraph out intent. If your counterpart jokingly suggests to you that they think you're only "*holding a pair of deuces,*" don't you think you're likely to sit up straight and wonder what they're really up to? On the other hand for example, if they suggest that "*we ought to be dancing more in sync,*" wouldn't that suggest that we might be headed towards a productive agreement that has good value for both sides?

Now, just **put yourself in your counterpart's shoes** and think about the metaphors that you might have uttered or employed during a negotiation. Ask yourself just what you might have been "*telegraphing*" to them! Were you suggesting a problem solving approach or a battle?

Conclusion

Language is everything. What you say and how you say it can be literally translated into how your counterpart will respond to you or vice versa. The business metaphors we employ in our negotiations can influence how either party is perceived by the other. We can also change the metaphors we use to influence the mood of a business negotiation and to bring about a result that is both positive and productive.

(From https://www.negotiations.com/articles/business-metaphors/)

Notes

1. Georg Christoph Lichtenberg (1 July 1742—24 February 1799) was a German scientist, satirist, and Anglophile. As a scientist, he was the first to hold a professorship explicitly dedicated to experimental physics in Germany. Today, he is remembered for his posthumously published notebooks, which he himself called *Sudelbücher*, a description modelled on the English bookkeeping term "scrapbooks", and for his discovery of the strange tree-like electrical discharge patterns now called Lichtenberg figures.

2. an icy glance, or nerves of steel：目光本身是没有"冰冷"的属性的，将冰的属性用在目光上，说明眼神反映出个人情感的冷漠；意志和钢铁也没有共性，但将钢铁的坚硬用在意志上，反映出意志的坚定。

Read the text and answer the questions.

1. What is *Metaphor*? What is it used for?
2. Why can metaphors be regarded as an Emotional Mirror?
3. What does "*combat*" metaphor mean?
4. Do you agree to the Negative Metaphors and Positive Metaphors listed in the text? Why and why not?
5. How can metaphors be used as a self-reflection?

要点小结

一、商务谈判语言的特征

在商务谈判中，无论采用何种谈判语言，都要具有以下特征：客观性、准确性、灵活性和逻辑性。

二、商务谈判语言的主要类型

从不同的角度，可以分出不同的语言类型，按语言表达的特征可分为：1. 礼节性语言；2. 专业性语言；3. 幽默诙谐式语言；4. 威胁、劝诱式语言。

三、选择谈判语言类型的原则

1. 根据双方关系选择语言；
2. 根据不同对象选择语言；
3. 根据不同的话题选择不同的语言。

Task 3　Language Skills in Business Negotiation Communication

商务谈判沟通的语言技巧

谈判是借助谈判者之间的信息传递来完成的，而在商务谈判中，信息的交流则需要通过谈判人员之间的听、问、答、说、辩等完成（这里的“说”是指说服）。在谈判过程中，必须仔细聆听对方的发言，捕捉到对方的意图，做出及时、灵活的反应，才能在谈判中占据有利的位置。

案例学习

Once there was a negotiation on herring between Norwegian government and Russian government. The offer of the Norwegian was extremely high, as it knew there was no other source of supply and the Russian had to purchase from it. Rounds and rounds of negotiations had passed but no result. Finally, Russian dispatched Alexandra Kollontai to negotiate, but there was still no agreement. Finally, Alexandra said, "Well, it seems I have to agree on your selling price. But if my government does not agree on the price, I have to compensate the difference with my salary, and I have to ask for installment as my salary is paid month by month." How can Norwegian men force a lady into such an embarrassed circumstance? Finally, the Norwegian gave in and decreased the offer price. Alexandra used her humor to realize the success of negotiation.

(From *Qiang Huang. Light-hearted Negotiation: the Skill of Wording in Business Negotiation*)

案例思考

1. Why did the Russian dispatch Alexandra to negotiate?
2. How did Alexandra solve the deadlock of the negotiation at last?
3. Why do you think Alexandra could succeed?
4. What does this case suggest?

案例解析

在该案例中，俄方和挪威方因价格问题使得谈判陷入了僵局。俄方派出 Alexandra 进行谈判，起初也并未有什么进展，直到最后，Alexandra 用了一句看似玩笑的话回答对方，却赢得了谈判最后的胜利。这句话字面意思是：如果对方坚持自己的价格，Alexandra 只能用自己的薪水填补其中的差价；实际上，是要告诉对方：俄方无论如何都无法接受这个价格，用一句玩笑话表明了俄方的底线和他们强硬的态度。挪威人为了将买卖做成功，只好降低自己的价格。

理论拓展

Negotiation Listening Skills
谈判中的倾听技巧

"*Do you hear what I hear?*" That's the flashing, neon question mark at crucial moments in our negotiations. When people, and this includes negotiators, gather together after hearing someone speak, we often hear dissimilar versions about what was said. People digest what others tell them and provide their own unique interpretation about what was said to them. This article explores how to go about boosting our negotiating listening powers.

What does listening mean?

First, listening is actually broken down into two specific functions. The first obvious function is the reception portion where we receive the message from the person speaking. The second function of listening is how we decode or interpret the message that we receive. This is the tricky one. Three categories of listening have been identified. All of us actively engage in these three forms of listening when someone is speaking to us, and it dissects each negotiation listening skill that we can effectively take advantage of to achieve our negotiation goals.

1) Passive Negotiation Listening Skills

Just as the phrase implies, we sit there like a sponge and absorb the message from the sender without any form of active engagement. We do not acknowledge what is being said to us, nor do we provide any feedback that we are absorbing.

Clearly, this **underscores** the importance of paying attention when we are listening. This strikingly illustrates why a negotiator should not be distracted by looking over or rifling through their notes and files, and not giving the speaker their full and undivided attention. We are being disrespectful to the speaker when we allow other things to distract us. Distractions will also cause us to miss some important information, or misunderstand a key section of the message. Passive negotiation listening skills require single-mindedness and concentration.

How else can this blaringly obvious **titbit** be of use to us?

Consider this possibility—there are people who cannot tolerate long silences. They need to fill in a lengthy silence gap with conversation. They simply can't keep quiet. When we encounter this sort of person in a negotiation, we may use the tactic of silence. It is highly likely that the person may begin a one way dialogue, or **divulge** information that we can use to our advantage. We can learn valuable information and perhaps enhance our agreement. Our negotiating counterparty may even talk themselves, into either accepting or deciding against a position, all on their own.

This type of negotiator is also susceptible to speak when, not having got a satisfactory response from him, all you need do, is remain silent and stare at the person expectantly. The talkative negotiator can no longer tolerate the silence and will begin to add or provide more information. This technique is also referred to as "*The Pregnant Pause*"[1].

2) Acknowledgement Listening Skills

Acknowledgement listening skills involve a slightly more active role in the listening process. It simply means that we provide a sign of recognition to the speaker, by sending them subtle messages. We accomplish this by telegraphing physical or other non-verbal signals to the narrator, to show that we are involved in the listening process. This is a visual clue that is a form of positive engagement and encourages the person who is speaking.

Using this listening skill, it is imperative that we make eye contact with the speaker as much as possible[2]. This will give the speaker validity and the confidence that their message is reaching us.

Other physical signals to show that we are tracking the relevant points, include nodding our head, saying "*mm-hmm.*", or "*I see*", or by making other physical gestures such as grinning at a pun.

Physical responses, like frowning or shaking our head, also inform the speaker whether we disagree with their position. This signifies that important issues are being resisted or disputed, and should perhaps be addressed immediately before proceeding further.

3) Active Negotiation Listening Skills

The final form of receiving the counterparty's message, involves verbal participation and is also referred to as "*reflective responding*". Essentially, the skilled negotiator listens and then repeats the phrase back to the speaker by re-phrasing what was said, best done using slightly different wording. For example, we might hear the speaker say something like "*I am particularly puzzled about how we are going to resolve the distribution conflict.*" You re-phrase it back to the speaker by saying "*I understand that you're stymied by this distribution challenge.*"

The majority of times that we use are reflective statements. We are making personal reference to the other party's feelings, positions or beliefs about something. In a sense, we **commiserate** with the speaker which acts as a bond or an abstract pat on the back as if to say, "*I hear you—I understand.*"

This type of active negotiation listening skills allows us to follow the speaker, without pressuring them, while permitting us to further explore this line of thought in greater detail. More importantly, we signal to the speaker that we are fully and actively engaged in what they have to share, and we often do so by responding to their feelings.

Summary

The listening process described above does not mean or suggest a negotiator should remain passive. We have our own business objectives and positions to put forward and persuade or defend. Effective negotiation skills in the arena of listening allow us to gain valuable information, information we can use to our benefit and advantage, at the same time, enabling us to learn more about the other party's positions and business objectives. Having more information at our disposal also allows us to reach our negotiation goals without conceding as much along the way. These negotiation skills require training in order to enjoy the results, and most of us develop effective listening skills rather than being born effective listeners.

(From https://www.negotiations.com/)

Notes

1. pregnant pause：耐人寻味的停顿

2. …, it is imperative that we make eye contact with the speaker as much as possible. It is imperative that sb. + (should) +谓语动词原形+其他成分。

Read the text and answer the questions.

1. What is the function of listening skills?
2. How many categories have listening skills been identified? What are they?
3. What will distractions cause?
4. What is the technique "The Pregnant Pause" referred to?
5. What are Acknowledgement Listening Skills? Give some examples.
6. What are Active Negotiation Listening Skills?

要点小结

一、商务谈判中“听”的技巧

（一）倾听的要点

1. 给对方创造发言的机会；2. 听取关键词；3. 反应式倾听。

（二）倾听的注意事项

1. 眼耳并用，弄清楚各种暗示；2. 边听边思考；3. 回顾和总结：在交谈时，回顾对方的话，整理出重点所在。

二、商务谈判中“问”的技巧

（一）提问的要点

1. 提问要有针对性；2. 提问态度要诚恳；3. 注意对手的状态。

（二）提问的注意事项

1. 提问的时间；2. 避免提出有关隐私、令人尴尬的问题。

三、商务谈判中“答”的技巧

（一）回答的要点

1. 留有思考的时间；2. 模糊回答；3. 重申和打岔：在谈判中，再次阐明对方所问的问题，实际上是争取思考的时间。

（二）回答的注意事项

1. 有所保留；2. 不知不答；3. 不留话柄。

四、商务谈判中“辩”和“说”

商务谈判中的“辩”和“说”，就是对听、问、叙等各种技巧的综合运用，因此，要灵活、多角度地运用以上的基本技巧。

Task 4 Non-Verbal Language in Business Negotiation Communication 商务谈判沟通的行为语言

交流分为有声交流和无声交流，商务谈判也是这样。无声交流在谈判中可为我们提供很多额外的信息，所谓无声交流，是指通过谈判者的行为、体态来反映谈判过程中谈判者的思想状态，主要包括眼神、表情、四肢的动作方式等。

案例学习

At the China Import and Export Fair (Spring Fair) in April 2016, a young Chinese businessman, Mr. Liu, was discussing the export of a chemical product with a young American businesswoman, Monica. After more than hours of intense negotiation, all other contract terms except for the price had been negotiated. When Monica asked for the final price, in order to win this new customer, Mr. Liu quoted the best price: USD2100 per ton FOB Qingdao port, China.

"Is this the lowest price?" Monica asked, her eyes fixed on Mr. Liu.

Never before had a foreign lady looked at herself this way, so close and so direct, especially a pretty young lady. Mr. Liu felt a little shy, lowered his head and said, "Yes, it's the lowest price."

To his surprise, the young American businesswoman stood up, left the negotiating table without hesitation, and never came back. Mr. Liu was very confused and puzzled.

A month later, Mr. Liu met with a Canadian client and asked the Canadian client about the reason for the incident. After listening, the Canadian client said, "Mr. Liu, you made a big mistake." Then, he told Mr. Liu the secret.

Fortunately, at the autumn fair in the same year, Mr. Liu met Lily, another American businesswoman. On the basis of learning from the last lesson, Mr. Liu was full of confidence this time. After more than two hours, other terms were negotiated. When Lily asked for the lowest price, Mr. Liu said: USD2300 per ton FOB Qingdao port, China, the lowest price! When the American businesswoman Lily stared straight at him, Mr. Liu also stared at her for more than a minute. To Mr. Liu's surprise, even though the offer was $200 per ton higher than the last time (the international market price did not change much during the same period), Lily accepted it happily instead of bargaining. The two sides shook hands **amicably** and signed the contract on the spot. The total contract price was $230,000.

(From https://wenku.baidu.com/view/)

案例思考

1. Why did Mr. Liu quote the lowest price at the Spring Fair and the American businesswoman did not accept it, but at the Autumn Fair, the American businesswoman accepted the price increase of $200 per ton?
2. The price offer given by Mr. Liu at Autumn Fair is obviously not the lowest price, but he claimed it was the lowest price. Is it dishonest behavior?

案例解析

本案例属于中美两国商人的价格谈判，而价格谈判受多方因素制约，譬如供求关系、产品质量、付款条件、品牌影响力、买卖双方的谈判力等等。而此案例的核心则是双方谈判力的非言语沟通因素：对目光接触的涵义，两个国家的商人有不同的理解。在中国，当男女之间沟通时，一般不直接看对方的眼睛，尤其不会盯得过久。否则，被视为不礼貌的行为；而在美国，则有一句俗语：不要相信不敢直视你眼睛的人。也就是说，在美国，如果你不敢直视对方的眼睛，那就意味着你没有说实话，你在撒谎。这正好解释了本案例第一次春交会上刘先生为什么失败的原因。当美国女商人莫妮卡问他是不是最低价时，他立刻移开了目光。对中国商人刘先生来讲，移开目光是因为出于对女士的尊重；而对美国女商人莫妮卡来讲，移开目光则意味着他在撒谎。于是，此次谈判失败。而在第二次秋交会上，刘先生从加拿大客户那里了解到了美国目光接触的含义，并巧妙地利用这个特点，每吨多报了 200 美元，并说是最低价格。当美国女商人莉莉双眼盯着他时，他双眼也紧紧地盯着对方，时间超过一分钟。敢于这么长时间地直视自己的眼睛，美国女商人就认为他说了实话，于是就愉快地签了合同。

另外， 刘先生在秋交会上的报价明明不是最低价，却谎称是最低价。从商务谈判的视角，刘先生的做法是对的，因为他掌握了中美文化差异中目光接触的不同涵义，了解了对方的特点，属于谈判力强的范畴。从企业视角，这样做也是对的，因为在法律许可范围内，追求利润最大化是企业的天职。从商业惯例来讲，这样做也符合要求，因为在谈判中，卖方常常说自己赔本了，买方却常常说自己买贵了，这些都属于正常的谈判技巧，不属于诚实和欺诈的范畴，只要双方合作，对双方都是有益的，只是利益大小不同而已。

理论拓展

Non-Verbal Communication—Actions Speak Louder than Words
非言语交流——行动比言语更响亮

Scenario 1—You are sitting in front of an interview **panel** with arms crossed. So far you have not been asked a single question, however, your crossed arms have spoken louder than the words.

Tip 1—Never keep your arms crossed especially during formal one-on-one meetings. It suggests you are not open to feedback and could also suggest that you are trying to dominate the situation.

Scenario 2—You are giving a presentation to a group of 20 people. You keep your gaze fixed at the centre of the class/room through the presentation—your gaze has spoken louder than your words.

Tip 2—Your gaze at one person should not be more than 4-5 seconds while delivering a presentation/communicating with a large group unless you are addressing an individual.

Scenario 1 and 2 clearly demonstrate the importance of Non-Verbal Communication.

What Is Non-Verbal Communication?

It is communication of feelings, emotions, attitudes, and thoughts through body movements/gestures/eye contact, etc.

The Components of Non-Verbal Communication Are:

- Kinesics: It is the study of facial expressions, postures & gestures. Did you know that while in Argentina to raise a fist in the air with knuckles pointing outwards expresses victory, in Lebanon, raising a closed fist is considered rude?
- Oculesics: It is the study of the role of eye contact in non-verbal communication. Did you know that in the first 90 sec-4 min you decide that you are interested in someone or not. Studies reveal that 50% of this first impression comes from non-verbal communication which includes oculesics. Only 7% comes from words—that we actually say.
- Haptics: It is the study of touching. Did you know that acceptable level of touching varies from one culture to another? In Thailand, touching someone's head may be considered as rude.
- Proxemics: It is the study of measurable distance between people as they interact. Did you know that the amount of personal space when having an informal conversation should vary between 18 inches[1]-4 feet[2] while, the personal distance needed when speaking to a crowd of people should be around 10-12 feet?
- Chronemics: It is the study of use of time in non-verbal communication. Have you ever

observed that while an employee will not worry about running a few minutes late to meet a colleague, a manager who has a meeting with the CEO, a late arrival will be considered as a non-verbal cue that he/she does not give adequate respect to his superior?

- Paralinguistics: It is the study of variations in pitch, speed, volume, and pauses to convey meaning. Interestingly, when the speaker is making a presentation and is looking for a response, he will pause. However, when no response is desired, he will talk faster with minimal pause.

- Physical Appearancc: Your physical appearance always contributes towards how people perceive you. Neatly combed hair, ironed clothes and a lively smile will always carry more weight than words.

Remember, "what we say" is less important than "how we say it" as words are only 7% of our communication. Understand and enjoy non-verbal communication as it helps forming better first impressions.

(From https://www.managementstudyguide.com/non-verbal-communication.htm)

Notes

1. inch：英寸，1 英寸相当于 2.5 厘米
2. feet：英尺，1 英尺为 12 英寸，相当于 30 厘米

Read the text and answer the questions.

1. Do you think Tip 1 and Tip 2 are useful for these two scenarios? Why?
2. Can you summarize the definition of "non-verbal communication" with your own words?
3. Which components of non-verbal communication listed above do you think is most important? Why?
4. Why is it said "Actions speak louder than words"?

要点小结

不同的民族、地区，不同的文化，其动作行为会传达出不同的信息，因此谈判者应在所处的具体环境中分析非语言信息。另外，我们在观察对方的行为动作时，不能只从某一个静止的、孤立的行为去判断，应该分析和观察连续的、一系列的动作，并结合对方的面部表情及语调、语气进行分析，这样才能得出可信、真实、全面的结论。

综合实训

Task 1 In the case study of task 1, Factors and Types of Business Negotiation Communication, if you were the representative of the U.S. company or the representative of the Japanese Company, how would you repair damaged relationships and present the scenario? Please work in pairs.

Task 2 Role-play: for this task, you need read the article *Use Clever Questions in Your Negotiations* first. Then display the negotiation scenario of asking good questions and bad questions based on the case following this article.

Use Clever Questions in Your Negotiations

"Are you simple or what?" Bet we now have your attention. Do you use and can you tell the various types of negotiation questions apart? How often can you tell when your chain is being pulled, in order to get a "fight or flight" response?

"The pen is mightier than the sword." This is only partially true. The power of the spoken word should be more powerful or impactful. The tone or volume we use in our voice can be as blunt as steel or as calming as a lullaby to a sleepy eyed child. We don't expect this is news to you. Yet, often we don't give particular thought to how we really effectively communicate. Language can be used and played like a melodious violin, or annoy our senses like itchy, irritating hives. Oft times, we neglect to use our communication skills in our negotiation to our best advantage.

Good Questions vs. Bad Questions

Asking questions the right way is both an art and a science. The negotiation experts answers our site visitors' question for free, but only those that we consider of value to our readers. Ask the question the wrong way and a person might act like a turtle, becoming defensive and withdrawing into their shell. Ask the questions another wrong way and a person might roar back at you like an enraged lion. Ask it the right way, and the person might "spill the bean" like they use to say in those old black and white movies. During a negotiation, we need to learn how to ask questions to get vital information, and we need to think about how to ask questions to get our counterparts to talk.

These really are the only two types of questions. Good questions produce results while bad questions don't. Sounds simple enough, doesn't it? But what's the real difference between the two? Let's take a look and hone our communications skills.

Effective and Useful Questions

The following are the most productive types of questions to ask in a negotiation. When you are attempting to elicit information, you need to phrase your question with the objective that you will obtain a beneficial and productive response that you can use to you advantage.

1. Open-ended questions

These are the kinds of questions that require a detailed answer in a negotiation and cannot be simply replied to with a "yes" or "no" response. They consist of using who, what, where, when, why, and how. The respondent has no alternative but to provide some detail.

Example—"How did you arrive at that particular price?"

2. Open opportunity question

This form of question invites the person to participate and offer their views.

Example—"What do you think of this option as a solution?"

3. Leading question

Just like it sounds, you try to guide the person to your point of view in a persuasive manner.

Example—"With all these advantages I've pointed out, don't you think that this package benefits us both and is the best way to go for both of us?"

Or, another form of leading negotiation question simply tails off and invites the other person to fill in the blanks.

Example—"And after we provide those documents that you just mentioned, you will...?"

4. Low key question

This is a gentle way to ask a question and not trigger an emotional or hostile response.

Example—"How much more will this cost if we chose this additional feature?"

5. Sequential questions

Sometimes, it can be very good strategy to ask a series of questions to lead up and achieve a particular result or conclusion. Generally, it might be a good idea to plan these in advance.

Example—"And after you complete the first delivery, how long will it take for you to have the second shipment ready and sent to us?"

6. Flattery question

This is an effective means to be both complimentary to your counterpart while eliciting information from them, both at the same time. Everyone responds well to a friendly compliment.

Example—"Could we draw upon your particular and specialized expertise to add some input into this particular issue?"

7. Probing deeper question

When you need to gain a better insight into a person's thought process to further illuminate their rationale or position.

Example—"Could you provide us with more detail in how you analyzed the data that you just described and how you reached your conclusion?"

8. Emotional thermometer

There are occasions when you will sense that something might be starting to boil beneath the surface. This might be a good time to address a pending emotional response that might de-rail the negotiation by simply checking out how the other person feels about certain issues. Example—"How do you feel about that aspect of settlement package?"

Landmine questions

These are the kinds of questions that can be very counter productive, confrontational and evoke negative emotional responses. When used in wrong stage of a negotiation, you might put your counterpart on the defensive or cause them to respond aggressively in return. Either way, your negotiation could end up being de-railed without your intending to self-destruct.

1. Aggressive

Certain kinds of questions can result in being too pushy, especially when used at the wrong stage of your negotiation.

Example—"You're not trying to pull a fast one on us are you?"

2. Loaded

This style of question puts the person on the hot seat regardless of their responding to the answer, and therefore in very defensive position. It is very aggressive.

Example—"Do you expect me to believe that this is the only acceptable solution that you will accept?"

3. Emotional trigger

Certain questions will definitely result in triggering a powerful emotional response particularly when posed with a tint of arrogance or insulting scorn. You are definitely not going to add to your knowledge base by adopting this type of question because it's like shooting yourself in the foot in the process.

Example—"Do you really think that this ridiculous proposal is worth wasting my time?"

4. Impulsive

This is the type of question that pops out of your mouth before you gave it any thought.

Always think—then ask, not the other way around.

Any inappropriate question can serve as an example here.

5. Tricky

These are the questions that are loaded with innuendo, and may imply a threat or some similar action.

Example—"Are you going to cede to the demands we've outlined, or take us to arbitration?"

This is not to say that occasionally the so-called bad questions aren't productive in prompting a necessary reaction or response in the right situation to move things along. However, they are not the kinds of question that will elicit badly needed information, or that can be positively used when you are trying to build a partnership or relationship with your opposite number.

Summary

When you are asking questions to get information you need to evaluate the circumstances of your negotiation, you want your counterpart to work with you and not against you. It is important to think about how to best use your communication skills to get the best results. The manner in which you ask your questions can have a powerful bearing on the results of your negotiation so, and as they say, "Think before you speak."

(From https://www.negotiations.com/articles/negotiation-questions/)

Now display the following negotiation scenario by asking good and bad questions.

Negotiation Scenario
吉利收购沃尔沃谈判

买方背景

浙江吉利控股集团是中国汽车行业十强企业。1997 年进入轿车领域以来，吉利公司凭借灵活的经营机制和持续的自主创新，取得了快速的发展，2009 年资产总值超过 170 亿元人民币，连续九年进入中国企业 500 强，连续七年进入中国汽车行业十强，被评为首批国家“创新型企业”和“国家汽车整车出口基地企业”。吉利旗下品牌有全球鹰、帝豪、英伦，分别代表了不同的品牌诉求。

卖方背景

福特（Ford）是美国著名的汽车公司（Ford Motor company），公司的创始人是亨利 • 福特（Henry Ford）。福特汽车公司是世界上最大的汽车生产商之一，成立于 1903 年，旗下拥有福特、林肯、马自达、沃尔沃等汽车品牌，总部位于密歇根州迪尔伯恩市（Dearborn）。1999 年，福特以 64.5 亿美元收购 VOLVO 汽车公司，与路虎、捷豹和阿斯顿马丁共同成为福特汽车公司首席汽车集团（PAG）旗下成员。

市场背景

吉利公司在 2009 年度净收益额从 2008 年度的 8.79 亿元人民币合每股净收益 0.14 元人民币增长至 11.8 亿元人民币（约合 1.73 亿美元），合每股净收益 0.17 元人民币。而当年公司的销售额也翻了三倍之多，从之前的 42.9 亿元人民币飙升到 141 亿元人民币。

沃尔沃，英文名为 Volvo，瑞典著名汽车品牌，由沃尔沃集团和沃尔沃汽车公司共同拥有。沃尔沃品牌于 1927 年在瑞典哥德堡创建，创始人是古斯塔夫 • 拉尔松和阿萨尔 • 加布里尔松。1999 年，沃尔沃集团将旗下的沃尔沃轿车业务出售给美国福特汽车公司。沃尔沃被收购前的盈利状况一直不理想，2008 年巨亏 15 亿美元，其销量比 2007 年降幅达 20%以上。但沃尔沃品牌价值较高，在 1972 年就向联合国提出了汽车的环保责任，几十年来持之以恒，在汽车环保和安全方面不断实现创造发明，其中包括汽车安全车厢、三点式安全带、安全玻璃、三元催化器、安全气囊、ABS、儿童安全座椅、侧撞保护系统、城市安全系统、全力自动刹车和行人探测的碰撞警示系统等。沃尔沃计划到

2020年实现零排放零伤亡。这是一家欧洲汽车公司为全人类做出的卓越贡献。

谈判背景与目标

此次谈判前我方已经与福特公司进行过多次交涉，因此，这次谈判主要的目标在于以下三方面：

（一）在收购价上与福特公司代表达成共识。

（二）明确包括知识产权等在内的股权以及在收购过程中沃尔沃与福特的知识产权分拆问题。

（三）展示我们完成这次收购的实力和信心以及帮助沃尔沃未来发展的能力（具体目标如下）。

1. 最优期望目标：16亿美元收购沃尔沃100%股权，吉利拥有其所有技术和知识产权的所有权，包括沃尔沃在安全与环保方面的知识产权。

2. 最低限度目标：21亿美元收购沃尔沃100%股权，吉利拥有其关键技术和知识产权的所有权，包括沃尔沃在安全与环保方面的知识产权。

3. 可接受目标：16亿—20亿美元收购沃尔沃100%股权，吉利拥有其关键技术和知识产权。

Task 3: Case Study

Dan Smith 是一位美国的健身用品经销商，此次是 Robert Liu 第一回与他交手。就在短短几分钟的交谈中，Robert Liu 立即感到这位大汉粗犷的外表，藏有狡兔的心思——他肯定是沙场老将，自己绝不可掉以轻心。

First round of talks

D: I'd like to **get the ball rolling** by talking about prices.

R: Shoot. I'd be happy to answer any questions you may have.

D: Your products are very good. But I'm a little worried about the prices you're asking.

R: You think about asking for more? (laughs)

D: (chuckles) That's not exactly what I had in mind. I know your research costs are high, but what I'd like is a 25% discount.

R: That seems to be a little high, Mr. Smith. I don't know how we can make a profit with those numbers.

D: Please, Robert, call me Dan. (pause) Well, if we promise future business-**volume sales**—that will **slash your costs** for making the exerciser, right?

R: Yes, but it's hard to see how you can place such large orders. How could you **turn over** so many? (pause) We'd need a guarantee of future business, not just a promise.

D: We said we wanted 1,000 pieces over a six-month period. What if we place orders for twelve months, with a guarantee?

R: If you can guarantee that on paper, I think we can discuss this further.

Directions: If you were Robert or Dan, how would you negotiate in the second round of talks to get the deal done? Discuss the question with your partner and role-play the

conversation with your own ideas.

Second round of talks.

R: Even with volume sales, our coats for the exerciser won't go down much.

D: Just what are you proposing?

R: We could **take a cut** on the price. But 25% would slash our **profit margin**. We suggest a compromise—10%.

D: That's a big change from 25! 10 is beyond my negotiating limit. (pause) Any other ideas?

R: I don't think I can change it right now. Why don't we talk again tomorrow?

D: Sure. I must talk to my office anyway. I hope we can find some **common ground** on this.

Directions: If you were Robert or Dan, how would you negotiate in the third round of talks to get the deal done? Discuss the question with your partner and role-play the conversation with your own ideas.

Next day

D: Robert, I've been instructed to reject the numbers you proposed; but we can try to come up with something else.

R: I hope so, Dan. My instructions are to negotiate hard on this deal—but I'm trying very hard to **reach some middle ground**.

D: I understand. We propose **a structured deal**. For the first six months, we get a discount of 20%, and the next six months we get 15%.

R: Dan, I can't bring those numbers back to my office—they'll **turn it down flat**.

D: Then you'll have to think of something better, Robert.

R: How about 15% the first six months, and the second six months at 12%, with a guarantee of 3,000 units?

D: That's a lot to sell, with very low profit margins.

R: It's about the best we can do, Dan. (pause) We need to **hammer something out** today. If I go back empty-handed, I may be coming back to you soon to ask for a job. (smiles)

D: (smiles) OK, 17% the first six months, 14% for the second?

R: Good. Let's **iron out** the remaining details. When do you want to **take delivery**?

D: We'd like you to execute the first order by the 31st.

R: Let me run through this again: the first shipment for 1,500 units, to be delivered in 27 days, by the 31st.

D: Right. We couldn't handle much larger shipments.

R: Fine. But I'd prefer the first shipment to be 1,000 units, the next 2,000. The 31st is quite soon—I can't guarantee 1,500.

D: I can agree to that. Well, if there's nothing else, I think we've settled everything.

R: Dan, this deal **promises big returns** for both sides. Let's hope it's the beginning of a long and prosperous relationship.

(From https://www.langfly.com/a/20100713/132126.shtml)

Group Work

Answer the questions.

1. How many types of business communication does this case present and what are they?
2. What factor is the key to the success of the negotiation? Why?
3. Do you think the non-verbal communication in this case is important? Why?

Task 4

选择当地某一正在销售的楼盘作为谈判情景，将学生分成小组，每两个小组之间进行商品房买卖的价格谈判。

（1）谈判中双方小组可以使用听、问、答、说、辩等各种技巧，阐述己方的立场和观点。

（2）双方互相进行身体语言的暗示，分析其含义。

（3）根据谈判的进程，实时记录对方使用各种语言技巧以及非语言技巧后给己方带来的心理、战术上的改变。

实践语句

在商务谈判中，有时不能给对方一个确切的答案，但是又不能一口否定，那么要使谈判有回旋的余地就得回避明确的答复。

1. I'm afraid I can't give you a definite reply now.
恐怕我现在无法给你一个明确的答复。
2. I can't make a decision right now.
我现在无法做出决定。
3. I just need some time to think it over.
我需要时间考虑考虑。
4. We are still a little unsure about the prospect, though.
不过，我们对于前景还是有点不能确定。
5. There are certain points that I'll have to consider very carefully.
有些问题我得慎重考虑。
6. That may well be so. I'm not sure.
很可能是这样的，我不敢确定。
7. We'll have to talk it over some more.
看来我们还得再谈一谈。

8. Let's see if we can work it out to your satisfaction.
我们来看看是否有什么办法让你满意。
9. When can you come around to discuss some details with us?
什么时候可以过来讨论细节呢？
10. It all depends.
这得看情况而定。

词语释文

amicably	*adv.* 友善地
commiserate	*vt.* 表示慰问；同情
connotation	*n.* 含义
divulge	*vt.* 泄露
howl	*vt.* 嚎叫；叫喊，吼叫；怒号；啸鸣
intimidation	*n.* 恐吓
jargon	*n.* 行话
panel	*n.* 评委小组；讨论小组
reverberation	*n.* 回响；回声；后果
tactic	*n.* 策略；战术，手段
titbit	*n.* 小片食物；趣闻
terminology	*n.* 专门用语；术语
underscore	*vt.* 在……下面画线；强调；*n.* 下画线
unravel	*vt.* 解开；澄清
vigilant	*adj.* 警惕的

a structured deal	阶段式合约
boil rage (*or* boil with rage)	形容发怒至极无法抑制
carte blanche	全权；具有/被授予全权（做某事）
common ground	共同信念
get the ball rolling	开始
hammer something out	敲定某事
in fits and starts	凭一时高兴
iron out	解决
profit margin	毛利润
promise big returns	实现高额回报
put oneself in one's shoes	设身处地为某人着想
reach some middle ground	互相妥协

shoot! colloquial (speak out)	说出来
slash one's costs	大量降低成本
take a cut	降低
take delivery	取货
turn it down flat	断然拒绝
turn over	售出
volume sales	大量销售
walk away with	轻松赢得；获得；错拿；顺手牵羊拿走

Unit 5 Strategies and Tactics for Business Negotiations

商务谈判策略与技巧

任务目标

1. Knowing the strategic considerations
2. Knowing and applying five common negotiation strategies
3. Knowing and applying negotiation tactics for five common negotiation strategies
4. Developing and practicing negotiation strategies and tactics under different situations

商务谈判本身是一个合作的利己主义过程，谈判双方在这个过程中，为了实现各自利益的最大化，需要展开一场综合的较量。这种较量不仅体现在实力上，更体现在心理和智力上。因此，双方会根据谈判形式的变化制定相应的谈判策略和技巧，不同策略和技巧的应用会导致不同的谈判结果，是影响谈判成败的重要因素。

Task 1 Strategic Considerations

策略思考

在商务谈判中，谈判人员的素质、经济实力、拥有的信息量、准备的情况等诸多因素会影响谈判形势以及谈判所使用的策略，从而导致谈判结果的不同。

案例学习

Orvel Ray wanted to shop for a used piano, the seller was asking $1,000, and it would have been a bargain at that price. In order to search for a negotiating advantage, Orvel was able to deduce several facts from the surroundings. The piano was in a furnished basement, which also contained a set of drums and an upright acoustic base. Obviously the seller was a serious musician. There had to be a compelling reason for selling such a beautiful instrument.

Orvel asked the first question: "Are you buying a new piano?"

The seller hesitated. "Well, I don't know yet. See, we're moving to North Carolina, and it would be very expensive to ship this piano clear across the country."

"Did they say how much extra it would cost?" Orvel queried.

"They said an extra $300 or so."

"When do you have to consider?"

"The packers are coming this afternoon."

Now Orvel knew where the seller was vulnerable. "Here's what I can do: I can give you $700 in cash right now, and I can have a truck and three of my friends here to move it out of your way by noon today."

The seller hesitated: "Well, I suppose that would work. I can always buy a new piano when we get settled."

Orvel left before the seller could reconsider. By the time the group returned with the truck, the seller had received three other offers at his asking price, but because he had accepted the cash, he had to tell them that the piano had already been sold.

（From J. C. Levinson, M. S. A. Smith, O. R. Wilson. Guerrilla Negotiating [M]. New York: John Wiley, 1999: 15-16.）

案例思考

1. Why do you think this negotiation can be concluded so fast?

2. Do you think this is dealing for one-time or long-term cooperation? What are the differences to deal with?

3. During this negotiation, which party do you think is in a relatively strong position? Why?

4. Do you think "time" is important in this case? Why?

案例解析

本案例是一次性交易，双方没有再合作的可能，谈判者无须过多考虑为维系双方关系而做出不必要的让步。因此 Orvel 利用对话套出卖方的信息，成功得知对方交易的底线在哪里，强势地结束了本次谈判并取得交易的成功。

理论拓展

Pre-Negotiation Strategy Check List
谈判前的策略审核清单

1) Assess the Situation

Each negotiation is going to be different, no matter how often we've addressed similar situations. We will always be negotiating with people who have different styles, goals and objectives, and who are coming from different circumstances and have different standards. So, always take stock and **gauge** each negotiation as something unique.

2) What Kind of Negotiation?

There are basically 3 circumstances to consider.

Is it a one-time negotiation, where we will unlikely interact with the person or company again?

Is it a negotiation that we are going to be repeating again?

Is it a negotiation where we are going to form some kind of long term relationship?

Most of our business negotiations are likely going to fall in the last two categories. We will be handling a lot of repeat negotiations, where we negotiate with regular suppliers, or engage in labor negotiations with the same union reps for example. Or, we will be seeking a long-term negotiated agreement such as a joint venture, where we will be mutually entwined over a long period of time.

3) What Does This Negotiation Mean to Us?

There are only two reasons why we enter into a negotiation.

The first reason occurs when out of necessity, we have to. This could be due to either some immediate need, such as urgency to find a particular supplier, or it could be that we face severe cutbacks in personnel, if we can't increase our business. The second reason occurs when we are seeking out an opportunity. This situation may arise simply because an opportunity has sprung up, where we can increase our overall business at an opportune time. The reason for entering into a negotiation will affect both our approach and strategy, and also our relative negotiating power in comparison to our counterpart.

4) Is the Clock Ticking?

Time has an impact on the course of negotiations from two perspectives. Firstly, there are deadlines that might be imposed, to either make or break an agreement. Offers with expiry dates may be tendered.

Secondly, we all know that “Time is money”. Negotiations use up time, and if a plant is shut down while the clock is ticking because of a strike, then this is costing money. Or, it could be due to some other resource issue, such as waiting for badly needed components, in order to resume production. The point to remember is that the longer the negotiations drag out, time will negatively affect the bottom line.

5) Who Is Going to Blink First[1]?

There are situations when we have to decide how a proposal or offer is to be presented, or in deciding who is going to go first. Will we make an informal proposal before we start the negotiations, or wait until we meet face to face? Will we be prepared to make an offer after listening to their proposal, or do we need more information? Will we respond right away, or refer the matter to our constituencies? Will it be to our advantage to be first in making an offer or proposal, to set an anchor around which the talks revolve? Or will it be better to hold our cards tight to our chest and let the other side go first? Of course, this will all relate to the issues, positions, goals and objectives that will determine our approach. These are very serious questions that we need to intelligently address, before we begin our talks.

6) Are We Strong or Weak?

Two or more parties who are about to engage in a negotiation, seldom operate from an equal power base. If one party has something that we desperately need, for our company's survival and we have no alternatives, then we may find ourselves negotiating at a disadvantage. This all relates to our BATNA and how we stack up against our potential counterpart. Size is not necessarily relevant, as we've all heard the old biblical account of “David versus Goliath”[2], and how that conflict turned out.

Weakness can be countered by strengthening our BATNA, or even by finding allies to support our position and add to our strength. Also, we should seek ways to diminish the power base of the opposing party where possible, before we begin our negotiations, or even during the negotiation process itself.

Summary

Negotiation strategies need to be developed by considering a whole host of factors that might have a powerful impact on our success. It is also wise to remember that our strategy has to be flexible and will need to be adjusted as the game plays itself out. We cannot know everything before we go into our first meeting, so we need to prepare to adjust our strategy and tactics, as the situations warps and changes shape. Flexibility is vital, but good preparation is essential.

(From https://www.negotiations.com/articles/negotiations-need/)

Notes

1. blink first：踏出第一步。

2. David versus Goliath：David 是圣经故事里的一个英雄，他年纪轻轻就上战场，对战 Goliath。Goliath 则是圣经故事里的一个巨人，他身形巨大，比 David 健硕。但最后，David 却把 Goliath 杀死。David versus Goliath 的意思是一个看起来弱小的人对战一个人高马大的人。

Read the text and answer the questions.

1. What strategic considerations does this text present?
2. Why should we enter into a negotiation?
3. Do you think blinking first is good or not during a negotiation? Why?
4. When you are in a weak position, what can you do?

要点小结

采取策略考虑的因素一般包括：

（1）是否属于能重复进行的谈判；（2）谈判双方的实力；（3）交易的重要性；（4）时间节点；（5）谈判的资源：谈判的资源也会对谈判策略的选择产生影响，比如，谈判之前对对方的信息搜集、备选的谈判方案等。

Task 2 Five Common Negotiation Strategies
五项基本谈判策略

策略指的是根据形势发展而制定的行动方针，是为谈判目标而制定，并随谈判形势发展而修改。谈判策略在商务谈判场合的应用，是谈判人员为实现预期谈判目标，在谈判过程中采取的各种战术、技巧、方法、手段的集合。

案例学习

"Hey Paul, would you come on over to my place a little before three?" Orlo asked his neighbor during a phone call. "I've got someone coming over to look at the old Cadillac, and I need some competition… just act interested."

When the prospect showed up, he saw two men poking around under the hood. Orlo greeted him, and introduced him to Paul who glanced up and grunted. After a quick tour of the car, the prospect was obviously interested. "You mind if I take it for a spin?" he ventured. Orlo looked at Paul. Paul shrugged his shoulders, "Sure. Remember, I was here first." The prospect returned, impressed with roominess and comfortable ride. "OK, how much do you want?"

Orlo quoted the price listed in the newspaper, and Paul objected, "Hey!"

The prospect stuck out his hand. "I'll take it!"

Orlo looked sheepishly at Paul and shook the now-buyer's hand.

After the new owner left, Paul said, "I can't believe that he paid you that much for that old car!"

(From Leigh Steinberg. Winning with Integrity [M]. New York: Random House,1998: 47.)

案例思考

1. Why do you think this negotiation can be successful?
2. What kind of strategies do you think Orlo has used to achieve this negotiation success?

案例解析

该案例采用的策略是典型的竞争型策略——要么赢，要么输。Orlo 为了实现自己的利益最大化，请自己的邻居来假装买家之一，让真正的买家误认为这场交易的竞争很激烈，从而在没有认真考虑的情况下就草草买下了这辆二手车。

根据不同的谈判形势，可供选择的谈判策略可分为以下五种：（1）合作（Collaborating）；（2）妥协（Compromising）；（3）随遇而安（Accommodating）；（4）竞争（Competing）和（5）回避（Avoiding）。

理论拓展

Negotiation Strategy: Seven Common Pitfalls to Avoid
谈判策略：可以避免的七个常见陷阱

Whether you're negotiating for your firm or for your position in it, you'll do better if you avoid some common pitfalls.

Successful bargaining means looking for positives in every possible circumstance. "If I can trade off issues that I care about more and you care about less, then we've been able to create value in a transaction," says Margaret Neale, professor of organizational behavior and director of two Stanford GSB executive education programs in negotiation. "That's the **silver lining**."

Sometimes negotiators fall into traps and leave resources on the table because they can't see that **silver lining**. Some common pitfalls are:

1. Poor Planning

Successful negotiators make detailed plans. They know their priorities—and alternatives—should they fail to reach an agreement. You must know your bottom line, your walkaway point. In addition, you need to understand time constraints and know whether this is the only time you will see your opponents in negotiation.

After preparing your own agenda, outline the same for your opponents: What are their preferences, alternatives, and bottom line? Once at the bargaining table, test your hypotheses to determine what the opposition's priorities really are. Prepare a written goal and analysis sheet for yourself.

2. Thinking the Pie Is Fixed

Usually it's not. You may make this common mistake when there is a "**congruent** issue," when both parties want the same thing. For example: In the context of an overall negotiation involving salary, bonus, and vacation, the boss wants to transfer a junior manager to San Francisco. The manager is eager for the San Francisco assignment. But frequently, the employee will look at the situation and believe that since the boss gave him a desired promotion the employee must compromise on the transfer location. The employee might actually suggest a transfer to Atlanta. His psychology is: "I can't expect to get everything I want, so I'll take the middle." The boss is **ambivalent** about the transfer and figures she can get someone else to go to San Francisco.

3. Failing to Pay Attention to Your Opponent

Negotiators need to analyze the biases their opponents bring to the table. How will they evaluate your offers?

One way to get inside your opponent's head and influence his attitude is to shape the issues for him, a technique called "framing." If you get your opponent to accept your view of the situation, then you can influence the amount of risk he is willing to take.

For example, you are a purchasing manager renegotiating an hourly wage contract with a subcontractor. The subcontractor currently makes $10 an hour. You are willing to elevate the subcontracting firm to $11 an hour. Another organization recently boosted its rate with your subcontractor to $12 an hour. You know that when the negotiators for your subcontractor hear your $11 offer, they may think they are going to have to give up a dollar an hour.

You must get them to focus on the point you are starting from—$10, not $12. You frame the issue positively by talking about all the ways your contract is different from the others. Your contract has some advantages outside of the hourly pay. The other side will be more willing to risk lower wages for the purported other benefits. A common mistake is negotiating from a negative frame: "The other firm's deal offers more, but we can afford only $11."

4. Assuming That Cross-Cultural Negotiations Are Just Like "Local" Negotiations

You need to remember that differences do exist, that they are not necessarily negative, and that these differences can create huge potential benefits—as well as big problems if ignored. Services and negotiations need to be tailored to enhance your position with the other side.

Neale uses a case study that centers on the construction of a large American theme park in Europe. To convince local government officials that an American park would be a great opportunity, the American developers brought the European officials to a theme park in the United States.

Unknown to the American executives, the Europeans were dismayed and shocked with what they observed: highly commercialized American culture blasting from every fast-food bar, bandstand, and gift shop. This was not what they had envisaged for their **quaint** countryside.

Trying to dream up more **enticements** during the negotiation, the clueless American executives offered more free trips to the U.S. park for an expanded group of local European officials and their families. It was a disaster.

Had the Americans had a sensitive negotiator on the ground in Europe, they could have capitalized on the differences in the two cultures and offered a detailed presentation of an amusement park tailored to local tastes, skipping the **junkets** to the U.S. park.

5. Paying Too Much Attention to Anchors

Anchors are part of a bargaining dynamic known as "anchoring and adjustment[1]." This involves clearly setting the parameters for negotiation. For example, a couple was selling their house for $500,000. The first offer came in at $375,000, which was too low to consider. If the couple had acknowledged the offer with a counter, they would have started bargaining somewhere between $500,000 and $375,000. Instead, they responded that it was not a reasonable offer and told the buyers to come back when they had a decent offer. The buyers came back at $425,000. The seller then countered at $495,000. The buyers then came up to $430,000, but the sellers still didn't accept the offer.

The buyers argued that they had come up $55,000 from $375,000. But the sellers were careful to remind them that $375,000 was not their starting point; rather, it was $425,000, the first reasonable offer. Using that anchor, the sellers argued that they had come down $5,000 from $500,000—and the buyer had come up $5,000 from $425,000. Both had moved the same amount in negotiations. One more round of bidding had the house sold—for a price well above the buyer's initial bid. "The point is: You've got to watch the anchors and where they are set," says Neale.

6. Caving in Too Quickly

Accepting a well-priced deal too quickly can cause anger on the other side, too. If you list a used car for $5,000, you might really be thinking of accepting $4,500. But when your first buyer has it checked by a mechanic and then immediately writes you a check for $5,000 without trying to bargain, how do you feel? Disappointed. You'll think you sold it for too little. The lesson is: No matter what the price, even if it's fair, always offer less—if only to make your opponent feel good about the deal. You may come up to full price in the end, but at least your opponent will feel as if he made you work for it. "Never give anyone their first offer; it makes them crazy," says Neale.

7. Don't Gloat

Finally, when you've cut a sweet deal, never do the dance of joy in public by turning to your opponents and telling them you would have done it for less. Gloating will only drive your opponent to extract the difference from you sometime in the future. Today, flagging corporate allegiances and rampant job hopping make it essential to keep on professional terms with your negotiating opponents. You may find yourself on the same side of the bargaining table one day.

(From https://www.negotiations.com/articles/#articles)

Note

anchoring and adjustment：锚定与调整法则，经济学术语，指在没有把握的情况下，人们通常利用某个参照点和锚（anchor）来降低模糊性，然后再通过一定的调整来得出最后的结论。

Read the text and answer the questions.

1. How do you understand the phrase "The pie is fixed"? What does the "pie" refer to?
2. How do you understand the technique "framing"? Please explain in your own words.
3. Why was it a disaster that the American executives offered free trips to the U.S. park for the local European officials and their families?
4. Which one do you agree most about the 7 pitfalls? Why?

要点小结

谈判是一个动态的过程，不宜在谈判开始之前对谈判全过程制定过细的策略。谈判过程随时可能会出现意想不到的变化，谈判者需要根据具体的情况采取相应的策略。谈判的策略大致分为竞争策略（Competing）、随遇而安策略（Accommodating）、回避策略（Avoiding）、妥协策略（Compromising）、合作策略（Collaborating）等。

Task 3 Tactics for Each Negotiation Strategy
谈判策略的技巧

一般来说，策略是在谈判过程中采用的各种技巧的组合，而技巧是实施该策略具体适用的方法。在谈判中，善于运用谈判技巧的一方，往往会得到交易中的大部分利益，而不善于运用者只能得到他本来应得利益中的一部分，这就是谈判技巧的效用所在。

案例学习

K. G. Marwin Inc. developed a particular technology, called the Trilliamp Process, that the Chinese government sought to buy and integrate into an ethylene facility in Lanzhou, the capital city of Gansu Province. Marwin recommended the Japanese company Auger-Aiso whose chief negotiator was Todman Glazer as most capable of producing the turbines, while the Chinese invited two U.S. companies—Federal Electric and Pressure Inc., which manufactured through the large Japanese trading company Mitsubo—to compete for the multi-million-dollar sales negotiation contract.

At the first sales negotiation meeting in Beijing, the Chinese insisted that custom required the visitor—Glazer—to make the first sales negotiation presentation. This he did, even though he was trained to allow his opponents to speak first. Glazer began by training his attention on the excellence of Auger-Aiso technology, explaining that the manufacturing would all be done in Japan to ensure product excellence. When the Chinese offered no indication of their position or sales price, Glazer's training taught him to quote an upper-range price that would allow flexibility. The Chinese still made no comment.

In the afternoon, the Chinese heard sales negotiation offers from the combined Mitsubo-Pressure team, then Federal Electric. By the end of the day, Federal Electric had dropped out of the sales negotiation race, accepting that it could not compete.

During the first week of negotiations, a pattern emerged. The Chinese would meet with Glazer and his colleagues in the morning and ask for a price, saying that their competitors had already bid such-and-such a price, which was invariably lower than the last Auger-Aiso bid. They would meet with Mitsubo-Pressure in the afternoon and use the same sales negotiation tactic, causing the latter to drop its price. Moreover, each meeting would end with the Chinese saying, "We will call you tomorrow."

But, because they never called, both prospective vendors became panicky and visited the Chinese office without notice to present an even lower bid. As the Chinese kept the vendors guessing and in the dark, Glazer understood how the Chinese had earned a reputation as master negotiators.

At the second meeting, sales negotiation tactics changed and there were different people representing the Chinese side. An antagonist would suddenly burst out in loud Chinese and harangue the Auger-Aiso side for some fifteen minutes, complaining about the quality of the machines they were offering. A protagonist would then intervene and, apologizing for his colleague, saying he had been upset about the current sales negotiation situation.

Glazer regarded these outbursts as no more than sales negotiation training rehearsed role playing, designed to make the protagonist (the good cop/guy) appear more trustworthy to the foreigners. But, Glazer realized, all the participants had likely been training in play-acting.

Then there was yet another change. The Chinese located the Auger-Aiso and Mitsubo-Pressure teams near the meeting room, in adjacent rooms. Mitsubo-Pressure would be called in and asked for its best sales price. After the team had returned to its room, Auger-Aiso would be called in, told the latest sales price, and asked if it could beat this. When the prospective vendors could drop their price no lower, they would add something to the package. Auger, for example, added oil gauges for its turbines, effectively a three-percent add-on. Even so, the Chinese's negotiation training meant that they still would not commit to placing a sales order.

Glazer could hardly believe that he had lowered his price twenty percent that week; to do so would have been out of the question in the United States. On the final day, Auger-Aiso made another sales negotiation offer—and, for the first time, the Chinese made a counter purchasing negotiation offer. Auger-Aiso accepted, and agreement was reached. A few hours later, Mitsubo-Pressure came back with an even lower sales negotiation price, but the sales deal had already been struck.

(From https://www.negotiations.com/case/bargaining-price/)

案例思考

At the first sale negotiation meeting:

1. Do you think Auger-Aiso occupied favorable position? If not, how did they counter it?

2. Why do you think Federal Electric had dropped out of the sales negotiation race?

During the first week of the negotiation:

3. What tactics did the Chinese use to keep the two prospective vendors guessing and in the dark? Why?

At the second meeting:

4. What tactics did the Chinese use? How did the two vendors counter?

At the end of this negotiation:

5. Compared with Mitsubo-Pressure, how did Auger-Aiso succeed in this negotiation? Please list the reasons.

案例解析

本案例是一则能体现中国智慧的谈判案例，谈判共经历了三个阶段。在首轮谈判中，中方采取竞争策略和拖延技巧，让两家公司在不知对方谈判底线的情况下互相竞争，以获得最好的谈判条件。最后取得成功的 Auger-Aiso 公司开始并未占据有利地位：在没有摸清楚竞争对手的实力和中方的要求的情况下被要求第一个发言是十分危险的。但是 Auger-Aiso 的首席谈判 Glazer 运用了较好的方法应对，将发言集中在讨论技术的优越性上，并提出了一个弹性范围较大的价格，为以后与中方的价格谈判做好铺垫。

在第二次谈判中，中方采取了“红白脸”的谈判技巧。虽然 Glazer 识别出该谈判技巧，并未被吓到而导致自乱阵脚，但是对许多新手谈判者来说，这一招还是很管用的。

在最后谈判中，Auger-Aiso 公司不仅给出了当时谈判的最低价格，还在价格最低时，给出了其他优惠条件，让中方通过此次谈判获得了最大的利润。

理论拓展

How to Succeed When Working with Tactical Negotiators
如何打败具有谈判技巧的谈判者

How do negotiators handle particular situations? For example, abruptly walking out of the session, not showing up on time, forcing you to sit in an uncomfortable chair, or asking for a “few more concessions” after an agreement has been reached?

Tactics and tricks can be combined into categories:

◆ Psychological games and individual attacks: criticizing your integrity, personal put-downs, uncomfortable surroundings, and threats (“I’ll pull my accounts if you don’t do this!”) are examples.

◆ Misrepresentation of information, or outright deception.

◆ Positional power: using tactics to pressure you to negotiate against yourself, make unneeded concessions, or even give concessions after the negotiation has concluded.

1. Psychological games and personal criticism

No one wants to be around anyone who is attacking them or causing them discomfort. In fact, it may cause a negotiator to give in, just to get out of there. Confident, skilled negotiators do not allow this to happen.

If a room is uncomfortable, request a change. Either another chair, or change rooms. If they refuse, tell them that the conditions are not satisfactory (not a personal attack, “You made me sit with the sun in my eyes!”) and we will have to meet at a different time or place to be able to have any chance at success.

If it is a personal **affront**, for example "Are you qualified to be here?", or "You look ill. Are you feeling OK?" recognize the attack. Bringing it up ("You know my qualifications, so can we proceed?", or "I've never felt better, but thanks for your concern.") is the way to alert the other party you know the game. Most of the time, it stops this from further recurrence.

Using threats is a frequently used tactic to acquire concessions. Statements like, "I'll move all my business" are common to try to use perceived power to get what they want.

Many negotiators, when attacked or placed in uncomfortable situations tend to overlook them and try to move on. This is the result the tactical negotiator needs.

2. Misrepresentation of facts

This can be very difficult to handle, as our emotional reaction would be to call them a liar. Remember, you cannot correct the person, only the situation. People issues have to be separate.

If you cannot trust the other party, you can still negotiate with them. Have your facts and confirm everything. If you cannot confirm something, ask to **confer**, or reconvene until you can to ensure that the facts are accurate.

If presented with contradictory information, present your facts as being in conflict with theirs, and ask for confirmation. Whenever possible, use third party sources as backup as those sources are unbiased towards this negotiation.

If the other party has represented themselves as the decision-maker and after an agreement has been reached advises you they "have to get it approved", let them aware that the agreement is now non-binding. Either side can now make alterations as needed. If the other negotiator does not have the authority to agree to the deal, there is no deal. Put this in writing, immediately.

3. Positional Power

These tactics are employed by negotiators who are trying to position the other party into negotiating with themselves. They place the other party into a position where they are the ones making concessions, many times unnecessarily. This is very common when negotiators start negotiating to save the relationship instead of trying to reach an agreement.

Examples of tactics used:

◆ Flinch: used when you submit your offer. The hope is that you might say something like, "Oh, is that too much? I have some room here." when your original offer was fine.

A simple reply is to dismiss the flinch. If there is a real issue, it will come out later and can be negotiated without the use of tactics.

◆ Hot Potato: the other side waits until the last minute to present their proposal, and allows no time to decide or prepare.

Take a recess, caucus, reconvene. If it's a "take or leave it" deal, let it alone.

◆ Walk out: a gambit to get you to concede something to get them to return to the table. Wait them out. If there are issues, they can be handled in due course in the negotiation.

◆ Nibblers: they return after the deal has been concluded asking for a small concession. It can be because they "forgot" something, or "something changed, can you help us out?"

The best way to reply to this is to say, "If we are going to reopen the contract, then it will be satisfactory to reopen the entire contract for further considerations. We would like a few small changes, ourselves." Usually, this stops the tactic.

NEVER give something away for free. Always obtain something in exchange that is of high value to you.

◆ Tag-team negotiators: typically this occurs when a deal has been offered. For example, a company is negotiating to do business with another and there are "two" decision makers on the other side. The first one says, "We can do this, but I can only pay a 5% commission[1] on your orders." The second negotiator gets an odd look on his face and says, "Come on, we can do better than that. Why don't you pay them 6%?" In reality, they pay 10%, and since you prepared your negotiation, you checked this out. What sounds like a concession is actually a tactic. A recommended way to respond to this is to say, "It looks like the two of you have a disagreement. How about I go out for a while so you can work this out?"

These are just several of the tactics used by negotiators. When faced with tricks and tactics, it is vital to remember some key points:

◆ If you prepare and plan your negotiations, you will be more equipped to deal with tactics. You will always know where you are going, where you are in the process, and will know what you can do if negotiations are unsuccessful.

◆ The objective of the negotiator is to obtain, efficiently, an agreement that is fair to both sides. We want to keep the relationship intact.

◆ Remember you can only correct and control the situation, not the other person. Our focus has to be on the problem and the process.

◆ A negotiator may not only require negotiating the issue, but also the ground rules of the negotiation process.

◆ Recognize when a tactic is being employed. Address the tactic with the other party. Do not personalize it ("You are lying to me!").

◆ Always have sufficient confidence to stop proceedings if they are not going well. This can be via a caucus, or even rescheduling for another day or venue.

◆ Always know what you will do if an agreement cannot be realized. Having that knowledge can and will prevent you from proceeding in a negotiation where tactics are muddying the issue. Know where you are in relation to what you will do if negotiations are unsuccessful, throughout the negotiation process. Do not allow the use of tactics to cause an agreement to be worse than what could have been done on your own.

Most of us have to negotiate on a regular basis for goods and services we require in our lives. Few enjoy the process, and many do not because they are not equipped to handle the use of tactics in the negotiation process. Understanding tactics and how to deal with them, coupled with more detailed and focused planning of negotiations will give negotiators better outcomes for both sides. This gives the negotiator the confidence to do what is necessary to alter the process so it will work, rather than focusing on the behavior of the other side. Last, when tactical negotiators learn how their tactics can be neutralized, they stop using them and begin to get better results.

(From https://www.negotiations.com/articles/negotiation-tactics/)

Note

Commission：佣金，是商业活动中的一种劳务报酬，是具有独立地位和经营资格的中间人在商业活动中为他人提供服务所得到的报酬。

Read the text and answer the questions.

1. What categories can tactics be combined into? Explain it in your own words.

2. How do skilled negotiators counter the psychological games and personal criticism? Give an example.

3. What's the most important issue about the category "Mispresentation of facts"?

4. As for the tactics "Flinch", "Hot Potato", "Walk Out", "Nibblers", "Tag-team negotiators", could you give some examples to illustrate them?

5. As for the 7 key points mentioned to face with tricks and tactics, which one do you think is the most useful? Why?

要点小结

适用于不同策略的谈判技巧：投其所好、疲劳轰炸、权力有限、欲擒故纵、声东击西、针锋相对、最后通牒、最大预算、减兵增灶、抹润滑油、折中调和、抛砖引玉、一揽子交易、步步为营、红白脸、积少成多、拖延战、先苦后甜、故布疑阵等。

综合实训

Task 1

Translate the following tactics into English.

虚张声势	红白脸	权力有限	主动示弱
沉默是金	积少成多	滚木策略	针锋相对
以退为进	拖延战	休会策略	蚕食战

Task 2

Scenario Simulation

In the case study of Task 1: Strategic Considerations, if you were the seller, now you regretted and want to break the deal. Consider the strategic considerations, how do you act and present the scenario?

Task 3

1. Role-play: In the case study of Task 3: Tactics for Each English Strategy, please act as Federal Electric, Auger-Aiso, Pressure Inc, and Chinese government, present the scenario that Federal Electric chose to drop out of the negotiation race.

2. Case Study

上海第一纺织厂李厂长与日本株式会社吉野先生就购买日本纺织机事宜进行谈判。在此之前，李厂长曾到进口国类似设备的大厂进行实地考察，了解该设备的性能及价格等情况。

日方报价："我方经销的设备是日本第一流的，代表了目前世界最先进的水平，全套240万元人民币。"并摆出一副舍我其谁的神情。

李厂长心中有数：中国进口的同类设备，最贵的只有180万元人民币，便宜的是140万元人民币。李厂长不卑不亢："据我方掌握的资料，与贵方产品完全一样，我方某厂购买的价格比贵方开价便宜一半。因此希望贵方重新出价。"

第二天，日方将各类设备的价格列出详细的清单，并报出180万元人民币。经过几番谈判，双方各不相让，一直停留在160万元人民币，与我方的目标价格相差太远，只有暂时休会。这时，李厂长得知正好有几家外商来谈此项目，于是马上和另一外商进行洽谈联系，这一动作被日方发现，价格降至140万元人民币。

谈判桌上气氛很紧张，李厂长要求对方再次报价，日方愤怒了："李先生，我方已经四次降价，你们还不满意，太无诚意了。"说完生气地把包摔在桌子上。我方代表站了起来，大声说："先生，请记住，这是磋商，你们的价格、你们的态度我们无法接受。"说完，也将提包摔在桌子上，这一摔，把里面另一个外商的设备资料和照片撒在桌子上。日方大吃一惊，急忙说："李先生，我们的权力有限，等我们向总经理请示后，再商量。"李厂长寸步不让："请转告总部，这样的价格我们不感兴趣。"说完转身就走。

果然不出李厂长所料，晚上，日方宴请了中方，并宣布总部同意降至120万元人民币。至此，李厂长最后表态如果再降5%则可成交。

1. 谈判中，日方和我方分别运用了哪些策略和谈判技巧，请完成下表。（该练习考查学生对谈判策略和技巧的实际运用能力和综合分析问题的能力。答案并非唯一，有理即可。）

	日方	中方
谈判策略		
谈判技巧		

2. 你认为此次谈判最终能否成功，为什么？
3. 中方在此次的谈判过程中体现出了什么样的中国智慧？

实践语句

1. What is it you are really looking for?
你们真正想要的是什么？（为了获取情报直接提问）
2. You have been listening carefully to our discussion, and so what do you think about it ?
你很认真地在听我们的讨论，那么你认为应当怎样？（打破沉默）
3. Of course, you realize that we are obliged to talk to other potential suppliers.
当然，你知道我们是被迫去找其他供应商的。（增加谈判力度）
4. We would like to get this problem solved quickly, but we are not stuck for time.
我们是非常乐于解决这问题的。只是我们没有那么多时间去做。（将弱点最小化）
5. You have made this statement. Can you tell me how you came to this conclusion?
这是你们所做的陈述。你是否可以告诉我们，你们是怎么得出这个结论的？（就结论提出问题）
6. There appear to be some inconsistencies between what you and your colleague said earlier. Perhaps you can clarify…?
现在看来，你与你的同事先前的说法有些矛盾。也许你应该澄清一下关于……（言行不一）
7. You have heard my proposal. Perhaps we should adjourn to let you consider it and then come back with a revised offer.
你已经听到我们的提议了。是不是我们暂时休会，给你们一点时间就此进行考虑，然后再重新就修订以后的议题加以讨论？（建议休会）
8. Last time I agreed to help you out. Well, it's your turn now, so give me a better offer on…
上一次我方同意在这个问题上帮你们解决困难。我认为现在该轮到你们这么做了。我觉得贵方可以在……上给我们一个好的出价。（提出道义上的要求）
9. When you said…, I thought you were referring to… I would never have made this claim if I had known that…
在你说……的时候，我以为你的意思是……。如果我知道你说的是……的话，那我是绝对不会提出这个要求的。（装糊涂）
10. If you change your offer on…, I am prepared to reconsider my demand for…
如果你们在……方面改变出价的话，我们准备重新考虑对于……的需求。（以附带条件开价）

词语释义

affront	*n.* 侮辱
ambivalent	*adj.* 矛盾的
confer	*vt.* 授予，赋予；商量，协商
congruent	*adj.* 一致的，合适的
enticement	*n.* 诱惑，诱惑物
gauge	*vt.* 精确测量；估计；判断
junket	*n.* 公费旅游
quaint	*adj.* 古香古色的，老派的，老式的
silver lining	（不幸或失望中的）一线希望；乌云周围的白光

Unit 6 Initiating Business Negotiations

商务谈判开局

任务目标

1. Understanding the importance of creating a positive atmosphere of negotiations
2. Mastering some emotional words and their roles in negotiations
3. Trying to use positive emotions or negative emotions to achieve good negotiation outcomes
4. Knowing some basic strategies in initiating negotiations
5. Learning to apply some strategies at the start of negotiations
6. Entering into negotiations with one or two companies if possible
7. Knowing the opening statements

在商务活动中，双方或多方都带着明显的目的性。商务谈判的开局就是谈判的起点，它起着引导谈判的作用，关系到能否取得谈判的控制权和主动权。双方的态度、诚意、情绪与行为都可能受影响，甚至决定着在未来判断中双方力量的对比和对于谈判局面的掌控。一场成功的谈判，无不与良好的开局相伴而行。

Task 1 Creating a Good Atmosphere of Negotiations
营造良好的谈判氛围

谈判气氛会影响谈判者的情绪和行为方式，进而影响到谈判的进展。一般而言，谈判需要信任、和谐、融洽、友好的气氛。营造适宜的谈判气氛容易取得一致，形成共识，从而有利于和谐融洽的谈判气氛形成。任何谈判都是在一定的氛围中进行的，谈判氛围的形成与变化将直接影响到整个谈判的结局，并最终关系到自身利益能否实现。

案例学习

In February 1972, US President Richard Nixon visited China, for the two sides would conduct an international negotiation of great historical significance. In order to create a **harmonious** environment and **atmosphere** of the talks, the Chinese side, **headed by** Premier Zhou Enlai, had made thorough preparations and **meticulous** arrangements about the variety of environments in the negotiating process. And they had even made careful selection of the Sino-American folk music that would be played at the **banquet**. At the welcome banquet for Nixon and his **entourage**, when the President heard the piece "America the Beautiful" selected by Premier Zhou and played by a military band skillfully, he was greatly surprised and moved. He had never expected to hear the musical piece he was so familiar with in Beijing, China, because that was his best favorite and the specified hometown music played on his **inauguration** day. When he **drank a toast**, Nixon went over to the band specially and expressed his gratitude. At that moment, the atmosphere of the state banquet reached its **climax**, and the American guests present were also **infected** with the harmonious and warm **ambience**.

案例思考

1. What did Chinese side do before this negotiation?
2. Is it necessary to make some preparations in advance? Why?
3. Why did Nixon express his gratitude?

案例解析

1972 年尼克松访华，在访华期间进行了数次会谈，取得的成果标志着双方关系的改善，建立彼此尊重的关系，推动世界和平与经济流通。这与良好的谈判氛围是息息相关的。在会谈之前，针对尼克松总统这一特定的谈判对手，事前在接待方案中专门插入了一个精心安排，选择美国最著名的爱国颂歌《美丽的亚美利加》(America The Beautiful)，取得了触动心弦的良好效果，赢得了和谐融洽的谈判气氛，这不能不说是中方高超谈判艺术的体现，为创造取得谈判成功的条件做好了铺垫。

美国总统杰弗逊曾经针对谈判环境说过这样一句意味深长的话："在不舒适的环境下，人们可能会违背本意，言不由衷。"英国政界领袖欧内斯特·贝文也说，根据他平生参加的各种会谈的经验，他发现，在舒适明朗、色彩悦目的房间内举行的会谈，大多比较成功。显而易见，为了更好地实现谈判目标而营造出良好谈判氛围，是一种有效的谈判策略。

理论拓展

Can Emotions Affect the Negotiation Outcome?
情感因素会影响谈判结果吗？

Negotiation is an important aspect of our daily life. One **definition** is that it concerns the process of getting an **agreement** regarding the exchange of goods and services. Although this definition has a strong flavor of economic rationality it can be used to describe diverse processes such as two parents trying to get an agreement on who will take the children to school, **do the groceries** and clean the house as well as having the world leaders negotiate CO_2[1] **emissions**. Some experts emphasize that negotiation is not just about money, but also about relationships, awareness of all issues, personal preferences, knowledge of your alternatives (if no deal is reached), and **reflection on** your performance and emotions.

Research has shown that emotions can affect the negotiation outcome. For example, the best negotiation outcomes are reached when people manage to create and maintain a positive and relaxed atmosphere. Negotiating is an emotional process, certainly for the **novice** negotiator. The more that depends on the outcome of the negotiation, the more intense the emotions. Negative feelings may cause the **phenomena** such as not being in control of the situation, not knowing what to expect, and fearing to inhibit the exchange of information about underlying concerns, whereas in a relaxed atmosphere the additional information **broadens** the scope of the negotiation. In fact, a bad atmosphere and a **lack of** information are structural

barriers to an agreement. Furthermore, human negotiators make mental errors, some of which are related to emotions; **biased** perception, **irrational** expectations, **overconfidence**, and **unchecked** emotions. Biased perception is the problem of perceiving the world with a bias to make it fit your view of the situation. These problems can be reduced by proper preparation, an effective negotiation style, a good dialogue with the **opponent**, timely **interventions** (such as a break). Interestingly, recent research shows that the display of negative emotions such as anger can in some cases enhance the negotiation outcome for the person showing the negative emotion. However, this **beneficial** effect **is dependent on** the strength of the alternatives of the opponent. The role of emotion and affect in negotiation is complex and **multifaceted**. We study questions such as: how do emotions influence perception and decision making of the one having the emotion, and how do they influence the other party? How do we **measure** emotions during a negotiation in a acceptable way for negotiators? And, how can we use emotions in a **constructive** way in the negotiation strategy? Generally speaking, preparation, negotiation style, good dialogue and training are important to enhance the negotiation outcome. One point most researchers seem to agree on[2] is that good negotiators try to create a harmonious atmosphere at the start of a negotiation.

Notes

1. CO_2：carbon dioxide 的缩写形式，意为“二氧化碳”。
2. most researchers seem to agree on 是一个定语从句，修饰前面的 point，关系代词省略了。

Team Work

Divide the class into two or more teams and debate against each other.

Team A's Position	Team B's Position
If a person shows positive emotions by creating and maintaining a harmonious and relaxed atmosphere, he will always succeed in the negotiating process.	If a person shows negative emotions, he can't achieve good negotiation outcomes at the negotiating table.

要点小结

本节的目标任务是希望学习者了解情感的基本概念，重视情感因素在商务谈判中的作用和影响，以便在竞争激烈的商场中获得更大成功。

一、情感的含义

情感是态度这一整体中的一部分，它与态度中的内向感受、意向具有协调一致性，是态度在生理上一种较复杂而又稳定的生理评价和体验。

二、情感的分类

人的情感复杂多样，我们可以从不同的观察角度进行分类。由于情感的核心内容是价值，人的情感主要应该根据它所反映的价值关系的不同特点进行分类：

1. 根据价值的正负变化方向的不同，情感可分为正向情感与负向情感。
2. 根据价值的强度和持续时间的不同，情感可分为心境、热情与激情。
3. 根据价值的主导变量的不同，情感可分为欲望、情绪与感情。
4. 根据价值主体类型的不同，情感可分为个人情感、集体情感和社会情感。
5. 根据事物基本价值类型的不同，情感可分为真感、善感和美感三种。
6. 根据价值的目标指向的不同，情感可分为对物情感、对人情感、对己情感和对特殊事物情感等四大类。
7. 根据价值的作用时期的不同，情感可分为追溯情感、现实情感和期望情感。
8. 根据价值的动态变化的特点，可分为确定性情感、概率性情感。
9. 根据价值的层次的不同，情感可分为温饱类、安全与健康类、人尊与自尊类和自我实现类情感四大类。

三、情感在商务交往中的作用

根据以上对情感的描述不难得知，如果能巧妙地利用好情感因素、处理好情感问题，将极大地有利于商务活动，反之就会阻碍正常的交往。

Task 2 Strategies in Initiating Negotiations
谈判开局策略

谈判开局策略是谈判者谋求谈判开局有利形势和实现对谈判开局的控制而采取的行动方式或手段。开局策略运用的恰当与否，直接关系到谈判的最终结果。

案例学习

A well-known Japanese motor company had just "landed" in the United States, **starving for** a US agent to sell their products, so that they could **make up for** their **deficiencies** of not knowing the American market well enough. One day, the negotiating representatives of the Japanese company were invited to negotiate with an American company. They were very excited and got themselves ready for it. Unfortunately, they were late on their way to the office of the American company because of **traffic jams**. The US negotiators held on to this event, hoping to **take advantage of** it and obtain more favorable terms. When the Japanese representatives found that there was no way back, one of them stood up, saying calmly: "We are very sorry to have kept you waiting and wasted your time, but that is not our **intention**. Our lack of the traffic situation in the United States led to this unpleasant result. I hope we should not consume our valuable time on this matter. If you doubt our **sincerity** of cooperation because of it, we have to **conclude** this negotiation. By the way, I think the favorable terms we have offered will be easy for us to find partners in the United States." Hearing the **remarks** of the Japanese **representative**, the American negotiators there became **dumbfounded**. Since the Americans did not want to lose the opportunity to make money, the negotiation went on smoothly.

案例思考

1. What does this case tell us?
2. Why did the US negotiators **hold on to** that event?
3. Why were the Japanese representatives late on their way to the office of the American company?
4. What strategies were employed in this negotiation?

案例解析

在这个案例中，为了让日本代表因为迟到而感到内疚，美国公司谈判人员选择了挑剔式的开局策略，不断指责日本代表参加谈判会议不守时，形成一种情感攻击的压力，目的在于让对方处于被动地位，美国代表希望利用这种压抑的开局气氛，从中获取对其自身更多有利的条件。

通常情况下，“过错方”往往会低调行事，做出一些让步，但此案例中的日本谈判代表在面对开局时挑剔式的尴尬氛围中，冷静而机智地采取了进攻式的开局策略进行反击，提出己方的条件很优惠，若对方没有合作诚意，也容易找到其他很多合作方。这种进攻式的开局策略使形势反转，破解了对方营造的低沉开局气氛，最终使双方真正顺利地进入了谈判的实质阶段。

以上案例主要体现了在谈判的开局阶段，双方谈判者为了谋求在谈判中的有利地位，运用了不同的开局策略。显而易见，开局策略的有效运用，对决定整个谈判的走向和发展趋势起着至关重要的作用。

理论拓展

The Importance of Good Skills in Initiating Negotiations
谈判开局运用好技巧的重要性

Negotiation process is influenced by various factors. The first such factor is the skill and ability of a negotiator. Another ability, which is a major factor in a negotiation, is that the negotiator should **keep control over** the process. A negotiator should review the progress of the negotiation process; time and again endeavor to build bridges between the parties[1]. He or She should try to create a positive attitude towards agreement. A great deal of skill and experience are necessary to control the entire process of negotiation, which can be gained by keen observation of strategies adopted by other parties.

People must be ready to negotiate for a dialogue to begin. When participants are not **psychologically** prepared to talk with the other parties, when adequate information is not available, or when a negotiation **strategy** has not been prepared, people may be reluctant to begin the process. For people to reach an agreement over issues about which they disagree, they must have some means to influence the attitudes and/or behaviors of other negotiators. Often influence is seen as the power to threaten or **inflict** pain or undesirable costs, but this is only one way to encourage another to change. Before you start a negotiation, asking thought-provoking questions[2], providing needed information, seeking the advice of experts, appealing to influential associates of a party, exercising **legitimate** authority, **finding fault with** your opponents or providing rewards are all means of **exerting** influence in other parties.

Using good skills or not in **initiating** negotiations can be the difference between success and failure in the business world. Those that know how to negotiate tend to rise to the top of whatever industry[3] they are in. At the same time, those that do not know how to negotiate tend to stay where they are or fall backwards.

If you want to be successful in the industry, a study of developing negotiation skills should be at the **forefront** of your mind. Here are a few strategies to consider about the importance of good skills to business success before your negotiation.

One of the **primary** benefits of having good negotiation skills is that you will be able to save money. If you represent your business or if you are negotiating for yourself, you will be able to negotiate a cheaper price when buying something. When making large purchases, you need to be able to negotiate with the sales representative and get a better price. If you simply take the price that is being offered to you, it is very possible that will get taken advantage of. Learning how to negotiate at the start will allow you to save **substantial** amounts of money over a period of time.

Another important reason for developing good negotiation skills is that you will be able to make more money for your business as well. If you are trying to sell a product or secure a contract, you need to be able to negotiate in order to make it happen. By doing this according to the circumstances, you should try different skills to secure a larger selling price and increase your profit margins[4]. Increasing profit margins is one of the biggest objectives for most businesses. If you can learn how to do this, you will be invaluable to your employer and this will be directly related to your business success.

In addition to being a better negotiator, you will also develop several other traits that are essential in business. Many of the same skills that you use in negotiations will translate[5] over to other areas of the business.

For example, when learning good negotiation skills, you will learn how to be an effective listener. In order to be successful in a negotiation, at first, you have to be able to listen to the other person to see what they want or what they think. This skill will be very valuable to you in other areas of the business. If you are a manager, you will need to be able to listen to your employees to see what motivates them. If you are dealing with customers, you need to be able to listen to what they are telling you so that you can find a product or service that matches their needs.

There are different styles of negotiation. Negotiating style is also a strategy. On some occasions the style reflects the attitude of the party and an experienced negotiator can guess the result from such a conduct of the party as becomes evident by the style. Negotiation style is reflected in communication skills, interpersonal behavior of negotiators, language, voice tones, choices, listening power, **non-verbal** gestures and judgment. When you are aiming to achieve business success, developing good skills in initiating negotiations should be at the top of your priority list. This is by far one of the most important skills that you can develop as a businessperson. It can easily take you from where you currently are to where you eventually want to be.

Notes

1. build bridges between the parties：此处是比喻用法，意为“搭建好各方之间沟通的桥梁”。

2. asking thought-provoking questions：问一些引人思考的问题。

3. industry：除了有“工业、产业”的意思外，还可以泛指“行业”，如：Representatives from across the horse *industry* will attend the meeting.（整个赛马业的代表都将参加这次会议。）

4. profit margins：此处意为“利润率”。例如：*Profit margins* have been slashed to the bone in an attempt to keep turnover moving.（为了维持资金周转，利润率已被降为最低。）

5. translate：此处不是通常情况下的“翻译”，而是引申为“转化、表达”之意。

Group Work

Work in small groups and discuss the following questions.

1. Why is negotiation process influenced by many factors?

2. Could you give some examples?

3. Do you think it is important to use some strategies or skills in initiating negotiations? Why so?

4. What primary benefits can we get by using good skills at the start of negotiations? Please name some of them.

要点小结

本节的目标任务是希望学习者了解商务谈判的开局策略，重视开局策略或技巧的运用对商务谈判过程的作用和影响，以便谈判中见机行事，掌握主动，使己方的利益最大化。

商务谈判的开局，就是指谈判双方第一次见面时，在讨论具体、实质性的谈判内容之前，相互介绍、寒暄以及就谈判具体内容以外的话题进行交谈的阶段。谈判开局是双方刚开始接触的阶段，是实质性谈判的序幕。谈判开局策略的好坏将直接左右整个谈判的格局和前景。商务谈判开局策略有很多，学习者不能机械地照搬，而应该根据谈判对象的不同、地点的不同、双方实力的不同、文化的不同、国际环境的不同、气氛的不同等诸多因素，创新性地灵活运用，比如必要时谈判开局策略还可以交叉使用。常见的开局策略方式有：挑剔式开局策略、协商式开局策略、坦诚式开局策略、慎重式开局策略、进攻式开局策略、劣势开局策略、优势开局策略、保留式开局策略等。

Task 3 Opening Statements
开局陈述

在实质性的谈判之前，谈判各方往往先要做一个正式的开局陈述，分别阐明本方所谈议题的基本原则，重点强调本方的利害所在。开局陈述的主要作用是亮明本方的观点，营造有利于本方的气势，探视对方的反应。

案例学习

At the Guangzhou Trade Fair, Mr. Smith, the President of the ABC Trading Company in New York, is talking with Miss Wang, the sales manager of Haier Group.

Smith: I've seen your exhibits and catalogues and I'm interested in your mini-refrigerators.

Wang: You have good judgment. Haier has developed mini-refrigerators, especially those lockable refrigerators for university students and auto-defrosting refrigerators for hotels in various designs and colors to meet the demand in the USA. You'll find that our mini-refrigerators will sell in your country.

Smith: Here is a list of my requirements. I'd like to have your lowest quotation.

Wang: Here is our latest price list for your reference.

Smith: Well, all your prices are on a CIF basis. We'd rather have offers on FOB prices.

Wang: That can easily be done. I'll work it out for you…Here you are. May I remind you that we always allow a quantity discount if your order is large enough?

Smith: Sounds good. If your price is reasonable, we will be prepared to place a large order, say 10,000 sets of lockable refrigerators and 20,000 sets of auto-defrosting refrigerators. By the way, do you allow any commission?

Wang: I'm sorry, sir. The prices are quoted on an FOB net basis. As a rule, we don't allow any commission.

Smith: But you know we are a commissioned agent. We do business on a commission basis. Commission transactions will surely help to push the sales of your products.

Wang: Well, since you are thinking of placing such a large order, we'll allow you a commission of 2% as an encourage for future business. We can't do more than that. You can see that our prices are the most attractive in the world market.

Smith: Good!

（From 张立玉. 商务谈判英语［M］. 武汉：武汉大学出版社，2009.）

案例思考

1. What is CIF, FOB?
2. What is commission?
3. Do you think Mr. Smith got enough information for the further negotiation? Why?
4. Do you think Miss Wang responded well in this negotiation? Why?

案例解析

在本案例中，美方的史密斯先生在陈述的开始就将谈判范围圈定在对冰箱的价格讨论上；中方的王小姐在谈判中对于一些非原则性问题，如报价是到岸价还是离岸价，根据美方的要求做出了积极的回应。但当涉及利益核心问题时，双方在陈述中始终保留自己的观点，美方认为：价格优惠则会大量购买；中方认为：大量购买才能给予折扣。另外关于佣金问题，中方本来是不允许任何佣金的，但考虑到美方是提取佣金的代理，有利于未来的长期合作，于是做出让步，同意给予2%的佣金。由此可见，双方在各自的陈述中，探明了对方的意图，最终提出了一个顾及双方利益的解决方案，让谈判得以顺利进行。

理论拓展

Dovetailing—Asking for Their Preference
利益融合——询问对方的偏好

One way to **dovetail** interests is to invent several options all equally acceptable to you and ask the other side which one they prefer. You want to know what is preferable, not necessarily what is acceptable. You can then take the option, work with it some more, and again present two or more variants, asking which one they prefer. In this way, without anyone's making decision, you can improve a plan until you can find no more **joint gains**. For example, the agent for the baseball star might ask the team owner: "What meets your interest better, a salary of $875,000 a year for two years, or $1,000,000 a year for three years? The latter? OK, how about between that and $900,000 a year for three years with a $500,000 bonus in each year if Fernado[1] pitches better than a 3.00 **ERA**?"

If dovetailing had to be summed up in one sentence, it would be: look for items that are of low costs to you and high benefits to them, and **vice versa**. Different in interests, priorities, beliefs, forecasts, and attitudes towards risk all make dovetailing possible. A negotiator's motto could be "Vive la différence![2]"

（From 邓忍. 商务英语谈判［M］. 北京：对外经济贸易大学出版社，2014.）

Notes

1. Fernado：美国著名垒球运动员，曾参加 2004 年雅典夏奥会，获得金牌。
2. Vive la différence！法语，意为“差别万岁”。

Team Work

Answer the following questions.

1. Could you please define "to dovetail interests"?
2. How do you understand the sentence "You want to know what is preferable, not necessarily what is acceptable."?
3. How do you understand the motto "Vive la différence"?

要点小结

开局陈述应注意以下三点：

一、陈述内容

- 本方对所谈问题的理解（圈定谈判范围）；
- 本方希望在将要进行的谈判中得到哪些利益或保障（包括不可让步的原则问题）；
- 本方愿与对方进行协商的部分（释放让步信号）；
- 过去的合作对对方带来的利益（隐含让对方感恩和让步的味道）；
- 未来合作中可能出现的机会或障碍等等。

二、陈述方式

针对不同的议题、不同的对手，表达方式也应有所不同。选择不同的陈述方式，可以营造出不同的谈判氛围（本章 Task 1 已做详细说明）。

三、聆听对方陈述时的反应

当对方陈述时，本方应做到：

- 弄明白对方的观点，遇有不懂之处要及时向对方提问；
- 聆听时尽量做笔记，记下对方的论据；
- 善于归纳对方的主要观点，突出谈判重点；
- 勿在对方陈述时向其提出挑衅性的问题。

最后做一个顾及各方利益的总结性发言，提出一个可行性很强和较为周全的解决方案，使谈判前景令人期待。

综合实训

Task 1

1. Think about what the following sentences imply and translate them into Chinese.

1) I cannot be your friend and your flatterer too.
2) If you make yourself an ass, don't complain if people ride you.
3) If you run after two hares, you will catch neither.
4) If you venture nothing, you will have nothing.
5) Industry is the parent of success.
6) It is easy to open a shop but hard to keep it always open.
7) It is hard to please all.
8) It is the first step that costs troublesome.
9) It is too late to grieve when the chance is past.
10) It takes three generations to make a gentleman.
11) Knowledge makes humble, ignorance makes proud.
12) Learn to walk before you run.
13) Life is not all roses.
14) It is easier to get money than to keep it.

15) It is easy to be wise after the event.

2. Fill in the table with some emotional words you can think out and tell the class their roles.

Words Concerning Emotions	
Emotions	Roles
1) 2) 3) ……	1) 2) 3) ……

3. Here are some words of emotional experiences. Choose some of them and discuss in pairs what experiences you may have in some cases.

Activation

Tense
Nervous
Stressed
Upset

alert
excited
elated
happy

Unpleasant

Pleasant

Sad
Depressed
Bored
Fatigued

contented
serene
relaxed
calm

Deactivation

4. Good negotiating skills are essential to the smooth running of your business. Negotiators should be aware of the role of emotions, moods, and conflicts in negotiations. The atmosphere of the negotiations determines the outcome. Work in small groups and draw up a plan according to the given situation, trying to create a good, friendly and positive atmosphere for your foreign guests.

Situation	
Party A's Personnel	**Party B's Personnel**
You are sales managers of International Department, Shanghai Trading Company.	Ms. Jane Smith is purchasing manager of Global Business Company, London. She comes to China with her two assistants, hoping to establish trade and cooperative relations.

Task 2

1. There are various strategies in initiating negotiations. Try to think out some strategies that are often employed in a negotiation and fill them in the table.

Strategies that are often employed
1)…………………… 2)…………………… 3)…………………… 4)…………………… ……

2. Discuss in pairs the roles of those strategies that you have thought out.

Strategies that you have thought out	
Student A's Strategies	**Student B's Strategies**
1)…………………… 2)…………………… 3)…………………… 4)…………………… ……	1)…………………… 2)…………………… 3)…………………… 4)……………………. ……

3. Analyse the following cases and tell the class what strategies are used.

Case 1

A Salary Negotiation Case Study

A friend of mine is a department manager at a large company. His secretary requested a 10 percent raise. She was worth it.

The problems was that 10 percent represented a large raise compared to the 5 percent other employees had received. **Was there a creative both-win way out of this problem?**

As they explored the possibilities, several ideas emerged. The company starts work at 8am and closes at 5pm.

The manager learned that his secretary encountered heavy traffic every evening on the way home. They agreed to have her work from 7:30am to 4:30am This saved her at least 20-25 minutes driving time. Certainly a benefit to her at little or no expense to the company.

They then studied her job in detail. Before long they jointly developed a new description which gave her more responsibility, and, at the same time, more interesting work.

Both parties benefited from the changed scope of work. The raise itself was then discussed. A **compromise** was reached by agreeing on a 6 percent raise for three months and then an additional 2 percent later if the new responsibilities were adequately **performed**.

Case 2

我国某工艺雕刻厂原是一家濒临倒闭的小厂，但经过不断创新和几年的不懈努力，发展为产值1 000多万元的规模，而且产品成功打入日本市场，战胜了其他国家在日本经营多年的一些厂家，被誉为“天下第一雕刻”。有一年，日本三家株式会社的老板同一天接踵而至，到该厂定货。其中一家资本雄厚的大商社，要求原价包销该厂的佛坛产品。这应该说是好消息。但该厂想到，这几家原来都是经销韩国、中国台湾地区产品的商社，为什么争先恐后、不约而同到本厂来定货？他们查阅了日本市场的资料，得出的结论是本厂的木材质量上乘，技艺高超是吸引外商定货的主要原因。于是该厂采用了“待价而沽”“欲擒故纵”的谈判策略。针对那家大商社，先是不明确表态，而是积极抓住两家小商社求货心切的心理，把佛坛的梁、榴、柱，分别与其他国家的产品做比较。在此基础上，该厂将产品当金条一样争价钱、论成色，使其价格达到了理想的高度，然后首先与小商社拍板成交，造成那家大客商产生失落货源的危机感。在这样的情形下，那家大客商不但更急于定货，而且想今后逐步垄断货源，于是大批量定货，以致定货数量超过该厂现有生产能力的好几倍，使谈判获得极大成功！

4. Divide the class into several groups. Each group should choose one or two negotiating strategies and get yourselves ready for a negotiation. You can refer to the following situation under the guidance of the teacher.

Groups Situation	Group A's Strategy	Group B's Strategy
Group A, seller, represents Premier Metals Inc. in California, USA. Group B, buyer, represents the Purchasing Department of Hongxin Trading Company in Chengdu, China.	1) ······	1) ······

Task 3

Role-play: work with your partners to design an Initiating Negotiation by “Asking Their Preference” and perform it.

实践语句

1. Good negotiators need to create an atmosphere of trust that both sides can feel during a negotiation.

优秀的谈判者需要能够营造一种谈判双方都能感受到的信任氛围。

2. I hear rock music really leaves the manager cold. What about her assistants?

听说那位经理对摇滚乐一点也不感兴趣，她的助手呢？

3. Our representative in your country faxed a letter that you showed an interest in some of our products on display at the Oct. Exhibition there. Now we'd like to know if you have any specific requirements in mind.

我们公司在你们国家的代理人发来一封传真说您对我们公司十月份在贵国的展会上

展示的产品有兴趣。现在我们想知道您心里是否对我们的产品有任何特殊的要求。

4. All right. When can we meet again for more specific details, Ms.Wang?

好的。王女士，我们什么时候再见面商讨具体的事宜呢？

5. You have a long head, I bet you will do well in your business.

您很有远见卓识，我敢肯定您会将生意做得很红火。

6. I'm so excited! We are finally here! The Great Wall! It is one of the wonders of the world. Thank you very much for your arrangement. He who doesn't reach the Great Wall is not a true man.

真激动，我们终于到了！长城，可是世界奇观之一呢！非常感谢你们的安排，不到长城非好汉！

7. I hope through your visit we can settle the price for our products, and conclude the business before long.

希望通过您的访问，我们可以解决产品的价格问题，并很快达成交易。

8. You know that the cost of production has risen a great deal in recent years while our prices are basically remain unchanged. To be frank, our products are moderately priced.

你知道，近年来生产成本上升太快，而我们的价格却基本保持不变。坦率地说，我方产品的定价是适中的。

9. I agree with what you say, but the price difference should not be so big. If you consider making some concessions in your price, we may place a larger order.

我同意你的说法，但价差不应该这么大。如果贵方考虑在价格上做些让步，我方可以多订购一些。

10. That sounds good. Looks like we can do business together. With our products, you'll be able to upgrade at relatively low cost to cover all your needs for the foreseeable future.

听起来不错，看来我们可以合作。用我方的产品，贵方可以在将来以低成本进行升级，满足你们的多方需求。

词语释文

agreement	*n.* 协定，协议；合同书
ambience	*n.* 气氛，布景；周围环境
atmosphere	*n.* 气氛；基调；大气层
banquet	*n.* 宴会，盛宴；筵席；宴请
barrier	*n.* 障碍；屏障；栅栏
beneficial	*adj.* 有利的，有益的
biased	*adj.* 有偏见的
both-win	*n. & adj.* 双赢（的），互利共赢（的）（与 win-win 同义）
broaden	*vt.& vi.* 变宽，加宽；扩展；扩大
climax	*n.* 顶点；高潮

compromise	*n. &v.* 妥协；折中解决；退让
conclude	*vt.& vi.* 结束，终止
constructive	*adj.* 建设的，建设性的；积极有益的
deficiency	*n.* 缺乏，不足；缺陷
definition	*n.* 定义；解释
dovetail	*vt.* 使……相吻合
dumbfounded	*adj.* 发愣的，哑然失声的
emission	*n.* 排放，辐射；排放物
entourage	*n.* 随行人员
ERA	垒球投手责任得分率（earned run average 的缩写）
exert	*vt.* 施加，发挥；运用
forefront	*n.* 前沿；首位
harmonious	*adj.* 和谐的，融洽的；协调的
inauguration	*n.* 就职；就职典礼
infect	*vt.* 使受影响，感染；传染
inflict	*vt.* 把……强加给，使承受，遭受
initiate	*vt.* 开始，发起
intention	*n.* 意图，目的
intervention	*n.* 介入，干涉，干预
irrational	*adj.* 不合理的，荒谬的；无理性的
legitimate	*adj.* 合法的，合理的；正规的；真正的
measure	*v.&n.* 测量，估量；尺寸
meticulous	*adj.* 谨小慎微的；重视细节的；
multifaceted	*adj.* 多方面的，多才多艺的
non-verbal	*adj.* 不使用语言的，非言语交际的
novice	*n.* 初学者，新手
opponent	*n.* 对手；敌手；反对者
overconfidence	*n.* 过度自信，自负
perform	*vt.& vi.* 执行；履行；表演；扮演；
phenomena	*n.* 现象（单数形式为 phenomenon）
primary	*adj.* 首要的，主要的；基本的
psychologically	*adv.* 心理地；精神上地
remark	*n.* 话语；评论
representative	*n.* 代表
sincerity	*n.* 真挚，诚意
strategy	*n.* 策略，战略
substantial	*adj.* 大量的；实质性的；结实的
unchecked	*adj.* 未经检查的；未受抑制的

(be) dependent on	依赖于，取决于
do the groceries	去杂货店买东西
drink a toast（to）	祝酒；干杯
find fault with	挑剔；找碴儿
headed by	在……带领下；以……为首
hold on to	坚持；紧紧抓住
in addition to	除……之外
joint gains	联合利益，共同利益
keep control over	控制住
lack of	缺乏；不了解
make up for	弥补，补偿
reflection on	反思，思考
starve for	急需；渴望得到
take advantage of	利用；占……便宜
traffic jams	交通堵塞
vice versa	反之亦然

Unit 7 Business Negotiation Consultation

商务谈判磋商

任务目标

1. Understanding the process of business negotiation consultation
2. Learning to apply some strategies of offer
3. Learning to apply some strategies of bargaining
4. Practicing the tactics of making concessions in business negotiations

谈判磋商是谈判的核心部分，也是谈判中最激烈、最困难的阶段。它不仅是谈判各方在实力、智力、技能和经验等领域的较量，也是求同存异、谋求合作、彼此理解和让步的过程。这一过程和结果直接影响谈判各方的利益关系，决定各方的整体满意度。谈判磋商的主要过程包括报价、议价和让步等环节。

Task 1 Strategies of Offer

报价策略

报价是商务磋商过程中非常关键的环节。它给谈判双方带来的第一印象是引起对方交易兴趣的前奏，也是影响谈判最终结果的开端。报价分寸掌握得当，则既能满足磋商者自我利益需求，又能把对方的期望值限制在一个特定的范围内，并且在以后的讨价议价过程中占据主动地位。影响报价的因素除了产品成本和产品质量外，主要还有市场行情、利益需求、交货期、附带条件和服务等。

案例学习

Case 1

Hugh Bradley was one of the excellent vodka companies in the world. Its famous product, the Smirnov wine, once covered vodka market shares as much as 23%. However, in the 1960s, another company launched a new product which tasted as good as the Smirnov wine. Because the new type vodka was sold at a lower price, it had a great impact on the vodka market position of Hugh Bradley. After careful consideration, the marketing staff of Hugh Bradley increased the price of the Smirnov wine by $1. At the same time, they launched a new vodka which was offered at the price as much as their rival's and another wine which was offered at a lower price. As a result, Hugh Bradley not only got through the difficulties, but also gained lots of profits. In fact, the three types of products launched by Hugh Bradley taste the same with same ingredients in.

案例思考

1. Which strategies did Hugh Bradley apply to make them get through the difficulties?
2. Why did Hugh Bradley offer their products at lower prices?

案例解析

按照惯例，休布雷公司有 3 条对策可选择：（1）降低一美元，以保住市场占有率；（2）维持原价，通过增加广告费用和销售支出与对手竞争；（3）维持原价，听任其市场占有率降低。但是，通过分析当时市场竞争态势可知，不论休布雷公司采取上述哪种策略，它都将处于市场的被动地位。该公司最终所使用的老产品提价策略及投入新产品策略，提高了公司史密诺夫酒的地位，同时使竞争对手的新产品沦为一种普通品牌，从而使公司渡过难关。

案例学习

Case 2

Someone read house-for-sale information on newspaper. It is known that a property owner was anxious to sell his house to go abroad. Many people came and offered 25-26 million, while the person proposed the price of 26.8 million after consideration. The owner, of course, was satisfied with the price of 26.8 million and turned down other potential buyers immediately. However, when the owner was looking forward for finishing the payment, the person began to find **flaws** on the house and delayed the contract signing with showing a tendency to drop the purchase. The date of departure for the house owner was drawing near, and no other one wanted to buy the house, the owner had to re-negotiate the price with the person and concluded a transaction with a lower price eventually.

案例思考

1. Why did the person start the price at 26.8 million, which was a little bit higher than others?
2. At which moment did the person begin to find flaws on the house? Why?
3. In which situation does the strategy not work?

案例解析

此人是真正的买家。开局中，他报出稍高于其他购房者报出的价格，独占这一交易（房主在较高叫价的诱惑下，拒绝了其他购房者）。接着，他开始挑剔房屋瑕疵，做出放弃购买该房屋的姿态。房主出国时间临近，急于售房，最终不得不降价销售。在这一报价策略的使用中，要注意价格不能虚高超出理性范围，以免降低购房意愿的表达。并且，先高价占领市场，再降价购买的策略，只有当卖家急于抛售的情况下才能奏效。

理论拓展

Japanese Offer and European Offer
日式报价与欧式报价

Japanese offer is also known as the lower price strategy whose basic approach is to launch the price from low to high. In detail, this offer is done in the following steps: the seller or the supplier first offers a price which is slightly lower to **attract** the buyers. The price is given not because of low product quality, but because of other kinds of factors, such as low laborer costs and quantity discounts. Then in the **process** of negotiation **consultation**, the seller would **add up** the price by various **reasonable** excuses including the **transportation** expenses[1] and the delivery period[2]. Japanese offer is more suitable when the transaction **involves** mass **contents** or sets of equipment, or the **opponents** do not understand the negotiation market conditions quite well and their experience is weak.

On the **opposite** side, there is another offer strategy, European offer, which is also called the high-**profile** strategy. The seller first offers a price which **allows** enough room to bargain. **Comparing** the strengths of sides, the current market condition and the external competitors, the seller gives various **incentives** including quantity discounts, price discounts, commissions[3] and payment concessions[4] to gradually get close to the buyer's requirement. Then ultimately, the negotiators achieve the purpose of transaction. European offer is typically used when the negotiators on the opposite side are not very familiar with the market, or when transaction price is not easy to grasp, or when the negotiations have plenty of time to practice. To apply this strategy, the **outcry** is **severe** and should be given slowly. The negotiators will take the opportunity to test each other's strength and **identify** each other's position.

Japanese offer is the traditional offer which is widely used in Japan and other Asian countries. European offer is generally **adopted** by the European and American countries. But now they two are both popular all over the world in the aspect of the negotiations.

Notes

1. transportation expenses：运费，是指支付货运所使用的船只、火车、飞机或其他类似运输手段的费用。

2. delivery period：交付期限。货物的交付期限是指货物交接的具体时间要求，它不仅关系到交易是否按期履行，还可能会出现货物意外灭失或损坏时的责任承担问题。一般在合同内应对交付货期限写明月份或更具体的时间。如果合同内规定分批交货时，还需注明各批次交货的时间，以便明确责任。

3. commissions：佣金。如果交易是由中间商介绍而为之的，卖方或买方就需给中间商为介绍成交而提供的服务支付佣金。

4. payment concessions：支付优惠是指对于某种支付所提供的价格折扣。例如，买方在支付货款时全额支付，卖方就可能在价格上做出让步，给予一定的折扣。

Group Work

Work in small groups and discuss the following questions.

1. What are the factors that influence choosing strategies of offer?
2. List the situations in which Japanese offer is suitable.
3. List the situations in which European offer is suitable.

要点小结

报价是商务谈判中的关键环节，在本节的学习中，要求掌握报价的方式和报价的基本原理，并操练报价技巧。

一、报价的方式

在商务磋商中，交易者常用的报价方式为日本式报价和西欧式报价。

1. 日本式报价

日本式报价的一般做法是将最低价格列在价格表上，以求首先引起买主的兴趣。

2. 西欧式报价

西欧式报价的一般模式为：首先提出留有较大余地的价格，然后根据买卖双方的实力对比和该笔交易的外部竞争情况，通过给予各种优惠来逐步软化和接近对方的市场和条件，最终达成成交的目的。

二、报价的基本原理

一般来说，报价应遵循以下基本原理：1. 报价必须合乎情理；2. 报价内容应该明确、完整、无保留。

Task 2 Strategies of Bargaining
议价策略

议价就是谈判双方的讨价和还价，其目的不仅仅是提供与对方报价差异的价格，还应力求给对方造成较大的压力和影响，甚至改变对方的期望。讨价还价应考虑到对方可能接受该价格，并愿意向互利性的协议靠拢。

案例学习

Case 1

One metallurgical company in China was planning to purchase a set of advanced equipment from the United States. A senior engineer was sent to make the consultation with the Americans. Taking full responsibility, the senior engineer fully prepared for the negotiation by finding related data and information. He spent a lot of time and efforts on understanding the international market of the advanced equipment and the background (such as status and operating situation) of the American company. At beginning, the Americans offered $2 million. After several rounds of bargaining, the price was reduced to $1 million and 280 thousand. The Chinese company still did not agree and insisted on biding $980 thousand. The Americans pretended to be angry and threw the contract on the face of the Chinese engineer. They threatened that the price could be 10 million lower only. If the price was dealt less than $118 million, they would go back to America **immediately**. For having done a detailed investigation, the Chinese engineer insisted on the price cuts. On the next day, when the Americans went back to America, the senior engineer was not astonished and calmed. As the engineer predicted, the Americans returned and continued negotiations a week later. At this time, the Chinese engineer showed out collected information: two years ago, the Americans sold the same equipment to Hungary for $88 million. The Americans were shocked and provided the inflation as an excuse to explain. The engineer said: "The price index does not exceed 6% every year. Can you calculate how much it rises in these two years?" Facing the fact, the Americans had to make concessions. Finally, the deal had been done at the price of $101 million.

案例思考

1. Why was the Chinese engineer not astonished when the American went back to America?

2. How did the Chinese company make the deal done?

3. What was the concession exactly made by the Americans?

案例解析

从中方来看，取得胜利的最关键的一点在于充分地收集和整理了对方信息，用大量客观数据给对方施加压力。从收集的内容看，中方不仅查出了美方与他人的谈判价格（援引先例），也设想到了对方可能会反驳的内容并运用相关数据加以反击（援引惯例，如6%），对客观标准做了恰到好处的运用。此外，中方的胜利还在于多种谈判技巧的运用：（1）谈判前，评估双方的依赖关系，对对方的接收区域和初始立场（包括期望值和底线）做了较为准确的预测，由此才能在随后的谈判中识破对方的佯装退出，而未予让步。（2）谈判中，中方依靠数据掌握谈判主动权，改变了对方不合理的初始立场。（3）在回盘上，从结果价大概处于比对方开价一半略低的情况可推测，中方的回盘策略也运用得较好。

Case 2

During negotiations at the height of the Cold War, Americans were amazed when a leader of **Soviet Union** became so angry that he started banging his shoe on the table. However, the photographs taken at the time show that while he did this, both of his shoes were still on his feet.

案例思考

1. Where did "the third shoe" come from?

2. What does this case tell you about the leader's negotiating strategy?

案例解析

很明显，这"第三只鞋"是苏联领导人事先准备的。谈判中，用"第三只鞋"愤怒地敲击谈判桌的行为也是有意为之。"霸凌"这一策略在谈判中经常被使用，具体而言是指用带侵略性的行为，逼迫对方同意和接受己方要求。

理论拓展

Multiple Equivalent Simultaneous Offers
多等效同时报价

Multiple Equivalent **Simultaneous** Offers (MESO[1]) is a **technique** used in negotiations. The principle behind MESO is, simply put, to make multiple offers which are mutually **equal** in your mind. By doing this, one can better understand one's partner in a negotiation—his or her interests, **expectations**, etc.

There are three steps to successfully applying the MESO strategy to your negotiation:

1. Identify and **Prioritize Issues**. **Estimate** their weights (**relative** value) to both parties. There may be some things that are important to you but less important to your **counterpart**.

2. Identify Different Likely **Outcomes** for Each Issue. Set one as the standard, and then set relative values of the others. Assigning point values is one way of determining whether one package is, on the whole, more **appealing** than another.

3. **Create** at Least Three Equivalent Offers. These offers should have **approximately** equal point values, according to the points assigned in step two.

MESO strategy requires multiple issues with realistic alternative outcomes. MESOs are better **utilized** if there are multiple interests, perhaps in a package deal. It would not be realistic if only one variable is under negotiation, such as a basic salary negotiation. This strategy can also be a **complex** process—discussing a variety of issues can lead to confusion. Lastly, a MESO is only **beneficial** if the party offering the multiple offers is honest—it requires that party to **reveal** some of its own interests.

There are **various** advantages to using a MESO in a negotiation. Not only does it help the negotiator gather information about the other side's relative priorities, but it also proves as an anchoring device. It also helps you to be aggressive while showing signs of cooperation and **flexibility**.

"Presenting more than one offer at a time increases the other side's satisfaction as well as the odds that an agreement will be implemented. Research shows that negotiators who use MESOs achieve better outcomes than those who make a single packaged offer, without **sacrificing** relationships or losing credibility."

"Making MESOs has a number of advantages over simply making a single package offer.

MESOs are beneficial because they allow negotiators to collect information while being **persistent** and aggressive at the bargaining table, but also to be perceived as being flexible and accommodating."

There are advantages for the counterpart in a negotiation when it comes to MESOs. Generally, others prefer to being given choices. Many options are preferable to one single offer. One MESO is likely to be more appealing, or of a greater value, than the other options. To the counterpart, this more appealing MESO can lead to further discussion and, ultimately, settlement. This also offers the counterpart an opportunity for input wherein they can discuss values, weights, interests, etc.

Note

MESO：这一词语的语源学起源在希腊，意味着“组合形式”和“中间”，表明国家之间的平衡。MESOs 策略的本意是让谈判人员收集和整合复杂的信息，将攻击与合作结合，将持久性与灵活性结合，从而获取谈判的成功。

Group Work

Work in small groups and discuss the following questions.

1. What are the advantages to using the MESO strategy during offer?
2. How can we successfully apply the MESO strategy in the negotiations?
3. Which situations could the MESO strategy be applied in?

要点小结

本小节主要内容是在商务磋商中议价的过程，价格谈判的策略，影响价格的因素和讨价还价应遵循的原则。讨价是指要求报价方改善报价的行为。谈判中，一般卖方在首先的报价和价格解释后，买方如果认为这一价格离自己的期望目标太远，必然要在价格评论的基础上要求对方改善报价。这种讨价要求既是实质性的，可迫使报价降低，也是策略性的，可误导对方对己方的判断，为己方的还价做准备。还价一般是针对卖方的报价买方做出的反应性报价。具体而言，还价以讨价为基础，是买方根据估算卖方保留价格和己方理想价格，按照一定的策略和技巧提出自己的还价。

谈判者在谈判前和谈判中应该根据实际情况的变化进行议价，考虑的主要因素有：（1）分析产品成本对价格的影响；（2）分析市场行情和竞争态势；（3）多渠道了解和判断谈判对手的战略意图和价格目标；（4）考虑交货期因素对价格谈判的影响；（5）分析产品的内在因素对价格的影响；（6）判定不同支付方式对价格谈判的影响；（7）确定价格谈判的目标体系。

Task 3 Making Concessions
让 步

让步是谈判者为了达成交易，在谈判中修改其原有目标，降低己方利益要求的做法。如果谈判双方都坚持自己的原始立场，那么协议将无法达成。让步是商务谈判中的普遍做法，其精髓是谈判者通过主动退让自己部分的利益以满足对方需要，从而换取自己的最低目标利益的策略。

案例学习

Case 1

On August 2nd, the European Commission announced the price commitment agreement on the formal approval of PV（光伏）between the EU and China. The program would be implemented on August 6th. This agreement marked that the Eu and China had reached a settlement on the PV anti-dumping case. However, the negotiation process was a tough marathon game. In May, the EU put forward a price commitment scheme with an extremely high price. The EU thought that the relatively fair price should be around 0.8 Euros/W or more on the basis of the market price last year (2012). After several rounds of consultation, the EU insisted to maintain the prices at 0.7-0.8 Euros/W, and the quota should be 5gw. Contrarily, China firmly refused the prices over 0.5 Euros/W. There was a great psychological **gap** between the two sides. After months of continuous bargaining seesaw battle, China put forward 0.55 Euros/W, and made a note: if the agreement was not reached, it would bring a crushing defeat which could be described as a loss-loss. That was to say that China's PV enterprises would lose the largest export market. Meanwhile, the PV downstream enterprises of Europe would not be able to obtain high quality and low price of PV products. Based on the above considerations, China made the biggest concession in terms of price, 0.55 Euros/W, which was almost the cost of Chinese PV products in the European market. There was almost no profit for Chinese companies. Out of a huge concession, the Chinese side increased the number of quotas, accounting for about 6 of the market share in the European PV market. Finally, the two sides reached the price at 0.56 euro/W, 7 GW of quota level. Even though, this price was not static because the two sides finally chose the third party, Bloomberg Data, as a benchmark for the price fluctuations.

案例思考

1. In order to reach PV trade price commitment agreement, what concessions did China make?

2. How did China make those concessions?

案例解析

经过几个回合的讨价还价，中方做出让步，最终将价格降到 0.55 欧/瓦，而这几乎是中国光伏产品在欧洲市场的成本价格了。在做出让步的同时，中方向欧盟客观陈述利害关系，分析协议失败对双方的危害，并且充分显示诚意，提出最低价格。当然，天下没有白吃的午餐，中方也得到了数量可观的市场份额。从中方的让步策略中不难看出，谈判者在做出让步的同时必须充分陈述理由，并应该得到其他相应的利益。

Case 2

There was a manufacturer of engine parts. After many consultations, the sale representative of the engine manufacturer had been given an interview with the boss of Europe's largest car firm. But the boss insisted that the representative met him at the airport a few minutes before he flies to Australia. This was a big chance! While walking towards passport control, the boss opened with a demand for the best price for a six-month contract to supply parts.

案例思考

If you were the representative, what would you do?

A. Give him the lowest price immediately.

B. Start slightly higher than your lowest price.

C. Start with a high price to give yourself room to negotiate.

D. Say "Have a nice flight!"

案例解析

This case is **adapted** from the book **Everything Is Negotiable** written by Gavin Kennedy who runs a consultancy firm specializing in negotiating. Gavin Kennedy says:

A. The boss eats people like this for breakfast. His intimidation has worked and he knows what the representative can do.

B. If you acting as the representative concede at the first meeting, what will you do at a longer meeting in six months' time?

C. A bit better, but this is still not the best move.

D. Yes. You should tell the boss to keep contact and say you will talk to his technical people about exactly what they need. After all, they may desperately want your engine parts and he can worry about that all the way to Australia—and back.

理论拓展

What's My Line?—The Reservation Price
最后底线是什么？——保留价格

The "**Reservation Price**"[1] is the point, place, or line where we will not pass. This is the place where the smart negotiator will make a stand and say, "No more!" This is the point where the smart thing should be done. The negotiators walk away from the deal because it no longer offers any value.

Reservation price often **refers** to a monetary price where the deal simply **makes no sense** to **pursue**. It can also refer to a **multiple** set of terms in a more complex negotiation. To a buyer, reservation price means the top price he would be willing to pay, for what he has determined as the **maximum** value of the product being purchased. From a seller's perspective, the reservation price would be the least amount he would be prepared to accept in terms of what he has determined as the least profitable amount acceptable to him. To go beyond the reservation price is that precarious line which will result in a financial loss to you and your company or interested constituents.

From a negotiation perspective, Max Bazerman and Margaret Neale, authors of the book, "**Negotiating Rationally**", describe the role of the negotiator as "Remembering the goal of negotiating is not to reach just any agreement, but to reach an agreement that is better for you than what you would get without one."

Here, they are referring to the root or foundation of what intelligent negotiation is all about. It's about knowing when to stop talking, and turn to your BATNA (Best Alternative to a Negotiated Agreement). Sometimes, this means that your best alternative is to simply walk away.

The key is to apply the best intelligence. You can muster to establish your reservation price. It is based on market demand, your budget or ability to pay. Keep your emotions and ego separate from your business dealings. If you don't, remember who's going to have to pay the piper afterwards.

A Few Guidelines

As a general rule, your reservation price is at least nominally somewhat better than your best alternative.

Don't ever reveal your reservation price to the other side. If your counterpart knows your reservation price, they will use it as a spear. As a result, the negotiations will revolve around the reservation price. If they're a buyer, they will try to pay the least. A seller will try to get the most.

Do try to get the reservation price from the other side. This game is a two-sided game after all. And we all want to get the best deal possible, don't we?

In more complex deals, consider what concessions or trade combinations you're willing to make or receive, before deciding to walk away. In multi-faceted negotiations, don't become too fixated on those price aspects, or your reservation price of a specific item. In particular, if there is something else of value which you might garner from your counterpart, you may treat it as an alternative component of the overall deal. In other words, always focus on the big picture.

Note

reservation price：保留价格，即买（卖）方能接受的最高（低）价。

Group Work

Work in groups and discuss the following questions.

1. What is the reservation price for a seller? What is the reservation price for a buyer?
2. What should the negotiators explain when they are making concessions?
3. List the situations in which the negotiators should make concessions.

要点小结

让步策略是谈判者在议价过程中为保持谈判继续进行的最常用策略。让步策略的运用需要考虑许多其他因素，每一次的让步都紧密关系谈判一方或多方的利益。虽然让步策略的运用主要依靠谈判者凭经验根据现场状况灵活运用，但让步策略的使用也是有一定的基本原则的：单方的一次让步应该与对方的让步相呼应；让步的步幅应该尽可能小，其幅度应该是到能让商务磋商继续进行的最低限度；让步是谈判者为推动谈判继续前行而做出的退让；不要轻易让步。

让步策略多种多样，如：以近谋远的让步策略、互惠互利的让步策略、以虚谋实的让步策略等。

综合实训

Task 1

1. Analyze the following cases and answer the questions followed.

Case 1:

Huayi Industrial and Trading Company in China deliberately dropped the price of the nail accessories from US$180 per dozen (the market price) to $165 per dozen, when they were in negotiation with a German company. The low price had attracted the German company a lot. So the German company gave up other nail sellers in order to focus on the negotiations with Huayi. In the negotiations, Huayi said if the German company expended retail sales, they could change the original paperback into hardcover, but the German company should add the price up to $167. Germen knew that such hard covered accessories were sold much better than the paperbacked ones. And then they accepted the price. On the delivery date, the German company required Huayi to complete the delivery task of 50 thousand dozen within two months. Huayi suggested to consider partial shipment because the factory couldn't accomplish large number of production in such a short time. But Germen insisted on two months. After further discussion, Huayi replied: the factories could work overtime to complete the export in order to meet the requirements of Germen's willing. But taking the small export profit margin into account, Huayi hoped that the Garman Company would pay some more for overtime-working. The Garman company was willing to pay US$3 more per dozen for overtime-working. Finally, Huayi said because the number of goods was large which made it difficult to get a loan, they hoped the German company would pay 30% in advance. In the end, the Garman Company agreed on a 20% advance payment. The negotiation reached. In fact, this batch of nail accessories was the **inventory**. In order to clear out as soon as possible, Huayi used bidding strategy successfully and made the deal beyond the expected profit.

Questions:

1) Which kind of offer did Huayi use, European offer or Japanese offer?

2) What are the key factors that Huayi used to affect the price in the negotiation?

Case 2:

In 1984, Los Angeles hosted the 23rd Summer Olympic Games and profited 150 million dollars, creating a miracle in Olympic history. The great success should be contributed to a famous young entrepreneur—Ueberroth. In addition to his excellent organizational skills and **superb** management skills, Ueberroth excellent negotiation skill also contributed the success a lot. The most negotiation strategy he used to solve the huge costs in the process of negotiation was the high-profile crane building strategy and open outcry.

At the beginning, Ueberroth proposed **rigorous** requirements, one of which was each

sustentation fund should not be less than 400 million. The famous Eastman Kodak Company which was proud of its centuries-old history was willing to sponsor only one million dollars along with a large number of films. Ueberroth gave no ground and absolutely granted the sponsorship to Fuji. This made Kodak Company bite its tongue off. Other sponsors learned a lesson from the event and were aware of the fierce competition in the Olympic Games negotiations. From then on, the sponsors became cautious and worked carefully. Finally, Ueberroth selected 30 sponsors among the competitors and easily solved the financing problem. The Los Angeles Olympic Games became the first profitable Olympic Games in the history, which enhanced not only the value of the Olympics, but also the Olympic hosts' confidence.

Questions:

1) Which strategies did Ueberroth use?

2) What did the strategies work out?

2. Practice the strategies of offer. Divide the class into several groups. Complete the following form and draft an offer plan for Company A.

A 公司与 B 公司就 PET 的购买进行谈判。A 公司的产品生产成本为 10 000 元/吨，市场平均价格为 12 000 元/吨，公司制定的保留价格为 11 000 元/吨，理想成交价格为 11 400 元/吨。本次谈判是双方第一次正式磋商，不会直接成交。此次谈判的成败关系到 A 公司能否进入海南市场。

根据国际石油价格行情和 PET 生产技术，PET 产品价格今后走势是稳中有升。目前 PET 在中国的市场行情为 12 000 元/吨，市场供求基本平衡，但 B 公司所在的海南省目前尚无生产 PET 的厂家，B 公司 PET 产品完全从外地采购。A 公司产品质量略优于同行。B 公司目前经营业绩下滑，迫切需要降低原料成本。此前，B 公司的 PET 的采购价格为 11 700 元/吨～11 800 元/吨。

报价策略策划表

报价依据	
报价方式	
报价时机	
报价起点	
报价陈述	
其他说明	

Task 2

1. Divide the class into several groups. Read the case and try to accomplish the exercises followed.

Case:

卖方：中国 SX 五矿进出口公司。中国较大的经营冶炼、铸造用焦炭产品的生产和出口商。

买方：印度 TT 贸易有限公司。印度著名的焦炭采购商之一。

印度 TT 贸易公司为改善高品质焦炭货源供给，通过多种渠道获得中国 SX 五矿进出口公司的资料，并通过函电表达了愿意与中国 SX 公司就冶金焦、铸造焦、增碳剂等冶金用炉料展开长期贸易合作的意向。中国 SX 公司也正好有扩大海外市场的想法，于是邀请印度 TT 公司的贸易代表来华进行实质性的谈判。

中国 SX 公司的工厂设在优质焦煤产地，生产设备和工艺水平处于国际领先水平，多年来在国际市场享有盛誉。据公司内部统计分析证明，中国 SX 公司的一级冶金焦产品的生产成本和销售成本分别低于同行业的 6%和 7%。中国 SX 公司的竞争对手主要来自国内，大约有 6 家国内企业对它构成不同程度的威胁。

印度 TT 公司在乌克兰和俄罗斯有两家长期供应商，但对这两家供应商的供应货品越来越不满意。印度 TT 公司最近正寻求成为世界最大的钢铁公司印度米塔尔钢铁公司（Mittal Steel）的焦炭采购供应商，米塔尔公司对焦炭原料的质量要求是出名得严格。

这次印度 TT 公司指定询价主导产品是一级冶金焦。当前，该产品的国际市场平均价格为 550 美元/吨，而中国 SX 公司发货的离岸成本为 495 美元/吨。目前供求基本平衡，但从长期看，该价格有下降趋势。印度 TT 公司提出的支付方式是以商业信用为基础的 D/P 或 D/A 计算方式。

1) There is a bargaining assessment model. Try to complete it on the basis of the case from the prospect of China Company SX.

中国 SX 公司价格谈判评估模型 单位：美元

一级冶金焦	情况描述	因素权重分析				加权平均 权重×估价
关键因素		有利因素		威胁因素		
		权重	估价	权重	估价	
产品成本	离岸价：495 美元/吨 成本低于同行业平均水平	0.12				
市场行情				0.10		
竞争态势				0.14		
买方战略意图		0.15				
交货期限		0.13				
产品内在因素		0.12				

续表

一级冶金焦	情况描述	因素权重分析				加权平均 权重×估价
关键因素		有利因素		威胁因素		
		权重	估价	权重	估价	
交易性质	长期的多品种交易			0.14		
交付方式				0.10		
总和		0.52		0.48		
算术平均价格						

2) Analyze the data in the assessment model and try to set up the price target system.

2. Role-play

A and B are having the negotiation consultation on a set of hi-tech equipment. Use as many bargaining strategies as possible. Then tell the class what strategies you have used.

Situation:

A: Your company wants to purchase a set of hi-tech equipment at the price of $1million.

B: Your factory invents hi-tech equipment. The technology of it is unique in the industry business.

Task 3

1. Work in pairs and try to make concessions during the bargaining.

A: Your company wants to buy a set of equipment. Its price is $1 million but you only want to pay $80 thousand.

B: You are a delegator of an equipment company.

A	B
1. Offer $80million	2. Refuse offer
3. Offer $82 thousand, condition: free delivery	4. Refuse offer
5. Offer $85 thousand, condition: free delivery and a two-year guarantee.	6. Agree to free car radio and two-year guarantee. condition: $87 thousand
7. Offer $86 thousand, condition: send the equipment immediately	8. Deal

2. Analyze the following case and answer the questions followed.

Case:

A China Machinery Import and Export branch company was ready to buy advanced equipment. After receiving numerous quotations, they took a fancy to a western company whose equipment and technology were more advanced. Then the Chinese company decided to invite the staffs of the western company to further negotiations.

The negotiation focused on the price issue: the westerners offered $200 thousand, and the Chinese side bargained $100 thousand. Both sides had estimated that the deal price would **range** from $140 thousand to $150 thousand. But according to the past experiences, the consensus could not be reached until several rounds of bargaining had been hold. In terms of the bargaining pace and magnitude, the Chinese side had different opinions which were mainly divided into two factions: (1) Considering the interests of both sides, the Chinese side was planning to bargain in two steps. In the first round of count-offer, they would bargain $100 thousand. It was the price to **eliminate** the gap and reach a consent. Then in the second round, they would bargain $140 thousand to make a **mutual** accommodation. (2) The Chinese side should not increase the price too fast and too sharply. In each round, their compromise should not be more than $5 thousand dollars and then generally increased the price to $105 thousand.

Questions

1) Which opinion of the counter-offer is better?

2) Is there any other strategy which is better than the two?

实践语句

1. Then in the process of negotiation consultation, the seller would add up the price by various reasonable excuses including the transportation expenses and the delivery period.

然后在商务磋商过程中，卖家会以运输成本和交货期限等各种合理借口加价。

2. Estimate their weights (relative value) to both parties. There may be some things that are important to you but less important to your counterpart.

评估双方实力（相对价值）。对于你方来说或许是很重要的方面，而对于对手可能就不是那么重要了。

3. That was to say that China's PV enterprises would lose the largest export market. Meanwhile, the PV downstream enterprises of Europe would not be able to obtain high quality and low price of PV products.

也就是说，中国的光伏企业会失去一个巨大的出口市场。与此同时，欧洲的光伏下游企业无法获得质高价廉的光伏产品。

4. I'd like to get the ball rolling by talking about prices.

我想从价格开始磋商。

5. That's not exactly what I had in mind. I know your research costs are high, but what I'd like is a 25% discount.

这不是我所想的。我知道你们的研发费用高，但是我要的只是 25%的折扣。

6. We could take a cut on the price. But 25% would slash our profit margin. We suggest a compromise, 10%.

我们可以降低价格。但是，25%的折扣大幅缩减了我们的毛利率。我们折中吧——10%。

7. At US$1,000 per piece, we'll make an average return of just 4%. That's too great a financial burden for us.

1 000 美元一件，那么我们的平均盈利只有 4%。对我们而言，这经济负担真的是太大了。

8. How about 15% the first six months, and the second six months at 12%, with a guarantee of 3,000 units?

前六个月（交付）15%，后六个月（交付）12%，保证（总共交付）3 000 套，如何？

9. But I'd prefer the first shipment to be 1,000 units, the next 2,000. The 31st is quite soon—I can't guarantee 1,500.

我希望先装运 1 000 套，然后 2 000 套。31 号很快就到了——我没法保证向贵方供货 1 500 套。

10. A three-year guarantee, not two. And a quality inspection tour after one year is fine, but we'd like some of our personnel on the team.

三年保质期，而不是两年。一年后（贵方）可以进行巡回质量检查，但是质检队中要有我方成员。

词语释义

adapt	*v.* 适应；改编
adopt	*vt.* 采用，采取，采纳；收养；正式接受，接受；批准
allow	*vt.* 允许；承认；给予；准许（做某事）
appeal	*vi.* （迫切）要求；有吸引力；求助（于）；提请注意
approximately	*adv.* 近似地，大约
attract	*vt.* 吸引；诱惑；引起……的好感（或兴趣）
beneficial	*adj.* 有利的，有益的
compare	*vt.* & *vi.* 比较，对照
complex	*adj.* 复杂的；合成的
consultation	*n.* 商议，磋商；商讨会
content	*n.* 内容；（书等的）目录；满足；容量
	adj. 满足的，满意的；愿意的；心甘情愿的
counterpart	*n.* 配对物；副本；相对物；极相似的人或物
create	*vt.* 创造，创作；产生
eliminate	*vt.* 排除，消除；淘汰；除掉

equal	*adj.* 相等的，平等的
estimate	*n.* 估计，预测；*vt.* 估计，估算；评价
expectation	*n.* 期待；预期
flaw	*n.* 瑕疵
flexibility	*n.* 柔韧性，机动性，灵活性；伸缩性
gap	*n.* 缺口；分歧；间隔
identify	*vt.* 识别，认出；确定
immediately	*adv.* 立刻，马上
incentive	*n.* 动机；刺激；诱因；鼓励
inventory	*n.* 存货清单；财产目录
involve	*vt.* 包含；使参与，牵涉
issue	*n.* 问题　*vt.* 发行；发布
maximum	*n.* 最大的量、体积、强度等
multiple	*adj.* 多重的；多个的；复杂的；多功能的
mutual	*adj.* 共有的；共同的；相互的
opposite	*adj.* 相对的；对面的；对立的
outcome	*n.* 结果；成果；出路
outcry	*n.* 高声叫喊，尖叫；拍卖，叫卖
persistent	*adj.* 持续的；坚持不懈的
prioritize	*vt.* 按重要性排列，划分优先顺序；优先处理
process	*n.* 过程；工序
profile	*n.* 侧面，半面；外形，轮廓
pursue	*vt.* 继续；追求；进行
range	*n.* 范围；类别
	vt. 排列；（按一定位置或顺序）排序；把……分类；徘徊
reasonable	*adj.* 合理的，公道的；适当的；有理性的
refer	*vi.* 提到；针对；关系到；请教
relative	*adj.* 相关的；相对的；相互有关的；比较而言的
reservation	*n.* 保留；预订，预约；保留地
reveal	*vt.* 显露；揭露；泄露
rigorous	*adj.* 严密的；缜密的；严格的；枯燥的
sacrifice	*vt.* & *vi.* 牺牲，把……奉献给……；廉价卖出
severe	*adj.* 严峻的；严厉的；剧烈的；苛刻的
simultaneous	*adj.* 同时发生的，同时存在的
Soviet Union	（前）苏联
superb	*adj.* 极好的；华丽的；丰盛的，豪华的；杰出的

sustentation	*n.* 生活资料；营养物；支持；维持
technique	*n.* 技巧，技术，手段；技能；手法
transportation	*n.* 运送，运输；运输系统；运输工具
utilize	*vt.* 利用，使用
various	*adj.* 各种各样的；多方面的；许多的

add up	加起来；总计
make no sense	毫无意义

Unit 8 Deadlock Settlement in Business Negotiation

商务谈判僵局处理

任务目标

1. Understanding the concept of deadlock
2. Analyzing the reasons causing deadlock
3. Practicing tactics and skills to settle deadlocks
4. Practicing making deadlocks

僵局不是商务谈判必然经历的阶段，而是谈判双方经过交锋和协商，彼此都不愿意让步，导致谈判难以继续的局面。实践表明，谈判中的僵局是一种客观存在，既不能避免也无谓惊慌失措。僵局一旦被突破，谈判就基本可以促成了。

Task 1 The Causes Leading to Deadlocks

僵局产生的原因

谈判可能不成功的原因有多种。谈判者应将每一个谈判僵局作为一个挑战，而不是视之为一个问题，并且有必要检视一些比较常见的原因，寻找克服、突破这些僵局的解决方案。在商务谈判中，谈判者只要认真细致地分析引起僵局的根源，然后对症下药，采取灵活而又有针对性的措施进行化解，就能化险为夷。

案例学习

The president of a multinational company visited a famous manufacturing enterprise in China to discuss about cooperation and development issues. In the negotiation, the general manager of the Chinese enterprise proudly introduced to the president about the Chinese company: "My company is a second level enterprise in China..." **Unexpectedly**, the president who once was **in the best of spirits** immediately changed his attitude and treated the Chinese general manager coldly. Then the delegators of the multinational company took leave in a hurry after several perfunctory words. On the way back to his own company, the president **complained**: "How can I **cooperate** with such a second-class enterprise in China!"

案例思考

1. Which kind of **conflict** causes the **deadlock**?
2. How to settle the deadlock?

案例解析

这一僵局显然是由于双方文化背景差异造成的沟通障碍，中方谈判者在沟通中没能注意关键词的细节描述。案例中提及的“中国二级企业”在英文文化背景中难以找到相关术语与之匹配，必须经过语言描述加以说明，才能阐述清楚，消除障碍。

理论拓展

Gender Negotiation Communication Style Differences: Women
性别在谈判交流中的风格差异：女性

By Dianna Booher[1]

Statistics tell the story: in the USA, women **compose** half the **professional** managerial workforce. Half the students who earned college degrees last year were **composed** of women. Of those who have a personal worth of more than $500,000, more than half are women. American women collectively earn more than $1 trillion a year. More than 7.7 million women who own businesses in the U.S. generate $1.4 trillion a year. Women **comprise** 35 percent of the country's 51 million **shareholders**. Researchers in the 1970s **predicted** the disappearance of **gender** communication differences. As women move into higher management **positions**, the gap or "disconnection" remains.

In organizations, one gender mainly sells to buyers of the same gender. Take stock brokers for example. For years, **male** stock brokers have been selling mostly to other males—their **comfort** zone. Another example is the **residential** real estate industry where **female agents** dominate the **scene**. A third example is the health-care industry. In fact, the **potential** for gender communication gaps are widest in those organizations where one gender takes up most of the **senior executive** positions.

As the **traditional** picture changes and both men and women must communicate in teams, and sell to the other gender, their **awareness** grows. In other words, they both experience the problem but don't know where to begin to expand their repertoire of communication skills.

Professionals and companies that create cultures which encourage both genders in their career paths, recognizing the accomplishments and contributions of both men and women, will be the most **productive** and satisfied. And that will be the competitive advantage at the turn of the century. Neither men nor women are better communicators. They're just different. We must learn to recognize these general differences in the way the two genders communicate and be more **effective** with the other half of the business community.

As females grow up in our culture, they are taught not to be confrontational, not to be aggressive or pushy. So how do they express opposition to an idea? Frequently they use indirect **channels** such as questions. They, of course, also use questions in the traditional way: to solicit information to make people rethink their positions, plans, or ideas.

Men, on the other hand, do not always recognize indirect messages or pick up on nuances in words or body language. In short, they don't always accurately "read between the lines"[2]; to understand a woman's meaning or question.

The results:

1. Women ask questions meant as indirect **objections**, men appear to **ignore** their objections and feelings.

2. Women ask questions meant only to solicit information to which men react defensively. Women's language tends to be indirect, **indiscreet**, tactful, and even manipulative. Women tend to give fewer directives and use more courtesy words with those directives. Example: "The approach is not precisely foreign to our designers"; meaning "They are **familiar** with it."; or "Mary may not be **available** to handle the project" meaning "Mary doesn't want to handle the project."

Notes

1. Dianna Boomer is CEO of Boomer Consultants, a Dallas-based communications consulting firm.

2. In short, they don't always accurately "read between the lines"：简而言之，他们（男性）总是不能在两性交流时领会言外之意。

Group Work

Divide the class into several groups and discuss the following questions.

1. What are the differences between men and women in negotiation communication? List the differences down.

2. How do men and women think differently? Give some examples.

3. There are many issues that may cause deadlock in negotiation, such as culture gap and gender gap. Think about what else can cause deadlock?

要点小结

商务谈判僵局是指在商务谈判过程中，当双方对所谈问题的利益要求差距较大，各方又都不肯做出让步，导致双方因暂时不可调和的矛盾而形成的对峙，致使谈判呈现出一种不进不退的僵持局面。

谈判僵局主要由三类冲突引发：第一类，假想冲突，由沟通、交流不充分造成；第二类，人为冲突，由谈判者故意制造，以迫使对方妥协、让步；第三类，真正冲突，这是谈判本质上的利益矛盾。

谈判中大量僵局是由假象冲突造成的。沟通障碍是指谈判双方在交流彼此情况、观点、洽谈合作意向、交易的条件等过程中，所可能遇到的由于主观或客观的原因所造成的理解障碍。

第一种沟通障碍是由于双方文化背景差异，一方语言中的某些特别表述难以用另一种语言描述而造成误解。

第二种沟通障碍是一方虽已知悉却未能理解另一方所提供的信息内容。这是因为接收信息者对信息的理解受其职业习惯、受教育程度以及为某些领域内的专业知识所制约。有时表面上看来，接收信息者似已完全理解，但实际上这种理解却常常是主观的、片面的，甚至往往与信息内容的实质情况完全相反。

第三种沟通障碍是一方虽已理解却不愿意接受这种理解。因为他是否能够接受现实，往往受其心理因素的影响，包括对对方的态度、与对方以往打交道的经历以及个人的偏见等。

Task 2 Strategies of Breaking a Deadlock
突破僵局的策略

谈判僵局对谈判双方的情绪和利益都会产生不良影响。谈判僵局会导致两种后果：僵局被打破，谈判继续；或谈判破裂，无法继续。后者当然是双方都不愿意看见的结果。

因此，僵局一旦出现，谈判者必须运用科学有效的策略和技巧打破僵局，使谈判重新顺利地进行下去。

案例学习

A foreign pharmaceutical company (Company A) negotiated with a large pharmaceutical agency (Company B) in China on the production of cardiovascular system drug. Because the business director of Company A was unavailable, the production director was sent to lead the delegation to meet with the staff of Company B. Company A firstly **proposed** the price for products to Company B. **Criticizing** the offer, Company B suggested that Company A should carefully consider the severe competition in drug market and the fact that the product made by Company A was almost unknown in China. They required Company A to reduce the price for supplies. But Company A insisted on the original price. As explanation, Company A cited the production costs, research and development costs and other price factors. In the end, Company A stressed that their price was very reasonable. Company B required Company A to cut the price by a further analysis on the market conditions and emphasized that Company B was one of the largest pharmaceutical agencies in China, who had channel resource advantages. A few rounds had been down without a result. Company B thought Company A was too stubborn. On the opposite, Company A considered that Company B acted in an **arrogant** attitude. Blaming each other, the two parted in **discord**.

案例思考

1. What are the reasons for the deadlock in the negotiation?
2. Can the deadlock be avoided?
3. What efforts can be done to settle the deadlock?

案例解析

造成此次谈判僵局的主要原因有三个：（1）只站在自身立场考虑问题。谈判双方在价格问题上都坚持己见，谁都不愿意做出让步。（2）有意无意地强迫。谈判过程中，B方以自己是中国大型医药商业公司，以渠道资源优势突出为由，要求A方降价。A方因受到强迫，更不愿退步降价。（3）谈判团人员素质问题。A公司商务总监因故不能参加谈判，派出以生产总监为首的谈判代表团与B公司谈判。生产总监在谈判技巧和策略方面难免缺乏经验。B方认为自己占有优势，语言态度难免傲慢，造成双方不快。以上种种都使得双方沟通困难，以致最后出现僵局。

这场僵局是有可能避免的。首先，双方应该客观评价自身利益，做出适当让步，化解僵局。其次，双方还可以从不同的方案中寻找替代。比如，A方可以采取在不降价的情况下向对方提供优惠政策和其他利益等策略，让对方接受。B 方也可以用提点等其他利润回报方式说服对方适当降价。最后，双方可以尝试站在对方角度看待问题。B 方要考虑到 A 方作为生产企业也必须有自己的利润空间。同时，A 方也应该考虑 B 方作为大型医药商业公司的地位和优势，适当降低自己的利润空间，实现薄利多销并提高自己产品的知名度。

理论拓展

Essential Negotiating Strategies for Consultants
商务磋商的基本技巧

1. HAVE A POSITION BEFORE YOU ENTER THE ROOM.

Good negotiation starts with knowing what you want and putting it forth in conversation. This requires a substantial amount of preparation and asking the right questions through the discovery process, rather than improvising responses in calls and emails. When you negotiate from a position of strong preparation, the other party will be more comfortable meeting you on your terms, based on your **expertise**.

2. UNDERSTAND WHAT KIND OF LEVERAGE YOU HAVE.

Design firms bring a range of skills and hard-fought experience to bear on **client** problems. This is expertise that our clients rarely have within their own organization. "The most important **leverage** any design firm has is expertise," says Ted Leonhard. "Each of us has our own **mix** of history, skills and experience. A client can only get the unique skills you provide from you."

Beyond expertise, you also have leverage with regard to schedule, **scope** and other variables that are necessary for client success.

3. MAKE SURE YOUR POSITION IS REALISTIC.

If you wanted two million dollars and a platinum-plated Rolls Royce, negotiations would be difficult. However, if you're presenting an estimate for a design project and have some strong **logic** behind your pricing, or some ground as to why your audience will prefer green **instead of** blue for their new **logo**, you shouldn't change your position.

4. COMPROMISES SHOULD BE AROUND SHARED INTERESTS.

Don't give up in your negotiations until you've **exhausted** possibilities that meet your shared interests and help your firm create a quality product. Push for your best-case scenario, preserving your project's schedule, budget, creative direction and so forth. Know what other cards you can place on the table or return to your hand before considering a **compromise**.

5. ALWAYS KEEP THE BIG PICTURE IN MIND.

Know which decisions require formal negotiation and which are just potholes in the road. Changing a headline or **swapping out** a photo shouldn't be a **drama**. Spiking a killer concept to play it safe? That's another story. If you have a strong creative brief and a strong contract, these points shouldn't become issues. Don't treat every single discussion and point of **feedback** with the client as a potential conflict.

6. DON'T AGREE TO A DEAL UNTIL YOUR TEAM AGREES.

Avoid saying yes on anything related to schedule, scope management and other contractually required action steps until you can review the discussion with your **internal** team. Make sure that your team's goals and your client needs are **aligned**. To **quote** Robert Solomon in his excellent book *The Art of Client Service*: "Make no commitment without consultation." [1]

7. BEWARE OF CULTURAL NUANCES.

I once worked with a foreign client whose **method** of negotiation was to state in every deliverable review that there were always things that could be improved. We found ourselves increasing the project scope and number of deliverables in order to compensate for the **perceived** lack in quality. Their negotiating position wasn't unusual in their country, but it was for our team. After a few nerve-racking weeks, we realized that the client's escalations were an opportunity to set up clear approval criteria to demonstrate how our design work had merit and was on brief. In our final presentation, the success of our project was clearly evident to everyone within their organization.

8. DON'T RUSH TO AGREE WITH A CLIENT NEED.

If the stakes are high, take your time and **hash out** the finer points in detail. The longer and more drawn out the negotiation, the more important it is to never show your "settling point". [2] Get some time and space to think it over. Don't jump on the phone and immediately try to iron it out. Otherwise, whomever you're negotiating with may think that they can push their position even further. These situations are very hard for designers; we love to solve problems as quickly as possible!

9. KEEP YOUR DIALOGUE HUMANE, RESPECTFUL, AND HONEST.

When negotiating with clients or your boss, make sure you don't turn your negotiations into an "us vs. them" scenario. Our clients and co-workers have the same set of human needs that we do, and relating with them on a human level will strengthen your continued working relationship. It will also cement the expectation that no matter what happens in your work, you'll always be on equal footing as people.

10. BE PREPARED TO LEAVE THE TABLE AT ANY POINT.

Be willing to walk away from a negotiation if you think the options available are going to hurt you in the long term. Being willing to say no is important in contract negotiations, and the natural human desire to avoid conflict is something that potential clients may **exploit**. It's okay to say no.

11. IF THE NEGOTIATION FAILS, DON'T TAKE IT PERSONALLY.

Hindsight is 20/20. If you don't land a project because it wasn't the right fit or the client overrules your beautiful color scheme because they dislike purple, learn from what happened and move forward. Don't let your conscience eat a hole in your gut.[3] Analyzing these failures can have a big **impact** on improving future negotiations.

12. FAILURE TO LAND A PROJECT CAN LEAD TO A FUTURE WIN.

Relationships between your co-workers and your clients continue, even if you fail in your first negotiations. If you've been cordial and truthful about your position and the experience that you bring throughout the entire negotiation process, you'll gain respect. Mutual respect comes from **establishing** clear **boundaries** and reinforcing them throughout the life of a relationship. This is the currency that will yield future work and support you when you get down to business.

Notes

1. Make no commitment without consultation. 译为“没有协商就没有承诺。” Robert Solomon 在他所著的 *The Art of Client Service* 书中提到这一理念。

2. settling point：沉降点。此处是指“关键点”。

3. Don't let your conscience eat a hole in your gut. gut 意为内脏，肠道。这句话的意思是：不要因为良心（让这件事）成为你的内心负担。

Group Work

Divide the class into several groups and discuss the following questions.

1. In the article above, the author mentions some essential negotiating strategies. Which strategies can be utilized to settle deadlocks?

2. If the deadlock which led to the failure of the negotiation can't be solved, which attitude should the negotiator hold?

要点小结

当僵局出现以后，必须进行迅速处理，否则就会对谈判顺利进行产生影响。出现僵局不等于谈判破裂，但它严重影响谈判的进程，如不能很好地解决，就会导致谈判破裂。想要突破僵局，必须对僵局的性质、产生原因等问题进行透彻的了解和分析，才能正确地加以判断，从而进一步采取相应的策略和技巧，选择有效的方案，使双方重新回到谈判桌上来。

突破僵局的策略主要有：

1. 回避分歧，转移议题。
2. 尊重客观，关注利益。
3. 多种方案，选择替代。

4. 尊重对方，有效退让。
5. 冷调处理，暂时休会。
6. 以硬碰硬，据理力争。
7. 孤注一掷，背水一战。

Task 3 Making a Deadlock
制造僵局

制造僵局策略就是有意识地制造僵局，给对方造成压力，为己方争取时间并创造谈判优势。这是一种带有高度冒险性的谈判战略。在实际操作中，谈判者必须认真考量谈判双方的优势和劣势，要充分分析在双方的资源、时间、利益等因素共同作用下制造僵局的可行性。

案例学习

A negotiation was held between an American company and a Japanese company. There was a big interest gap between the two sides which might meet the Japanese company with a concession. Since at the very beginning, the Japanese knew that the American representatives had to leave after two weeks, so they spent more than one week on travelling with the American representatives and arranged parties at night instead of keeping the negotiation on. Finally, they continued the negotiation at the twelfth day, but the negotiation ended early so as to let the American representatives play golf. At the fourteenth day, they began to discuss the part which was relevant to the interest gap. But it was the time that the Americans should go back. Therefore, the Americans had no time to negotiate in details and had to accept the terms that Japanese referred. Then the American representatives signed the contract **perfunctorily**.

案例思考

1. What deadlock strategy did the Japanese apply?
2. What benefits did the Japanese gain by utilizing this strategy?

案例解析

这里使用的是最常见的策略——时间限制法。在商务谈判中，谈判者在得知对手的谈判时间底线的前提下，故意在某一具有重大经济利益谈判主题上坚持不让步，延缓谈判进程。最终，使得对手在利益和时间的双重压力下不得不屈服。这是谈判者故意制造僵局，搞突然袭击。当对手为僵局导致的利益问题而着急，并且同时又感受到时间的压迫时，就是解开僵局，谈条件的最佳时机。

理论拓展

How Time Pressure Affects the Outcome of a Negotiation?
时间压力如何影响谈判结果？

By Roger Dawson[1]

That was putting extreme time pressure on the negotiation, and people become pliable under time pressure. When do children ask the parents for something? Just as the parent is hurrying out of the door, right? Children are not especially **manipulative**, but instinctively, over all those years of dealing with adults, they learn that under time pressure people become more flexible.

Power Negotiators know that an interesting question is raised when both sides are closing in on the same time deadline. Think of this in terms of you renewing your office lease for example. Let's say that your five-year lease ends in six months, and you must negotiate a **renewal** with your landlord. You might think to yourself, "I'll use time pressure on the landlord to get the best deal. I'll wait until the last moment to negotiate with him. That will put him under a lot of time pressure. He'll know that if I move out the place will be vacant for several months until he can find a new tenant." That appears like a great strategy until you realize that there's no difference between that and the landlord refusing to negotiate until the last minute to put time pressure on you. So, there you have a situation in which both sides are approaching the same time deadline. Which side should use time pressure and which side should avoid it? The answer is that the side that has the greatest power could use time pressure, but the side with the least power should avoid time pressure and negotiate well before the deadline. Fair enough, but who has the most power? The side with the most options has the most power. If you can't reach a negotiated renewal of the lease, who has the best **alternatives** available to them?

To determine this you might take a sheet of paper and draw a line down the middle. On the left side, list your options in the event that you can't renew the lease. What alternative locations are available to you? Would they cost more or less? How much would it cost you to move the telephones and print new stationary? Would your customers be able to find you if you moved? On the right hand side of the page, list the landlord's options. How specialized is this building? How difficult would it be for him to find a new tenant? Would they pay more or would he have to lease it for less? How much would he have to spend on improvements or remodeling to accommodate a new tenant?

Now you must do one more thing. You must compensate for the fact that whichever side of the negotiating table you're on. You always think you have the weaker hand. After all, you know all about the pressure that's on you, but you don't know about the pressure that's on the leaseholder. One of the things that make you a more powerful negotiator understands that you always think you have the weaker hand and are learning to compensate for that. So, when you list each side's alternatives in this way, you'll likely end up concluding that the landlord has more alternatives than you do. So, compensate for that, but if you do so, and clearly the landlord still has more options than you do, he's the one who has the power. You should avoid time pressure and negotiate the lease renewal with lots of time to spare. However, if clearly you have more alternatives available to you than the landlord does, put him under time pressure by negotiating at the last moment.

Time is comparable to money. They are invested, spent, saved, and wasted. Do invest the time to go through every step of the negotiation; do use time pressure to gain the advantage, and don't surrender to the temptation to hurry a conclusion. Power Negotiators know that time is money.

Note

Roger Dawson is a negotiation consultant and a sales and management speaker. He is the author of *Secrets of Power Negotiating*.

Group Work

Divide the class into several groups and discuss the following questions.

1. What is the deadline?

2. When you are planning to make a deadlock by time-pressure, what tasks should you prepare to do?

要点小结

任何商务谈判中都会遇到僵局，其产生原因和解决方案各异，如核心价值产生的僵局、沟通障碍导致僵局、谈判人员的偏见或成见导致僵局等。有的僵局是人为制造，是谈判者故意为之，使得对手在利益和时间的双重压力下不得不屈服，从而达到获利目的。在商务磋商过程中，谈判者常采取商务谈判策略，制造僵局，如制造产品价值僵局、制造人员精力僵局、制造强硬作风僵局、制造时间僵局等。

制造僵局是一件操作难度高、风险大的策略。一般没有超高谈判水平的人不敢轻易运用。在故意制造僵局时应注意以下几点：（1）使用需谨慎；（2）选择时机条件应成熟；（3）表现应坚决；（4）僵局形成后应积极向对方人员施加影响。

综合实训

Task 1

In the following, there are some classic cases. Learn them by heart.

Case 1: Michael Bloomberg versus the New York Teachers' union

New York City stood to gain about $250 million in aid and $200 million in grants if it reached agreement on a new evaluation system with its teachers' union, a 4% overall increase in state aid. But as 2012 drew to a close, talks between New York's United Federation of Teachers (UFT) and New York mayor Michael Bloomberg were deadlocked. On the deadline date of January 17, 2013, the two sides separately announced that a final, late-night negotiating session had collapsed. Ultimately, New York governor Andrew Cuomo imposed an evaluation system on the city.

Case 2: Simon & Schuster versus Barnes & Noble

When months of negotiations with publishing house Simon & Schuster reached a **standoff** in January 2013, Barnes & Noble attempted to gain leverage by significantly reducing its orders of Simon & Schuster titles and engaging in other hardball negotiation tactics, such as refusing to book the publisher's authors for in-store readings. Given that Barnes & Noble sells about 20% of consumer books in the United States, Simon & Schuster editors and their associated agents and writers were "apoplectic" about the bookseller's decision to use them as a bargaining chip, *The New York Times* reported in March 2013.

Case 3: A Temporary Agreement with Iran

The negotiations between Iran and the United States to limit the Islamic Republic's nuclear weapons program reached an impasse in November 2013 when Iranian President Hassan Rouhani persisted in his assertion that Iran had a sovereign right to enrich uranium. While the United States did not accept this argument, the Obama administration did engage in concessions with the Iranian side regarding enrichment which led to more creative bargaining options for both parties.

Task 2

1. In the following, there are some cases. Read the cases and complete the exercises followed.

Case:

我国某集团公司下属的一个玻璃厂就玻璃生产设备的有关事项，与德国自动化生产线公司进行谈判。谈判在中方玻璃厂举行。在谈判过程中，双方就全套设备同时引进还是部分引进的问题产生分歧，中方代表因为公司资金和外汇额度有限，希望引进部分关键设备，其余附加设备由于技术含量不高，准备在国内以低价格定制。而德方从来就是成套设备出口，如果仅仅出口关键设备，将会大大影响公司的整体利润。双方代表各执一端，互不相让。德方首席谈判代表库克先生坚持整套设备出售。而中方首席谈判代表，玻璃厂厂长张强先生认为德国人历来固执己见，趾高气扬，态度令人无法忍受，于是拍案而起，把德国人晾在谈判桌上扬长而去。德国代表团也很生气，决定购买机票返回法兰克福。

一场刚刚开始的谈判已经到了濒临破裂的边缘。当天中午，中方集团公司领导召开紧急会议商讨对策。通过分析，得出结论：德国艾肯自动化生产线公司的生产设备、工艺先进，而且价格实惠，最适合本公司需要。为打破僵局，集团公司领导层决定临时由公司的营销副总裁韩涛先生担任中方首席谈判代表，并且在德国代表团订购飞机票前将他们拉回了谈判桌。

中方在新一轮谈判开始，就提出两套不同的方案供对方选择：A 方案，中方同意购买整套设备，但是出价极低。B 方案，中方选择进口生产线中的关键设备，作为回报，中方给出比较优惠的价格。德方经过考虑，愿意就 A 方案与中方展开磋商。经过几轮商谈，双方终于达成了协议。

Exercises:

1）评估谈判双方在谈判中所处的地位。

2）分析谈判中买卖双方僵持不下的具体原因。

3）中方在打破僵局方面运用了哪些策略？

2. Divide the class into several groups and analyze the following case in groups.

Case:

In 2011, two American customers came to visit Zhongshan Auman Lighting Technology Co. Ltd.. Considering the two American were big buyers, Zhongshan Company sent 4 persons (the Deputy General Manager, the Foreign Trade manager, the Director and a salesman) to welcome them. As it was lunch time when the two American customers arrived at the company, the Chinese Deputy General Manager politely asked if they would like to go for lunch. In advance, both sides had learned about the culture of each country. The Chinese Manager knew that Americans were more direct than Chinese people. So the manager of Zhongshan Company followed American style and asked directly. However, the two Americans, in accordance with the Chinese customs, euphemistically replied: "We are not very hungry. Take it casually." Finally, the American customers followed the enthusiastic Chinese staff to visit the factory in hunger. The negotiation ended in an unhappy and uncomfortable atmosphere. The American customers could not adapt to the situation and held no hope for cooperation. While on the other side, the Chinese were full of doubt about the American customers' attitude.

Questions:

1) What was the deadlock?

2) What caused the deadlock?

3) Could the deadlock be settled? And how to solve it?

Task 3

1. There are many negotiation strategies that can be used in making deadlocks. Match the strategies to its description below.

Bullying　　Appeal to a higher authority　　A last-time claim　　The deadline

1) an aggressive demand for a concession to be made

2) saying that only your boss can offer the concession that is being asked for

3) applying pressure by saying that you have to leave at a certain fixed time

4) a demand which is made after it appears that agreement has been reached

2. Read the following extracts from negotiations and decide the strategy used in each case. Then, practice the conversations with your partners.

Extract 1:

A: Right then, I think that just about **wraps it up**. Do we have a deal?

B: Absolutely. It's been a pleasure doing business with you.

A: And you.

B: Oh, just one last thing—it won't be a problem if we increase my discount by half a per cent, will it?

A: Um…

B: Only I have been thinking, it's going to make my life so much easier…

Extract 2:

A: Well, in principle, I like the sound of the idea, but the devil's always in the detail, isn't it? Now, what I'd like to do is talk through some of the small print.

B: Ok, here's the situation. I've got a flight back to New York at half past four, which means that I'm going to have to leave in half an hour…forty minutes at the very latest.

A: So, what are you saying?

B: I've got to tie up this deal before I leave. You know what's on offer—it's your decision.

Extract 3:

A: Well, it looks great. It's just the kind of service we want.

B: Fantastic.

A: But for me, the problem is the level of discount. As I said, I need seven percent.

B: Hmm. That is a problem. I'm afraid I can't take any kind of decision about discounts. I'm going to have to speak to my boss about this. But, well... she's not going to like it.

Extract 4:

A: Well, I must say that I think six percent is a perfectly fair discount.

B: Frankly, I don't think there's any point in us continuing with this discussion. There are lots of other people out there offering exactly the same services as you and at much better prices.

A: I'm sorry, but...

B: Just listen to me for a minute, will you? Either you give me ten percent, or I take my business elsewhere. Am I making myself clear?

A: Perfectly...

B: Am I making myself clear?

3. Divide the class into several groups and answer the questions followed.

Case 1:

A group of Chinese negotiators went to a country in Middle East for a project. When they chatted, a member of the Chinese team who was responsible for the commercial clause made a comment purposelessly on Islamism which was prevailing in the Middle East. The negotiators of the Middle East country were not happy about it. When it came to substantive issues, the radical business negotiators of the Middle East country did not compromise and repeatedly revealed the intention of withdrawal from the negotiation.

Questions:

1) What's the barrier in the case?

2) What situation did the barrier lead to?

3) What measure should be taken to break the deadlock?

4) What lessons should Chinese negotiators learn from the case?

Case 2:

At the end of the 1980s, a new type of integrated circuit product had been developed by a certain electronic company in Silicon Valley. The advantage of the IC product was not yet understood by the public. At this time, the company was going bankrupt in a heavy debt. This IC was appreciated to be the last hope of the electronic company. Fortunately, a European company had the discerning eye and sent three representatives to fly thousands of kilometers to discuss matters relating to the transfer. The European company offered the price as less as only 2/3 of the research funds. The representative of the electronics company stood up and said, "Gentlemen, let's stop here today." Then on the next few days, the negotiations lasted only three minutes from the beginning to the end each time. Unexpectedly, in the afternoon the Europeans asked to reopen the negotiation and showed a more cooperative attitude. Finally, the circuit had been transferred in a high price.

Questions:

1) Why did the Silicon Valley Company dare to cut off the negotiation?

2) Which kind of pressure did the Silicon Valley Company put on the opposite side?

实践语句

1. I can't bring those numbers back to my office—they'll turn it down flat.

我不能把这个价格带回公司——他们会打回票的。

2. Why don't we talk again tomorrow? I must talk to my office anyway. I hope we can find some common ground on this.

我们何不明日再谈呢？无论如何，我必须报备办公室。我希望在此方面我们能够达成共识。

3. I've been instructed to reject the numbers you proposed; but we can try to come up with something else.

我奉命拒绝贵方所提出的数字，但我们可以试着想出别的办法。

4. My instructions are to negotiate hard on this deal—but I'm trying very hard to reach some middle ground.

我所得到的指示是以强硬态度对待这笔交易——但我很努力地去达成一些共识。

5. We'd like to weigh the pros and cons with you.

我们想和贵方权衡一下利弊得失。

6. If we can settle a number of basic questions, I'm confident in saying that we are the most suitable for your needs.

如果我们能够解决一些基本的问题，我相信我方最适合贵方需求。

7. The most important leverage any design firm has is expertise.

任何设计公司最重要的力量是专业经验。

8. Analyzing these failures can have a big impact on improving future negotiations.

分析这些失败经验对提升未来的谈判水平会产生巨大影响。

9. Don't treat every single discussion and point of feedback with the client as a potential conflict.

不要把每一次与客户的讨论和反馈当作一个潜在的冲突。

10. Don't give up in your negotiations until you've exhausted possibilities that meet your shared interests and help your firm create a quality product.

在谈判中不要放弃，直到你用尽一切可能性，满足你的共同利益，并帮助你的公司创建高质量的产品。

词语释文

agent　　*n.* 代理人；代理商

align　　*vt.* 使成一线，使结盟；排整齐

alternative	*n.* 可供替代的事物；可供选择的事物
arrogant	*adj.* 傲慢的，自大的
available	*adj.* 可用的；有空的；可会见的
avoid	*vt.* 避开，避免；[法律] 使无效，撤销，废止
awareness	*n.* 察觉，觉悟，意识
boundary	*n.* 分界线；范围
channel	*n.* 频道；渠道；途径；海峡 *vt.* 引导，开导
client	*n.* 顾客；当事人；诉讼委托人
comfort	*n.* 安慰；舒适 *vt.* 安慰，使舒适
complain	*vi.* 抱怨，诉苦；申诉，控诉，抗议
compose	*vt.* 组成，构成
comprise	*vt.* 包含，包括；由……组成；由……构成
compromise	*n.* 妥协；妥协（或折中）方案 *vi.* 折中解决；妥协，退让
conflict	*n.* 冲突；战斗；相互干扰；矛盾 *vi.* 抵触；争斗；战斗；冲突
cooperate	*vi.* 合作，配合，协助
criticize	*vt.* & *vi.* 分析，评估；批评；挑剔
deadlock	*n.* 僵局；停顿，停滞 *vt.* 停顿；相持不下 *vi.* 成僵局
discord	*n.* 不和；不调和；嘈杂声 *v.* 不一致
drama	*n.* 戏剧，剧本；戏剧效果
effective	*adj.* 有效的；起作用的
establish	*vt.* 建立，创建；确立
executive	*n.* 总经理；行政部门 *adj.* 执行的；管理的
exhaust	*vt.* 用尽，耗尽；使筋疲力尽；排出；彻底探讨
expertise	*n.* 专门知识或技能；专家的意见；专家评价，鉴定
exploit	*vt.* 开采；开拓；利用（……为自己谋利）；剥削 *n.* 功绩；功劳；勋绩
familiar	*adj.* 熟悉的；通晓的
feedback	*n.* 反馈
female	*adj.* 女性的；雌性的 *n.* 女人；雌性动物
gender	*n.* 性别
ignore	*vt.* 忽视，不顾；[法律] 驳回（诉讼）
impact	*vi.* 冲撞，冲击；产生影响
indiscreet	*adj.* 不慎重的；轻率的；不明智的；不警觉的
internal	*adj.* 国内的；内部的 *prep.*（机构）内部的 *n.* 内脏，内部器官；本质，本性
leverage	*vt.* 使（某一公司）举债经营；补充（如金钱）支持；杠杆作用
logic	*n.* 逻辑，逻辑学
logo	*n.*（某公司或机构的）标识，标志，徽标

male	*adj.* 男性的；雄性的；有力的　*n.* 男；雄性动物
manipulative	*adj.* 善于操纵的；会控制的
method	*n.* 方法；条理
mix	*vt.* & *vi.* 混合；（使）结交；相容
objection	*n.* 反对；反对的话，异议
perceive	*v.* 意识到；察觉，发觉；理解
perfunctorily	*adv.* 敷衍；马马虎虎；潦草地
position	*n.* 位置，方位；地位，职位；态度；状态 *vt.* 安置；把……放在适当位置
potential	*adj.* 潜在的，有可能的
predict	*vt.* 预言，预测；预示，预告
productive	*adj.* 富有成效的；多产的；生产性的；具有创造性的
professional	*adj.* 专业的；专业性的　*n.* 专业人士
propose	*vt.* 提议，建议；打算，计划；推荐，提名
quote	*v.* 引用；报价；引述
renewal	*n.* 恢复；更新；续订；改进
residential	*adj.* 住宅的，适于作住宅的；与居住有关的
scene	*n.* 场面，现场
scope	*n.*（处理、研究事务的）范围；眼界，见识
senior	*adj.*（级别、地位等）较高的；资深的；年长的　*n.* 上级；较年长者
shareholder	*n.* 股东；股票持有者
standoff	*n.* 对峙；僵局；僵持
statistic	*n.* 统计数据；统计量　*adj.* 统计（上）的，统计学（上）的
traditional	*adj.* 传统的；口传的
unexpectedly	*adv.* 未料到地，意外地；竟；居然；骤然

hash out	具体讨论
instead of	（用……）代替……，（是……）而不是……
in the spirits	在内心
swap out	换出
wrap up	圆满结束

Unit 9 Business Contracts

商务合同

任务目标

1. Practicing the tactics of closing negotiations
2. Practicing strategies to bring to sign a contract
3. Approaching the content of a business contract
4. Learning the process of signing a business contract

谈判双方经历多个回合的讨价与还价、较量与让步，就商务交往中的各项重要内容完全达成一致以后，为明确彼此之间的权利和义务，同时也为以后的履行提供一个标准，取得法律的确认和保护，一般都要签订商务合同。商务合同的签订是交易者用文字的形式把双方或多方在商务交易中的权利和义务加以肯定和明确的法律行为，它是商务谈判是否取得成功的判定，是谈判活动的最终落脚点。合同的签订意味着全部谈判工作的结束。

Task 1 Strategies to Bringing to Sign a Contract

合同签订促成策略

有经验的谈判者总是善于在关键、恰当的时刻，抓住对方隐含的签约意向或巧妙地表明自己的签约意向，趁热打铁，促成交易的达成。如何洞察、把握签约的意向，如何抓住最佳时机，当机立断，立即签约，这是谈判者应该掌握的基本技巧。

案例学习

A foreign enterprise (named as Company A in the following) needed to **purchase** a number of new accessories. They headed to China and started negotiations with a **private** factory in Yiwu (named as Factory Y in the following). In the first few rounds of negotiations, the performance of the foreign enterprise was very enthusiastic. They repeatedly consulted information about the product they wanted. The staff of Factory Y answered them in detail and patiently. The two sides talked for more than two hours happily each time at the very beginning of several rounds of negotiation consultations. However, even until the last round, Factory Y still didn't ask Company A for orders, thinking the other party had not got a thorough understanding of their products yet. Factory Y decided to **contact** Company A more and then. A few days later, Factory Y contacted Company A again, and introduced some of the advantages that they missed last time. Company A was very happy. The foreigners carefully negotiated on the price issue and said they tended to buy. Since then, the two sides had **conducted** a number of negotiations in which Company A showed the good faith several times. Factory Y thought this transaction was as sure as a gun.

However, a week later, the **enthusiasm** of Company A slowly faded. Later, they found a few problems in the products made by Factory Y. Dragged on for another month, the deal which should have been made was **canceled** in the end.

案例思考

Why did the factory fail to make the deal done?

案例解析

The factory did not **grasp** the **opportunity** in the negotiations. The **satisfaction** of both parties couldn't be timely contributed to the **signing**. The deal dragged on, and then finally Factory Y lost the order. Therefore, in business negotiations, if both sides agreed on the **basic** conditions where there were not huge differences, the negotiators should **seize** the opportunity and contribute to the signing as soon as possible.

理论拓展

9 Essential Contract Negotiation Strategies
9 条合同谈判基本策略

Contracts are a necessary part of life, an **integral** part of many **transactions** and most deals—whether they are business-to-business or business-to-consumer contracts, employment agreements, car leases, real estate transactions, **prenuptial agreements**, and on and on. There is no doubt that at some point in your life you are going to be negotiating a contract. It is, therefore, critical that you understand the most common negotiating mistakes and most successful negotiation strategies.

1. Don't make the first major concession.

Although one can make the first minor concession, when it comes to major issues it is best that you not be the first to give in. Making a major concession too quickly sends an early message to the other party that they ought to raise their expectations. At the very least, hold back and find out just how strong their position is.

2. If you are a buyer don't give the seller a quick counter-offer to the asking price.

Whether you are a buyer or seller, my advice is that you make the other party work for every counter-offer they get, including the first one. They will appreciate your counter-offer more if they have to wait for it. The difference between getting a counter-offer and not getting one is vast, from a psychological standpoint. To the person waiting, it represents the difference between a negotiator who might be willing to deal and one who probably won't.

3. Be stingy with your concessions[1] and leave room to negotiate.

Whether you are selling, buying, or negotiating anything, this rule should be carefully considered: leave room to bargain when you open talks, and give in grudgingly as you move towards agreement. Your opening offer should be higher than what you expect to get and concessions should be made in smaller increments. Concessions, carefully controlled, lead the other party toward closure and provide them with a higher level of satisfaction with the final outcome.

4. Don't say "yes" too quickly.

The other party will always appreciate the settlement price more if they believe they have worked for it and gotten closer to the bottom line. If not, their self-esteem will be **bruised**. They may be angry at you and themselves, perhaps for a long time. Instead of saying "yes" right away, use phrases like, "I'll have to take it to my partner and get back to you," or "We'll have to run the numbers to see if this makes sense for us."

5. Plead to a higher authority[2].

While it may seem like having more authority during a negotiation is better, this is often not the case. In fact, having limited authority is a source of negotiating power. Having a higher authority to plead to allows you to say "no" gracefully, since really someone else is saying no for you. It also puts pressure on the other party to negotiate around your limits. And if you threaten to take the issue being negotiated to your higher authority (be it your boss, the legal department, etc.), this creates even more pressure on the other party—as the higher authority creates a new unknown factor. There is sometimes greater strength in not having authority than in having it.

6. Shut up.

The less the other person knows about you, the better off you are. The more you know about them, the stronger your bargaining power is. Of course, some information must be exchanged in the give and take of negotiating. The problem is that what you say and what you show may be used against you if it reveals your weaknesses. How much you choose to reveal is a matter of business judgment. Less is better than more in most cases.

7. Be skeptical. Things are not what they appear to be.

The information provided by the other party may not be **complete**. Their expert may not be an expert at all. What you are not told may be more important than what you are told. The product or service you receive after an agreement is reached may not be what you bargained and fought so hard for. If this harsh view of business negotiation offends you, it is not meant to—but it is realistic. Be smart and do your due diligence on the party you are negotiating with, as well as the terms that are proposed.

8. Watch your concessions as the deadline approaches.

In a formal experiment with 120 professional negotiators, both parties controlled their concession behavior for most of the hour-long session. Towards the end of the hour is when most of the concessions were made and deals were reached. The next time you are in a negotiation, recognize that your tendency will be to give away too much as a deadline comes close. Discipline yourself to make smaller concessions and spread them out a bit longer. Also remember that most deadlines are themselves subject to negotiation. There is usually time enough to make another concession if you must.

9. What is our next choice if this negotiation breaks down?

Good negotiators will always ask themselves these questions before going to the table: "What will I do if this deal fails? What is my next best alternative?" The willingness to walk away and start over gives you more flexibility and lets you negotiate from a stronger position. Put in a more commonly, "Don't put all your eggs in one basket."

Like any skill, the more you practice the better you get. Negotiation is no different. Comprehend these strategies and play out different scenarios before you enter into any contract negotiation. And remember, before you sign a complex contract it is a good idea to have a qualified attorney or professional look it over.

(From https://www.karrass.com/)

Notes

1. Be stingy with your concessions：不轻易做出让步

2. Plead to a higher authority 指的是商务谈判中经常使用的一种策略——“权力有限策略”。“权力有限策略”是指谈判者为了达到降低对方条件、迫使对方让步或修改承诺条文的目的，采取转移矛盾，假借其上司或委托人等第三者之名，故意将谈判工作搁浅，让对方心中无数地等待，再趁机反攻的一种策略。从某种意义上说，受了限制的权力才会成为真正的力量，一个受了限制的谈判者要比大权独揽的谈判者处于更有利的状态。例如，可以优雅地向对方说“不”，因为未经授权，这往往使对方大伤脑筋，迫使对方只能根据他们所拥有的权限来考虑问题。如果对方急于求成，虽然明知会有某种损失，也不得不妥协拍板。否则，就会冒谈判失败的风险。

Group Work

Divide students into several groups and discuss the following questions in groups.

1. How would you bring the negotiation into signing a contract when the other party is reluctant to close the negotiation?

2. Practice the following negotiation situation and try to use more than three of the negotiation strategies listed in the above passage.

3. The negotiation of a business contract is into an impasse, and no party is willing to make a further concession on the price of the commodity, and the negotiation breaks down finally. What should you do ?

要点小结

成交和签订协议是谈判的最后一个重要阶段，也是衡量谈判成功与否的关键标志。谈判者需要了解和熟悉成交所具备的基本条件和影响成交的因素。

影响成交的因素

影响成交的因素主要包括谈判者的因素和商品的因素。学会表达和捕捉成交的信号，成交时机的把握、从语言信息中有效识别成交信号、从行为信息中有效识别成交信号、从表情信息中有效识别成交信号。在成交前筹划的基础上，掌握促成交易的策略和方法，学会应用成交策略和技巧，提高谈判能力。

促成签约的策略

促成签约的策略主要有期限策略、优惠劝导策略、行动策略、主动征求签约意见策略、表明签约结束的行动策略等。

Task 2 Format and Content of a Business Contract

商务合同格式与内容

商务谈判的圆满结束，仅仅意味着买卖双方在交易的主要条件方面达成了一致，而商务合同条款远比双方谈判中所涉及的问题要多。商务合同的格式和内容都必须仔细检查和确认，甚至再次谈判和磋商，以免出现纰漏致使利益受损或在合同执行中出现不必要的纠纷。

案例学习

SALES CONTRACT

NO.: 2010026
DATE: Feb. 28, 2010
SIGNED IN: NANJING CHINA

SELLER: DESUN TRADING CO., LTD.
HUARONG MANSION RM2901 NO.85 GUANJIAQIAO, NANJING 210005, CHINA
TEL: 0086-25-4715004
FAX: 0086-25-4711363

BUYER: NEO GENERAL TRADING CO.
P.O. BOX 99552, RIYADH 22766, KSA
TEL: 00966-1-4659220 FAX: 00966-1-465921

This contract is made by and agreed between the BUYER and SELLER, in accordance with the terms and conditions stipulated below.

Commodity & Specification	Quantity	Unit Price & Trade Terms	Amount
ABOUT 1,700 CARTONS CANNED MUSHROOMS PIECES & STEMS 24 TINS X 425 GRAMS NET WEIGHT (D.W. 227 GRAMS) AT USD7.80 PER CARTON.	1,700 CARTONS	USD7.80	USD13,260.00
	With: More or less of shipment allowed at the sellers' option		
Total:	1,700 CARTONS		USD13,260.00

continued

Total Value	USD THIRTEEN THOUSAND TWO HUNDERD AND SIXTY ONLY
Packing	EXPRTED BROWN CARTON
Shipping **Marks**	ROSE BRAND 178/2010 RIYADH
Time of Shipment & Means of Transportation	Not Later Than Apr.30, 2010 BY VESSEL
Port of Loading & Destination	From : SHANGHAI PORT, CHINA To : DAMMAM PORT, SAUDI ARABIA
Insurance	TO BE COVERED BY THE BUYER.
Terms of Payment	The Buyers shall open through a bank acceptable to the Seller an Irrevocable Letter of Credit payable at sight of reach the seller 30 days before the month of shipment, valid for negotiation in China until the 15th day after the date of shipment.
Remarks	
The Buyer	The Seller
NEO GENERAL TRADING CO.	DESUN TRADING CO.,LTD
(SIGNATURE)	(SIGNATURE)

案例思考

1. Who is the buyer? Who is the seller?
2. What is the product that has been sold? And how many?
3. Where will the commodity arrive at?

案例解析

这是一份销售合同，该合同所列为基本条款，可以有一些其他条款，如：检验：中国天津进出境检验检疫局出具的质量和重量证书作为交货的质量和数量依据。Inspection: The certificates of quality and quantity issued by Tianjin CIQ (Tianjin Entry-Exit Inspection and Quarantine Bureau) shall be taken as basis for the shipping quality/quantity. 单据要求：卖方应提供议付银行名称、已装船清洁提单、进出境检验检疫局出具的质量和数量证明、商业发票、装箱单、保险单。Documents Requirement: The seller shall present to the negotiating bank, Clean on Board B/L, Certificate of Quality and Quantity issued by CIQ, Commercial Invoice, Parking List, and Insurance Policy. 除此之外，还有异议及索赔

（Discrepancy and Claim），不可抗力（Force Majeure），仲裁（Arbitration）等对出现状况处理的条款。

理论拓展

How to Write a Business Contract?
如何起草商务合同

Business Contracts Overview

Knowing how to write a business contract can be very helpful in navigating the business world, as little can be done without the completion and acceptance of such contracts. A business contract is an agreement made between two or more parties that defines the terms of, and legally binds each party to, the agreement. A business contract may cover such business dealings as:

Entering into a joint venture or partnership.

Buying or selling material items or services.

Buying or selling any kind of real estate.

Franchising.

Services involving freelancers or independent contractors.

No matter the topic of the contract, written contracts are always preferable because they provide a record of what was agreed to, should the contract be **disputed** and perhaps be sent before a court of law. Oral, or spoken agreements, may be technically binding, but they are far more difficult, if not impossible, to enforce. One should also be sure they understand every **aspect** of a contract before they sign it. If one does not understand any aspect of a contract, legal counsel[1] should be **obtained**.

Basics of Writing a Business Contract

Although business contracts will vary depending on what is being dealt with in the contract, the following basic elements are likely to appear in most contracts:

1. Basic information. The contract will start by stating the names and addresses of the parties involved and how such parties will be referred to in the contract.

2. The terms. Any **pertinent** terms used throughout the contract whose definition is useful to state should be stated near the front of the contract, as well.

3. The scope of the work or materials clause. A business contract should state what product or service a party will be providing in exchange for a payment or any other form of compensation. The product or service should be covered in specific detail.

4. The term clause. This will cover how long the contract will be in effect for.

5. The payment clause. This will state what compensation a party will receive for their product or services as well as when it will be received.

6. The acceptance clause. What criteria will be administered to deem a product or service acceptable and a sufficient fulfillment of the contract will be set out here.

7. The intellectual property clause. If intellectual property is involved, how the rights and usage of this will be handled should be defined, including if any such agreement involving it will be exclusive or non-exclusive.

8. The confidentiality agreement clause. If trade secrets or other sensitive information are dealt with in a contract, a confidentiality agreement is recommended to maintain their secrecy.

9. The claim clause. If there are to be conditions under which one party will not hold the other responsible for any type of injury, physical, financial, or otherwise, then a claim clause should cover the terms of this.

10. The notices clause. If information pertinent to the contract needs to be exchanged, the proper manner for this exchange should be explicitly stated.

11. The entire agreement clause. This will define the overall scope of the entire agreement and define how the agreement may be amended.

12. The termination for **breach of** contract clause. What conditions will constitute a breach of contract and the penalties for doing so will be stipulated here.

13. The force majeure clause. This allows for a party not to be held liable for unfulfillment of a contract if it is caused by forces reasonably believed to be outside the party's control (often referred to as "Acts of God[2]").

14. The choice of law clause. This states what state law or other **jurisdictional** law the contract in question will be entered under and bound to resolution under.

15. Signatures and dates. The signatures of the parties involved and the dates of their signatures should be provided at the end of the contract.

In writing up a business contract with these elements or any other elements, it is not necessary that you use technical "**legalese**," especially if you do not understand it. The most important thing is that the contract is clear and specific on what is being agreed to. Short, clear sentences and orderly, numbered paragraphs are preferred. There is no need to make the document **impenetrably** complex[3] just so it appears impressive.

(From https://www.upcounsel.com/)

Notes

1. legal counsel：法律顾问
2. Acts of God：天意、天灾。一般用来指代不可抗力。
3. impenetrably complex：这里指合同文本极其复杂，用来博人眼球。

Group Work

Divide students into several groups and discuss the following questions in groups.

1. Read the above passage carefully, and tell each other how to draft up a business contract.

2. What should the negotiator check before signing the contract?

要点小结

通过商务谈判过程，双方达成一致意见，对达成的一致意见签署协议，签订合同。通过本节学习，要求掌握商务合同的基本形式，熟悉商务合同的内容以及签约过程。

商务合同的形式

商务合同的形式主要有三类：口头合同、书面合同和推定形式。

商务合同的格式及主要内容

商务合同的格式及主要内容：首部、正文和尾部。

合同有效的条件

合同有效的条件：合法性、严密性和可行性。

Task 3 Strategies for Signing a Business Contract
签订商务合同的技巧

在将商务谈判结果转化为文本式合同的过程中，有大量的文字工作要做，可能会因为文字的疏漏导致合同条款产生歧义，也可能由于缮制合同的一方故意进行文字处理而导致对方利益受损；还有可能，一些谈判中没有涉及的非主要条款，在形成合同文字之后买卖双方不能够达成共识。因此，在正式签订商务合同前需再次认真审核，仔细核对，千万不可掉以轻心。合同的签订过程有许多应该注意的事项。

案例学习

The following conversation happened when both sides decided to sign the contract.

N: Now that we have agreed on all the matters, let's sign the contract. Please go over it and see if everything is in order.

W: Okay. Let me read it over. Don't you think we should add a sentence here like this: "If one side fails to observe the contract, the other side is **entitled** to cancel it, and the loss for this reason should be charged by the side breaking the contract?"

N: That's OK. I think all the terms should meet with unanimous agreement. Do you have any comment on this clause?

W: It is acceptable, but the time of payment should be prolonged two to three months.

N: Usually we are accustomed to payment within one month, but for the sake of the friendship between us, we'll fix it at two months.

W: You are so considerate. No wonder everyone speaks highly of your **commercial** integrity.

N: Thank you for your compliment, you know, it is our **permanent** principle that contracts are honored and commercial integrity is maintained. Anything else you want to **bring up** for discussion?

W: Yes, one more thing I would like to point out, that is timely **delivery**. You know our customers are in urgent need of the goods. If you fail to deliver the goods at the time stipulated in the contract, they may turn elsewhere for substitution. In the way, we just can't stand the loss.

N: Well, you may rest assured that the shipment will be duly delivered, we must have your L/C at least one month before the time of shipment.

N: Good, one more to say, the **stipulations** in the **relevant credit** should strictly confirm to the terms stated in the contract in order to **avoid** subsequent amendment. If that does happen, shipment will possibly be delayed.

W: I see. We will check terms and conditions carefully.

N: Any other questions?

W: No, nothing more. The contract contains basically all we have agreed upon during our negotiations. I think there's no question about the terms. We can sign the contract now. I'm glad our negotiation has come to a successful **conclusion**. I hope this will lead to further business between us.

N: Yes, have a cordial working relationship!

(Shake hands…)

案例思考

What details of the contract did they discuss?

案例解析

在这场谈判中，双方人员主要商讨了违约责任、付款期限、货物装运和货物数量信用证。

其中，违约责任是指双方在合同中明确约定的违约方应承担的具体责任。付款期限应详细到最后付款时间。譬如，在何种条件下，付款可以推迟或停止。货物数量和信用证之间的关系一般为：一般来说，在信用证中的货物描述中会规定货物的数量。对于溢短装条款，有的是在合同中标明可以有上下浮动的交货数量，或者在 ADDITIONAL CONDITIONS 里标注。根据 ISBP 65 条规定：信用证要求的货物数量可以有 5%的溢短装幅度。但如果信用证规定货物数量不得超量或减少，或信用证规定的货物数量是以包装单位或商品件数计量，则此规定不适用。当然，货物数量在 5%幅度内的溢装并不意味着允许支取的金额超过信用证金额。

理论拓展

Tips for Reading a Business Contract
审核商务合同的实用技巧

You are handed a business contract and told, "Sign here." Don't do it! Before you sign, read the contract carefully, following these guidelines, to avoid problems later.

Contracts are legal documents and if they are valid, they can be taken to court. That means you can be taken to court to uphold your end of the contract[1]. Whether it is a real estate contract, business sale agreement, employment contract, or contract between you and a customer or vendor, you can use these guidelines.

Agree on Definitions

All major terms must be defined completely. Much difficulty in contracts comes from incomplete or missing definitions. In one case, an unclear definition of "**overhead**" in the calculation of payment to an independent contractor caused a lawsuit. Overhead usually means expenses for administration and operations. But what's included in overhead can differ from business to business. Spell out exactly what is meant by terms like overhead.

Check Identification of the Parties

Make sure you are identified correctly. In most cases, it should be your business that's entering into the contract, not you personally. If your business has subsidiaries or is part of a holding company, make sure that this is noted. Also, check the identity of the other party. Is this who you think it is?

Don't Assume—Ask for Clarification

Assumptions are really the most difficult part of any contract. You read a contract that includes a section on how the value of property is determined. Even if you think you know what has been written, ask for an example, or ask a question like, "Just to clarify, I think this means X. What do you think it means?"

Don't worry about appearing **dumb** or difficult; it's better to clarify now than find out later you and the other party were thinking of two different meanings.

Ask "What Is Missing?"

This part is **tricky**; it is difficult to know what should be in a contract but isn't. In employment contracts, for example, there should be a section describing how the employer can terminate the contract and what notice must be given.

But sometimes there is no language about how an employee can terminate the contract and what notice must be given. For example, some contracts have no effective date or which do not completely identify the parties.

Take a look at this Employment Contract Terms article for an example of the sections in a typical contract. If you don't see something that should be in the contract, make sure it gets in.

Read "Boilerplate" Carefully and Don't Be Afraid to Change It

Boilerplate is so-called "standard" language that is in many business contracts.

An example of boilerplate might be language having to do with indemnity (holding someone harmless for their actions). An indemnity clause attempts to keep one party from being sued. It also might prevent you from bringing a lawsuit against the other party.

Another example of boilerplate is a mandatory arbitration clause. This clause attempts to **mandate** that any dispute is to be settled by arbitration instead of going to court.

What happens if one party doesn't meet the obligations of the contract? This is called "breach of contract" and the answer to the question may be in boilerplate. Read carefully.

Read those long boilerplate sections, even if your eyes cross and you start to nod off. Ask that the section be simplified or that it be shortened. Or ask that it be changed or taken out if you don't agree with it. Don't hesitate to make changes that clarify or which are to your advantage. Remember that in a contract, everything is negotiable, even "standard" language.

Finally, Get a Second Opinion[2]

If you are reading a contract prepared by the other party, don't rely on yourself or other non-attorneys to read the contract and find all the problems. Take it to an attorney who knows the law in your state.

Don't let the attorney re-write it (they love to do that and charge you for it!), just ask for comments on what might need to be changed. Then decide if you want the changes, and take the list of changes back to the table and negotiate.

Following these guidelines to reading contracts may not prevent you from making a mistake and signing a contract that will cause you problems, but it can eliminate some of the most obvious problems and provide clarification, which is always a good thing.

(From https://www.thebalancesmb.com/)

Notes

1. That means you can be taken to court to uphold your end of the contract：这意味着

你可能会被告上法庭，要求履行合同。

2. Get a Second Opinion：征求下别人的意见。

Group Work

Divide the class into several groups and discuss the following question in groups.

What is "Boilerplate"? Please find more examples to show it.

要点小结

商务谈判签约就是谈判双方或者多方就相关条款的议定情况达成协议的法律行为，其结果就是商务谈判合同的订立。

合同条款的审核

合同文本形成之后，审核的内容主要包括：商品的品质规格条款；货物的数量条款；货物的包装条款；货物的价格条款；货物的装运条款；货物的保险条款；货物的支付条款；其他相关条款。

合同签字

商务合同的签字形式不拘一格，多种多样。签约阶段的程序与礼仪注意事项如下：

签约仪式的准备；签字场所的选择；座次排列；文本准备；正式签约。

综合实训

Task 1

1. There are many negotiation strategies that can be used to bring to sign a contract. Match the strategies to its description below.

the deadline　　　　the last-minute claim　　　　scarcity

1) applying pressure by saying that you have to leave at a certain fixed time.

2) saying that this is your only chance to buy the product or service.

3) a **demand** which is made after it appears that agreement has been reached.

2. Read the following conversations from negotiations and decide the strategy used in each case. Then practice the conversations with your partners.

Conversation 1:

A: So, that's the deal. Believe me, you won't find a better offer anywhere else.

B: Well, perhaps I'll think about it.

A: Look, I don't want you to feel that you're under any pressure, but this offer's not going to be here forever.

B: What do you mean?

A: Well, this is the very last machine that we've got in stock. If you don't order today, I simply can't guarantee that it'll be here tomorrow.

B: I see.

A: And all the pieces are going up next week anyway.

B: Hmm.

A: So, what do you say?

Conversation 2:

A: Right then, I think that just wraps it up. Do we have a deal?

B: Absolutely. It's been a pleasure doing business with you.

A: And you...

B: Oh, just one last thing—it won't be a problem if we increase my discount by half a percent, will it?

A: Um...

B: Only I've been thinking, it's going to make my life so easier...

Conversation 3:

A: Well, in principle, I like the sound of the idea, but the devil's always in the detail, isn't it? Now, what I'd like to do is talk through some of the small points.

B: Ok, here's the situation. I've got a flight back to New York at half past four, which means that I'm going to have to leave in half an hour... forty minutes at the very latest.

A: So, what are you saying?

B: I've got to tie up this deal before I have. You know what's on offer—it's your decision.

3. Role-play.

Situation One:

In a department store, the customer was satisfied by one refrigerator. He intended to **present** an "unsatisfactory" and "defective" one. After several rounds of bargaining, the customer said: "Here are many places that I am not satisfied with, but I like this style. But the price is pretty high and delivery is not required. Can the price be lower?"

A: You are the manager of the department store. Try to bring to deal without any discount.

B: You are the moderate customer. Try to convince the manager and get the refrigerator with a discount of 7.5%.

Situation Two:

Three companies, Australian Company A, German Company G and Chinese Company C are negotiating on the issues about a mine investment. Company C who wants to control the export goods can contribute human resource and intangible assets, instead of offering cash to the cooperation. Then Company A and Company G send their representatives to China to inspect the mine. The whole agenda is considerately planned and well prepared which meets those three companies' demands in a limited period of time. All the three partners have discussed about the modes of the cooperated investment in the initial preparation meeting and summary meeting.

1) Company A brings the negotiation to sign a contract.

2) Company G brings the negotiation to sign a contract.

3) Company C brings the negotiation to sign a contract.

Task 2

1. Translate the following terms and sentences into Chinese. And try to learn them by heart.

1) Entry-Exit Inspection and Quarantine Bureau

2) Clean on Board B/L

3) Certificate of Quality and Quantity issued by CIQ

4) Commercial Invoice

5) Parking List

6) Insurance Policy

7) Inspection: The certificates of quality and quantity issued by Tianjin CIQ (Tianjin Entry-Exit Inspection and Quarantine Bureau) shall be taken as basis for the shipping quality/quantity.

8) More or Less of Shipment

9) Force Majeure

10) Liability for Breach of Contract

2. Translate the following Chinese items into English.

<table>
<tr><td colspan="4" align="center">销售合同

NO.: 2010026
DATE: Feb. 28, 2010
SIGNED IN: NANJING
CHINA</td></tr>
<tr><td colspan="4">SELLER: DESUN TRADING CO., LTD.
HUARONG MANSION RM2901 NO.85 GUANJIAQIAO, NANJING 210005, CHINA
TEL: 0086-25-4715004
FAX: 0086-25-4711363</td></tr>
<tr><td colspan="4">BUYER: NEO GENERAL TRADING CO.
P.O. BOX 99552, RIYADH 22766, KSA
TEL: 00966-1-4659220 FAX: 00966-1-465921</td></tr>
<tr><td colspan="4">This contract is made by and agreed between the BUYER and SELLER, in accordance with the terms and conditions stipulated below.</td></tr>
<tr><td>1. 品名及规格</td><td>2. 数量</td><td>3. 单价及价格条款</td><td>4. 金额</td></tr>
</table>

continued

ABOUT 1,700 CARTONS CANNED MUSHROOMS PIECES & STEMS 24 TINS X 425 GRAMS NET WEIGHT (D.W. 227 GRAMS) AT USD7.80 PER CARTON.	1,700 CARTONS	USD7.80	USD13,260.00
	With: More or less of shipment allowed at the sellers' option		
Total:	1,700 CARTONS		USD13,260.00
5. 总值	USD THIRTEEN THOUSAND TWO HUNDERD AND SIXTY ONLY		
6. 包装	EXPRTED BROWN CARTON		
7. 唛头（运输标志）	ROSE **BRAND** 178/2010 RIYADH		
8. 装运期及运输方式	Not Later Than Apr.30, 2010 BY VESSEL		
9. 装运港及目的地	From : SHANGHAI PORT, CHINA To : DAMMAM PORT, SAUDI ARABIA		
10. 保险	TO BE COVERED BY THE BUYER.		
11. 付款条款	The Buyers shall open through a bank acceptable to the Seller an Irrevocable Letter of Credit payable at sight of reach the seller 30 days before the month of shipment, valid for negotiation in China until the 15th day after the date of shipment.		
12. 备注			
买方		卖方	
NEO GENERAL TRADING CO.		DESUN TRADING CO.,LTD	
(签名)		(签名)	

Task 3

Divide the students into several groups. Try to complete the following practice.

A: a nail-beauty **accessory** factory in China

B: a nail-beauty store in Germany

1. You two just get an agreement. Try to **draft** down a business contract and consult the details of the contract from the perspective of Company A.

2. Tell your classmates what strategies you are going to use when you are drafting the contract.

3. You are the negotiator of Company B. Check the contract and discuss about it with Company A in details.

实践语句

1. This contract is made by and agreed between the BUYER and SELLER, in accordance with the terms and conditions stipulated below.

买卖双方同意以下条款达成交易。

2. With: More or less of shipment allowed at the sellers' option.

允许溢短装，由卖方决定。

3. This deal promises big returns for both sides. Let's hope it's the beginning of a long and prosperous relationship.

这单生意一定能让我们双方赚大钱。让我们共同期望这是我们长期共同繁荣的开端吧！

4. Now that we have agreed on all the matters, let's sign the contract. Please go over it and see if everything is in order.

既然我们就所有事项达成一致，现在我们签约。请仔细检查，确定是否所有事项都记入订单。

5. We need to hammer something out today. If I go back empty-handed, I may be coming back to you soon to ask for a job.

我们必须今天就敲定。如果我空手而归的话，我可能很快就会回来找你要一份工作了。

6. If one side fails to observe the contract, the other side is entitled to cancel it, and the loss for this reason should be charged by the side breaking the contract.

若任一方违反合同，另一方有权终止合同，因此产生的损失由违反合同一方负责。

7. I think all the terms should meet with unanimous agreement. Usually we are accustomed to payment within one month, but for the sake of the friendship between us, we'll fix it at two months.

我认为所有的条款都应达成一致。我们付款期通常为一个月，但为了我们之间的友谊，我们将在两个月内付款。

8. If you fail to deliver the goods at the time stipulated in the contract, they may turn elsewhere for substitution.

如果你方未能在合同规定的时间内交货，他们可能寻求其他供货商进行替换。

9. You may rest assured that the shipment will be duly delivered, and we must have your L/C at least one month before the time of shipment.

请放心，货物将按时装运，我们必须在装船前一个月收到贵方信用证。

10. I'm glad our negotiation has come to a successful conclusion. I hope this will lead to further business between us.

很高兴我们的谈判圆满结束。我希望这会使我们之间的业务进一步发展。

核心词汇

accessory	*n.* 附件；（衣服的）配饰
appear	*vi.* 出现，显现；出庭，出场；演出；发表
aspect	*n.* 方面；面貌；方位，方向；形势
avoid	*vt.* 避开，避免；撤销，废止
basic	*adj.* 基本的；首要的
boilerplate	*n.* 样板文件；文件模板
brand	*n.* 商标，牌子
bruise	*v.* 挫伤；（使）出现伤痕；撞伤； *n.* 青肿；瘀伤
cancel	*vt.* 取消，注销；抵消，偿还
commercial	*adj.* 商业的；贸易的；营利的
complete	*vt.* 完成，使完满；结束；填写（表格）
conclusion	*n.* 结论；结局；断定，决定；推论
conduct	*vi.* 引导；带领；控制；传导 *vt.* 组织；安排；实施；执行
contact	*vt.* 使接触；与……联系；与……通信（或通话）
content	*n.* 内容；（书等的）目录；满足；容量
credit	*n.* 信誉，信用；［金融］贷款
demand	*vt.* 要求，请求；需要
deliver	*vt.* 发表；递送；交付
dispute	*v.* 辩论，争论
draft	*vt.* 起草；制定；征募 *vi.* 拟稿；绘样
dumb	*adj.* 哑的；不能说话的 *vt.* 使变哑；使沉默
enthusiasm	*n.* 热情，热忱；热衷的事物；宗教的狂热
entitle	*vt.* 使有资格；给……定名；给予……权利；称作
grasp	*vt.* 抓住；了解；急忙抓住 *n.* 控制；控制力
impenetrably	*adv.* 顽固的；冥顽不化的
insurance	*n.* 保险，保险业；保险费

integral	*adj.* 完整的；不可或缺的
jurisdictional	*adj.* 司法权的，管辖权的
legalese	*n.* 专业术语
mandate	*vt.* 强制执行；授权；委任，命令
mark	*vt.* 做记号 *n.* 斑点；记号；成绩
obtain	*vt.* 获得，得到
opportunity	*n.* 机会；适当的时机，良机；有利的环境，条件
overhead	*n.* 日常开支；营运费用
pertinent	*adj.* 相关的，有关的
permanent	*adj.* 永久（性）的，永恒的，不变的，耐久的，持久的
present	*adj.* 现在的；目前的；出席的 *n.* 现在；礼物 *v.* 提出，陈述；正式提交
private	*adj.* 私有的，私人的；秘密的
purchase	*v.* 购买；采购；换得 *n.* 购买；购买行为
relevant	*adj.* 有关的，中肯的；相关联的
satisfaction	*n.* 满足，满意，舒服；妥善处理
seize	*v.* 抓住；逮捕；捉拿；俘获 *vt.* 夺取；占领；起获；没收
sign	*n.* 记号；信号 *v.* 签名，签字
stipulation	*n.* 契约，规定，条文；条款说明
transaction	*n.* 交易；处理；业务；买卖
tricky	*adj.* 狡猾的；诡计多端的

breach of	违反（义务）
bring up	教育；把……带到楼上/更高处；恶心；使突然停住
prenuptial agreements	婚前协议

Unit 10 Business Negotiations on Settling Disputes

商务谈判纠纷处理

任务目标

1. Identifying disputes in business dealings
2. The ascription of liability of business disputes
3. Mastering ways to settle business disputes

国际商务活动经常涉及不同的文化、理念、传统以及法律体系，因此争议分歧在所难免。企业通过谈判处理商务纠纷时，要充分考虑自身的条件、企业间的商业关系、纠纷处理成本以及各国法律对国际商务纠纷处理的差异，合理、理性地选择纠纷的解决方法，维护自身的经济利益。

Task 1 The Identification of Business Disputes

商务纠纷事故认定

国际商务活动中，买卖双方应该严格遵守合同约定，避免争议、纠纷的出现。然而，一旦出现商业纠纷，首先应该对争议进行认定。

案例学习

BLACK Corporation imported 3,000 sets bicycles from ANITA LIMITED. Both parties agreed the terms in the contract "Black-1,000 sets, Red-1,000 sets, Green-1,000 sets; Partial shipments are not allowed". In the shipment, ANITA LIMITED found that they only had 950 green bikes in stock, then replaced 50 sets with black.

案例思考

1. Is it reasonable for ANITA LIMITED to do so?
2. What consequences will be caused?

案例解析

卖方交货数量应该严格遵守合同条款，否则由此产生的一切后果应由卖方承担。本案例中，ANITA 公司的做法不妥。应该事先征得 BLACK 公司的同意后才能以 50 辆黑色自行车替代绿色的自行车，而不得擅自行事。否则，可能会遭到 BLACK 公司反对，轻则要求降低原价，重则拒绝收货付款并进行索赔。

理论拓展

Steps to Business Dispute Resolution
解决商务纠纷的步骤

The process of resolving a dispute or conflict expects you to follow a five-steps methodology to help you re-achieve that atmosphere of peace which existed before the dispute came to the surface.

1. Dispute Source Identification

It is true that half of your problems will automatically get solved if you focus highly on the accurate identification of the causes which gave rise to the disputes. For the purpose, ask both of the parties share their side of what they experienced and what made them unhappy and listen to both of them with extreme care.

Breaking down the incident into smaller questions, like when did it happen or what part of the incident hurt you most, and encouraging the response from both parties can surely help a lot in determining a solution to the disturbance.

2. Looking under the Surface[1]

Most of the times, just scratching the surface is not going to be enough and you will have to dig a little deeper to locate the original cause of the controversies and cut them down by roots. This step is important since it might also be a possibility that the **feud** is not a recent product, instead, it might be there for a long time in its dormant state but it has grown big enough to initiate quarrels either verbally or physically. As a mediator, it is your responsibility to look beyond the incident and for this, you can ask both of the parties that if they remember anything which resulted in all the mess.

3. Requesting Solutions

Requesting suggestions from the arguing parties is a well-understood step for putting forward a permanent and effective solution to the disturbances. After you get the point of view of the disputes and conflicts, you can ask the parties that what they think can make the situations better than they are now. Be an active listener and pay full attention to the body languages since you want them not to repeat the words that can hurt the other, and you are there to make the disputants start cooperating with you and not fighting again.

4. Identifying the Ideal Solution

Once you gather up the ideas from both sides, then focus on thinking about merits and demerits[3] that each of these suggestions can have. Then, if possible, combine two or more ideas to give rise to that ideal solution that is not only beneficial to the arguing parties but also to the brand.

5. Agreement on the Solution

Being a mediator, your job is not over yet because there's still one thing left to do and that's making the parties agree on the solution devised. For the purpose, write a contract which binds up the groups to a particular set of time frames from keeping back from actions that can again lead to disputes and conflicts in the future.

(From https://www.businessstudynotes.com/)

Notes

1. Looking under the Surface：进行更深入的调查研究
2. dormant state：休眠状态
3. merits and demerits：利与弊；优缺点

Read and discuss

1. Who should be responsible for the dispute?
2. What advice should you give to avoid such a dispute?

A computer programming company ("C") landed a large cost-plus contract with a bank to develop some customized database software. Midway through the project, the bank's project manager asked C's project manager to make some additional changes to the software. C's project manager explained that the changes would require a lot of rework, extra labor and additional time. The bank's project manager told him to proceed with the work so as not to slow down the project, and they would discuss any extra charges later.

C submitted a bill for the work, which included an extra $10,000 for the changes. A few months after C submitted the bill, the bank had still not paid the invoice. Upon inquiry, it was learned that the bank was denying that its project manager had authority to direct changes to the work, and accordingly the bank was refusing to pay the portion of the bill pertaining to the extra work.

要点小结

本节的目标任务是希望学习者了解商业纠纷的概念及出现的原因，以便在商业纠纷出现后对事故进行认定，在随后的事故处理中赢得主动。

争议，又称争端、纠纷，指在国际贸易中，交易的一方认为对方未能部分或全部履行合同规定的责任与义务而引起的业务纠纷。交易中双方引起争议的原因很多，大致可归纳为以下几种情况：卖方违约、买方违约、买卖双方均负有违约责任等。

Task 2 Liability Ascription
责任归属

在国际贸易中，合同一经成立，当事人各方就应受合同的约束。任何一方当事人如不履行合同中所规定的义务或履行合同义务不符合约定的条件均构成违约。违约发生后，首先要弄清事实，明确责任归属，然后才能向有关责任方提出索赔要求。

案例学习

A Russian exporter signed a CFR contract with an American importer on canned food for an amount of US$50,000, with payment by D/P at sight. On the morning of June 15, 2017, the goods were all loaded onto the named vessel. The Russian salesperson in charge of this contract was so busy that he forgot to send the buyer the shipping advice until the next morning. Unexpectedly, when the American importer went to the local insurance company to insure the goods, the insurance company had already learned that the ship suffered a wreck on May 6 and refused to insure the shipment. The American importer immediately sent a fax to the Russian exporter saying "owing to your delayed shipping advice, we are unable to insure the goods.

Since the vessel has been destroyed in a wreck, the loss of goods should be for your account. At the same time, you should compensate our profit and expense losses which amount to US$50,000." Soon all the shipping documents sent through the collecting bank were returned to the Russian exporter, for the reason that the importer refused to take up the shipping documents.

案例思考

Who should be responsible for the loss and why?

案例解析

CFR 术语项下，卖方负责办理租船订舱，买方办理投保手续；而且卖方负有在装船完毕后及时向买方发出装运通知以便买方办理保险的责任；否则，卖方应承担因其延误通知而产生的风险。本例中，出口方虽在规定的时间内完成了货物的装运，但其未及时发出装运通知，导致进口方无法及时办理投保手续，未能将风险及时转移给保险公司，所以本案中造成的损失应该由卖方承担。

理论拓展

Common Business Dispute Causes
常见的商务纠纷起因

Business disputes are a part of running a business, and our lawyers have seen them all. To protect your business and plan for how you will resolve business disputes, it is helpful to understand the most common causes of business disputes and different ways to resolve them.

Breach of Contract[1]

Contracts are used to hold businesses together and to outline agreements with service providers and other businesses. But when one party does not uphold their end of the bargain[2], the result is a breach of contract. Breach of contract disputes can come from lack of payment, missed deadlines, or obligations that were not performed.

Resolving a breach of contract dispute will depend on the type of agreement that was breached and the motivations of the parties involved.

Shareholder Disputes

Business owners may disagree about the direction the business is taking, misuse or abuse of company funds, breach of fiduciary duty[3], conflict of interest, disagreements over hiring or other management decisions, or financial issues and debt. These disagreements can arise in businesses large or small.

Some shareholder disputes can be resolved with little disruption to the business. One partner may choose to leave, and the business will carry on. Other times the business will **dissolve** and cease operations. Depending on the complexity and severity of the dispute, legal steps will need to be taken to ensure the governance procedures and applicable laws are followed.

Negligence

If your business hires a professional and their work is not performed with the appropriate level of quality or violates a professional standard, the professional may have been negligent. The business may claim that the professional breached their duty of care and the business was damaged as a result.

Some claims of negligence can be resolved quickly without the need for legal action. But when the professional claims they did nothing wrong or is unwilling to compensate the company to fix the problem, the only option may be legal action.

Confidentiality

If confidential information or other trade secrets are stolen by a competitor or misused by a former employee or business partner, a business may have a claim whether or not there is a confidentiality or non-compete agreement[4]. Business owners need to act quickly with sound legal guidance to protect the valuable intellectual property of the business. This may require filing an action with a Court to immediately stop the other party from using or disclosing the business' **proprietary** information.

Labor and Employment

When running a business with employees, labor and employment issues are bound to come up. Each company has unique needs and risks that can change over time and growth. A business lawyer will be able to assist with proactive planning steps that fit your company culture—like employee handbooks or employment—but even then, there is no guarantee that an employee will play by the rules. When problems with employees arise, sound counsel is essential to know how to navigate those issues and keep the company's workforce going strong.

(From https://www.rkpt.com/)

Notes

1. Breach of Contract：违约；违反合同

2. one party does not uphold their end of the bargain：合同一方不遵守协议规定

3. fiduciary duty：信用义务；信托责任

4. non-compete agreement：非竞争性协议/条款，也被称为“竞业禁止协议”。主要是指在技术转让合同中规定限制技术受方购买或销售非经技术供方指定的且与转让的技术和技术产品处于竞争地位的技术和产品。这一限制性商业条款的目的在于防止技术供方的竞争地位受到削弱，是各国立法所禁止的。

此外，当雇主和雇员之间的关系结束并且雇主希望阻止雇员在下一个岗位上与他们竞争时，无论是为同一市场的竞争对手工作，还是在同一领域启动另一项业务，都会执行非竞争协议。

Group Discussion

Could you please find more causes of Business Disputes besides these listed in the above passage?

要点小结

本节的目标任务是希望学习者了解违约的概念，明确违约责任的归属以及国际法律法规对违约的不同处理方法。

违约是指合同的一方当事人没有履行或没有完全履行合同规定的义务的行为。违约发生后，首先应该明确违约责任的归属。一般来讲，违约责任主要包括卖方责任、买方责任、承运人责任以及保险公司责任等。

Task 3 Claim and Settlement
索赔与理赔

在国际贸易交易过程中，买卖双方往往会由于彼此的权利和义务问题而引起争议。争议发生后，因一方违反合同规定，直接或间接给另一方造成损失，受损方向违约方在合同规定的期限内提出赔偿要求，以弥补其所受损失，这就是索赔。违约的一方，如果受理遭受损害方所提出的赔偿要求，赔付金额或实物，以及承担有关修理、加工整理等费用，或同意换货等就是理赔。如有足够的理由，解释清楚，不接受赔偿要求的就是拒赔。可见，索赔和理赔是一个问题的两个方面。

案例学习

A Chinese exporter signed a CIF contract with a foreign importer. Payment was to be made by irrevocable sight L/C. Both the contract and the L/C prohibited transshipment. Within the validity of the Credit, the exporter shipped the cargo on board a liner sailing direct to the port of destination, and presented the direct B/L for negotiation. Later the foreign issuing bank also made payment against the direct B/L forwarded by the negotiation bank. However, in order to collect some other cargoes, the carrying vessel unloaded the cargo at an intermediate port without authorization. The cargo was instead reloaded on to an old vessel, and thus arrived at the destination two months late. As a result, the buyer lodged a claim against the Chinese side for fraud, since the cargo was actually transshipped even though the direct B/L was issued. Finally the exporter accepted the claim and made compensation as requested.

案例思考

1. Do you think the settlement of the case appropriate?
2. Who do you think should be liable for the loss? And why?

案例解析

本案例中，买卖双方合同以 CIF 条件成交，根据《国际贸易术语解释通则 2020》规定，CIF 下卖方在指定装运港将货物装到指定的船上即完成交货，货物灭失或损坏的一切风险在货物装上船时转移。因此，买卖双方的风险转移以货物被卖方送到指定船上为界，货物在装运港装上船后的风险应该由买方承担；而且船方擅自转船造成的损失也应由买方承担。另外，CIF 属于象征性交货，只要卖方按照合同规定在装运港将货物装船并提交全套合格单据，就算完成了交货义务，无须保证到货。所以，本案中，国外买方应凭直达提单向船公司提出索赔，并凭保险单向保险公司进行交涉。

理论拓展

Claim and Settlement

索赔和理赔

Disputes arise in international trade to many reasons, for instance, a buyer may breach a contract by wrongfully refusing to accept goods or failing to pay for the goods when payment is due; a seller may violate a contract by failing to make an agreed delivery, delivering goods that do not conform to the contract etc. Usually a claim will be made, after the disputes, by the injured party against the other party.

Usually, most of the claims are related to imports. A claim is usually filed by the buyer against the seller who has delivered goods that does not accord with the contract.

Claims against the seller.

A claim may be filed by the buyer against the seller where the seller fails to make timely delivery or refuses to make delivery; where the goods delivered by the seller is not in accordance with the contracted quantity, quality, specification; and the goods are damaged due to improper packing etc.

Claims against the shipping company.

The shipping company is responsible for the relevant losses and damages where shipping company is responsible for circumstances such as: the quantity of the goods is less than that stated in the relevant B/L; the goods have traces of damages under a clean B/L.

Claims against the insurance company.

Under circumstances such as: goods in transit incur losses or damages that are caused by natural calamities, accidents and other events that are within the coverage of insurance, then the insurance company shall be responsible for the losses and damages.

When a buyer files a claim, attention should be paid to the following:

Proofs for claiming: When filing a claim against the seller, the buyer should present adequate proofs and give sufficient reasons, and documents such as statement of claim, inspection certificate issued by the inspection authority, invoice, packing list, copy of B/L etc. should be presented. When lodging a claim against the shipping company, the buyer should also present a **tally**[1] report issued and signed by the master or tally clerk of the harbor authority and a damage and/or short-landed memo issued and signed by the master. And additional document such as combined inspection report issued and signed by the insurance company and the buyer should be included for any claim that may be filed with the insurance company.

Claim amount: Claim amount should include invoice value of a contract and incidental damages such as inspection fees, loading and unloading expenses, bank charges, storage charges and interest etc.

Claim period: Claim should be made within the validity of the contract. If extension of the validity is necessary for commodity inspection, then the claim period can be extended after getting approval from the other party.

If a buyer files a claim, then the seller should:

Carefully check the documents presented by the buyer so as to ensure that the documents are authentic, inspection result is correct and the issuing party is competent.

Make a thorough investigation so as to find out the responsible party. If the shipping or the insurance company is responsible, the claim should be handed over to them. The seller should compensate the buyer for his losses or damages where the seller is held responsible, and the seller should reject claim that is unreasonable and **ill-founded**.

Correctly and reasonably decide the losses or damages incurred and work out a rational settlement to the claim.

(From Practice of International Trade, 2010)

Note

tally：理货，指船方或货主根据运输合同在装运港和卸货港收受和交付货物时，委托港口的理货机构代理完成的在港口对货物进行计数、检查货物残损、指导装舱积载、制作有关单证等工作。

Pair Work

Work in pairs and discuss as many causes as you can for customers' complaints and claims.

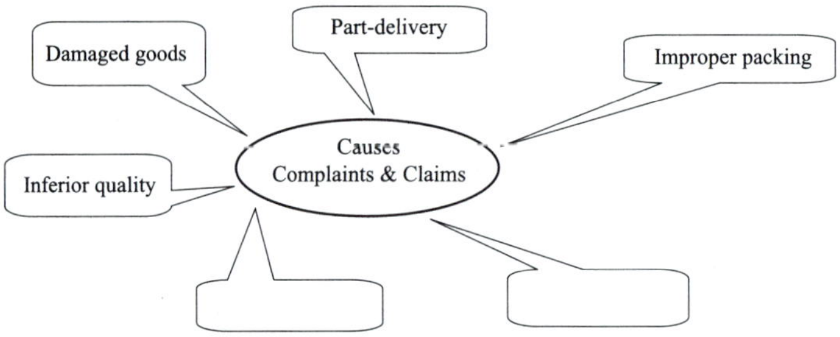

要点小结

本节的目标任务是希望学习者了解索赔和理赔的概念以及涉及索赔谈判的知识要点。

在国际贸易中，根据原因和责任的不同，索赔通常有三种情况：如果是合同当事人的责任造成的损失，向相关责任方提出索赔；如果是承运人的责任所造成的货物损失，向承运人索赔；凡属于承保范围内的货物损失，向保险公司索赔。

理赔（settlement）是违约方对于对方提出的索赔要求进行处理，即违约方受理受损方提出的索赔要求。

Task 4　Mediation and Arbitration
调解与仲裁

在国际贸易中，合同双方在履约过程中可能发生争议。由于买卖双方之间的关系是一种平等互利的合作关系，所以一旦发生争议，首先应通过友好协商的方式解决，以利于保护商业秘密和企业声誉。如果协商不成，则当事人可按照合同约定或争议的情况采用调解、仲裁或诉讼等方式解决争议。

案例学习

A dispute arose from the transaction between Company A from China and Company B from Japan. The amount involved is up to USD$ 120,000. As stipulated in the contract, Company A then launched an arbitration application in **CIETAC (China International**

Economic and Trade Arbitration Commission), and obtained the winning **award** with arbitration expense about RMB40,000. According to the award, Company A tried to proceed a settlement with Company B, but it was in vain for three months.

案例思考

How does Company A deal with the situation?

案例解析

国际贸易仲裁是终局裁决，即裁决一经做出即具有法律效力；当事人对裁决不服的，也不得再向人民法院起诉。负有义务的当事人应当依照裁决自觉执行；逾期不执行的，对方当事人可以向被申请人住所地或者财产所在地的人民法院申请执行。如果被申请执行人或者其财产不在我国境内，那么申请执行人应当向有管辖权的外国法院申请承认和执行。因此，本案中 A 公司可以向日本法院提交执行申请。

理论拓展

Resolution of Business Disputes
商务纠纷的解决方式

Resolving a business dispute will depend on the nature of the disagreement and the objectives of the disputing parties. The methods used to resolve disputes often **overlap**. For example, a failed negotiation may lead to arbitration or litigation, and then a breakthrough occurs and the disputing parties will ultimately arrive at an agreement through negotiation.

To successfully resolve a business dispute, it is helpful to understand different methods of dispute resolution.

Negotiation

In the early stages of business disputes, communication is key. Business owners, often with the assistance of their lawyers, can negotiate a solution to the disagreement, and the matter will be closed. A meeting to discuss the disagreement may be all that is needed to make necessary changes, and the business can continue moving in the right direction.

Mediation

A slightly more formal method of resolving business disputes involves the use of mediation. In mediation, disputing parties work with a **neutral** third party to help negotiate the dispute. A mediator is trained in dispute resolution strategies and can help the disputing parties find a middle ground that allows them to move forward.

Arbitration

Other times, a business may need to submit a dispute to arbitration. In arbitration, the disputing parties present their side to a panel of impartial arbitrators[1] who evaluate the case and make a decision. Sometimes arbitration is binding, while other times it is not. Oftentimes, arbitration proceedings are private and confidential.

In an arbitration, the rules of evidence do not apply and there is no formal discovery. Arbitrators may ask to review relevant documents and to hear from representatives of both sides of the dispute.

Some business contracts include an arbitration that requires disputing parties to submit to arbitration.

Litigation

Litigation is the formal process of taking a dispute to court. A complaint is filed, the parties exchange information through the process of discovery, and the case is scheduled for trial[2].

As the parties learn the strengths and weaknesses of their cases, they may consider trying to resolve the issue through mediation or arbitration. During litigation, negotiations are often ongoing.

Litigating business disputes can be expensive. It also offers very little privacy, as documents filed in court become matters of public record. But in some cases, a trial is the only way to resolve a disagreement.

(From https://www.rkpt.com/)

Notes

1. a panel of arbitrators：仲裁小组
2. trial：法庭的审判、审理

Group Discussion

What are the differences between negotiation, mediation, litigation and arbitration?

要点小结

本节的目标任务是希望学习者了解国际贸易争端的解决方式如调解、仲裁等的含义、方法等知识要点。

综合实训

Task 1

1. Read the following sentences and translate them into Chinese.

1) They have lodged a claim with the insurance company on the goods under order No.111 for loss in weight.

2) We are not in a position to entertain your claim.

3) I'm afraid you should compensate us by 5% of the total amount of the contract.

4) Claim on delayed shipment is that sellers fail to make the delivery according to time schedule.

5) Any dispute, **controversy**, or claim arising out or relating to this Agreement, or the violation, normal and early termination or invalidity thereof, shall be settled by negotiation or **conciliation**.

6) The award of the arbitration shall be final and binding on the Parties concerned. The Parties hereto shall recognize and execute the award in their country.

7) Any complaint about the quality of the products should be lodged within 15 days after the arrival.

8) We are very sorry to inform you that your last shipment is not up to your usual standard.

9) A claim for damage will be filed on us together with your surveyor's report as evidence.

10) We hold the goods at your disposition.

Task 2

1. Analyze the following case and talk about how to settle claims properly.

A Chinese import and export company concluded a Sales Contract with an England firm on August 20, 2017, selling a batch of certain commodity. The contract was based on CIF Liverpool at USD2,000 per metric ton. The Chinese company delivered the goods in compliance with the contract and obtained a clean-on-board Bill of Lading. During transportation, however, 100 metric tons of the goods got lost because of rough sea. Upon arrival of the goods, the price of the contracted goods went down quickly. The buyer refused to take delivery of the goods and effect payment and claimed damages from the seller.

Questions

(1) Who should be liable for the damages? Why?

(2) How would you deal with this case?

Task 3

1. Read the following paragraphs and fill in the blanks with proper words.

In business, if the buyer can prove that it is the seller's ________ for the loss of the goods, he can make a ________. The seller is obligated to compensate the buyer. Generally speaking, claims arise because the wrong goods may have been ________; the quality may have been found ________; the ________ may have been found damaged, short, missing, late; the prices charged may be excessive or not as agreed.

There is also another kind of claim. It is made by buyers who find fault with the goods as an ________ to escape from the contract, either because they no longer want the goods or because they can get them ________ elsewhere.

If a claim has to be made by the buyer, the matter should be ________ in detail and these details should be laid before the party charged. We must ________ claims with the principle of "on the first grounds, to our advantage and with restraint" and settle them amicably to the satisfaction of all ________ concerned.

2. Role-play activity: work in pairs and practice Role A and Role B to make a dialogue and see how to handle properly the following business dispute.

Role A: Several weeks ago you placed this order with ABC Company. The delivery arrived today. When you unpacked the goods you found the goods were not what you had ordered. They are microphones. Phone the company and explain. You need the goods urgently.

Order No: 12345

Quantity	Description	Price
1,000	P1357 Electronic Calculator	$10
	TOTAL	$10,000

Role B: You work in the Sales Department of ABC Company. A customer phones you to complain about a delivery. Find out what the problem is and try to handle it. This is part of your catalog.

Description	Price
M1156 Pocket Radios	$20
W1738 Microphones	$ 7
P1357 Electronic Calculator	$10

Task 4

Divide the class into several groups and conduct a simulated negotiation based on the following dispute.

A 与 B 于 2022 年 12 月 8 日签订大麦购销合同，合同号为 555。由于市场变化，买方认为合同中的价格过高，希望卖方可以降价，并且没有开立信用证。此后，双方进行了多次谈判，最终没有达成有效解决方案，且经过卖方催告买方仍未开立信用证，卖方以买方拒绝履行合同造成违约为由提起仲裁。

实践语句

1. We would like to submit this claim to arbitration.

本公司要将索赔一事提出仲裁。

2. If the cargoes cannot be found within a few days, we will file our claim for the full settlement of them.

若数日内货物不能运到，我们就提出全额清偿索赔。

3. A claim for damage will be filed on us together with your surveyors report as evidence.

具体索赔要求，将随同公证行的检验报告一起提交我方。

4. However, the B/L shows that when the shipping company received the goods, they were in apparent good condition. The liability is certainly not on our side.

但货运提单显示船公司收到货时，货物外表良好。因此，该损害我方并无责任。

5. Since this claim was filed two months after their arrival at your port, we regret that it cannot be accepted.

你方于该货抵达你港两个月以后才提出上述索赔，故我方歉难受理。

6. On examination we found that the goods do not agree with the original sample.

经过检查，我们发现货物与原样品不一致。

7. When unpacking the case, we found the color unsatisfactory.

开箱后，我方发现颜色不令人满意。

8. We find that the quality of your shipment is not in conformity with the agreed specification.

我们发现你方来货的质量与所协定的规格不完全一致。

9. Upon examination, we found you had sent us the wrong goods.

通过检查，我们发现你方发错了货。

10. We should settle the dispute through negotiations without **resorting** to legal proceeding.

我们应该通过仲裁解决争议而非法律途径。

11. We prefer to resolve disputes by amicable, non-bonding conciliation between two parties.

我们愿意双方友好、互相谅解地解决争议。

12. If any dispute should arise over the inspection, we may submit it for arbitration.

如果是检验引起的任何争议，我们可接受仲裁。

13. If you aren't prepared to compensate our loss, we suggest that case be submitted for arbitration.

若你们不赔偿我方损失，我们建议提交仲裁。

核心词汇

award	*n.* 判决，裁决
conciliation	*n.* 和解
controversy	*n.* 争论，辩论
dissolve	*vt.* 溶解，解散
feud	*n.* 争执，争斗
mediation	*n.* 调解
overlap	*vt.* 与……重叠，与……同时发生
proprietary	*adj.* 所有的，所有权的
resort	*n.* 手段，方法
shareholder	*n.* 股东
tally	*vt.* 理货

CIETAC China International Economic and Trade Arbitration Commission	中国国际经济和贸易仲裁委员会（CIETAC）
ill-founded	无正当理由的，无根据的

Unit 11 Business Negotiation Etiquette 商务谈判礼仪

任务目标

1. Learning the criteria for a good negotiator
2. Understanding the rules for proper negotiation etiquette
3. Learning how to apply proper etiquette in business negotiations

谈判双方人员具备良好的礼仪是商务活动中必不可少的素质，也是商务活动取得成功的基本保证。谈判者掌握良好的个人礼仪和主、客座礼仪会给谈判对手留下良好的印象，形成和谐的谈判氛围，使谈判在互相尊重、互相理解的气氛中进行。

Task 1 General Requirements of Business Negotiation Etiquette 商务谈判礼仪的一般要求

商务谈判礼仪一方面可以规范自己的行为，表现出良好的素质修养；另一方面可以更好地向对方表达尊敬、友好和友善，增进双方的信任和友谊。因此，商务谈判礼仪要求商务谈判人员应从自身的形象做起，在商务活动中给人留下良好的第一印象。

案例学习

A Chinese enterprise discussed the export business with a German company. As usual, the Chinese party arrived at the meeting room ten minutes ahead of schedule, and all Chinese members stood up and applauded while the German delegation were stepping into the room. All men and women in German delegation dressed in business attire, on the contrary, only the manager and interpreter in Chinese delegation were in suit, others wore jacket, jeans or even overalls. The German personnel showed a kind of unhappiness and the negotiation ended in half an hour unexpectedly, and the German delegation left in a hurry.

案例思考

1. What caused the problem during the negotiation?
2. What lessons should business negotiators learn?

案例解析

从中方人员提前十分钟来到会议室，可以看出中方还是比较重视这次谈判的，并且在德方人员到达时全体起立，鼓掌欢迎，这些并没有问题。但实际上一见面德方人员就不愉快，其原因在中方代表的着装上，因中方代表着装混乱，在德方看来，中方不重视这次谈判，因此心中产生不快，只好匆匆结束谈判。

商务谈判中，礼仪是商务人员个人素质、修养的体现，它贯穿于谈判的整个过程；良好的仪态有助于减少谈判的阻力，推动交易的成功。

理论拓展

Etiquette in Business Negotiation
商务谈判礼仪

Business negotiations can be a complex balancing act. Etiquette in business negotiation is not hard to earn. With practice and attention, you can attain etiquette in business negotiation skills, and do not want to be pressed so hard that you are reluctantly putting the business away, but you also do not want to be so soft that you lack confidence and patience. This passage will share suggestions for achieving etiquette in business negotiation.

Stay Genuine and Respectful

Keep a respectful attitude toward investors and business contacts, regardless of whether you're able to solidify a deal[1]. This is the No.1 rule of etiquette. Even though negotiation might require you to firmly state your position or valiantly persuade others to support your goals, it's not time to jest[2], complain, attack or belittle. When you negotiate, you're not just selling a product, promoting an idea or marketing your services—you're selling yourself. You want investors and potential partners to see you as a sincere, honest, and likable person who is approachable and easy to work with. Express sincere gratitude, stay humble and don't beg for financial resources. The goal is to prove that not only are your products valuable, but your skills, passions and expertise are worth the investment.

Be Patient and Listen

Take time to listen. You might feel like you're on the hot seat—especially if your boss says you're on the line to make the negotiations work—but don't rush the process. If you don't take time to listen to other viewpoints, goals and intentions, you might make wrong assumptions. Ask questions, such as "What are you hoping to get out of these negotiations?" or "How do you think our company can help you meet your goals?" Take time to listen, even if it tests your patience. You'll likely learn something important in the process that could help you finalize a win-win contract.

Stick to Your Bottom Line

Always know your bottom line before entering business negotiations. Otherwise, you'll waste everyone's time if you have to terminate the meeting to rethink your options. Plus, you don't want to get swept away in the process and overbid or oversell. You want to make financial decisions, including offers and counter offers, based on realistic numbers, not emotions. For example, if you're trying to get a business loan or financial support from investors, be honest about how long it will take you to pay back the funds. Or, if you're trying to buy out a competitor, offer a fair market value and stick to it.

Know When to Back Down[3]

Be polite and back down if negotiations become heated. Angry words and threats damage the negotiation process and often force business associates to respond defensively. Business negotiation etiquette always trumps[4] ugly deal-making. Try to re-establish common ground, review similar goals, and avoid being competitive or argumentative. The main objective of business negotiation is to find solutions that satisfy both parties. Don't offer ultimatums[5] or try to trap the other party in a corner. You'll come across as unprofessional. If you've approached negotiations from every angle and no resolution is in sight, be prepared to walk away with your head held high[6].

Observe International Business Etiquette

Research cultural norms before engaging in international negotiations. Most countries have specific guidelines that govern business negotiations, and you don't want to risk offending anyone. For example, in negotiations with Chinese associates, rank is extremely important. Your senior staff members should always sit across from senior-level Chinese associates. Only the senior Chinese negotiator will speak, so you may want to appoint one person from your team to do most—if not all—of the talking. In China, being late for a meeting is seen as disrespectful and insulting. When working with French business associates, stick to a rigid agenda but retain a welcoming tone. Expect probing questions and follow up with intellectual details to support your proposal. Be clear, concise and well-prepared to earn respect.

(From https://work.chron.com/)

Notes

1. solidify a deal：确保达成交易
2. jest：开玩笑，嘲笑
3. back down：让步，放弃
4. trumps：赢得，比……更重要
5. ultimatums：最后的通牒，最后的结论
6. walk away with your head held high：昂首离开

Group Discussion

As a new business negotiator, what etiquette should one acquire?

要点小结

在商务活动中，礼仪发挥着越来越重要的作用。本节的目标任务是希望学习者了解商务谈判礼仪的一般要求，如对商务人员在形象设计、着装、仪容仪表、语言、行为等方面的基本要求。它贯穿于谈判的整个过程，不仅体现着谈判者自身的教养与素质，而且还会对谈判对手的思想、情感产生一定程度的影响。另外，任何事物都有自己的规则，商务谈判礼仪也不例外，谈判中应遵循一些基本原则：如“尊敬”原则、“真诚”原则、“谦和”原则、“宽容”原则、“适度”原则等。

Task 2　Telephone Communication Etiquette
电话沟通礼仪

电话是一种常见的通信、交往工具，电话沟通礼仪是公共关系礼仪的重要内容，它不仅反映了电话接听人员的情绪、修养、礼貌和礼节，更代表了整个公司的形象和素质。

案例学习

Miss Chen graduated and found a job as sales clerk in Lihua Company. One day, the sales manager was on business, the phone rang and Miss Chen answered. The followings are the dialogues between the caller and Miss Chen:

Caller: Is this Lihua Company?

Chen: Yes.

Caller: The manager is there?

Chen: No.

Caller: Are you a company producing plastics gloves?

Chen: Yes.

Caller: How much for one dozen?

Chen: USD1.8.

Caller: What about USD1.6?

Chen: No.

Then Miss Chen finished the conversation and hung up the phone.

案例思考

Do you think there is any telephone etiquette problems of Miss Chen?

案例解析

现代商务活动中，电话的作用越来越重要，掌握商务电话联系礼仪也成为每一位商务人士的必修课。电话作为通信工具已经存在很长时间，通过电话交流你可以想象到对方的外貌，感受到对方的态度，对于商务人士来说，一次电话的成败直接关系到工作的成败。所以作为一名商务人士，在接打电话时一定要注意自己的礼仪。

本案例中，陈小姐在电话沟通礼仪方面犯了以下几个错误：(1）铃响了没有自报家门；(2）通话过程中该记的没有记录（对方的姓名、公司、电话号码)；(3）该问的一些信息没有问（如对方的情况，手套的需要量等)；(4）电话里不该说的却说了（如价格上的自作主张，不向上司请示)；(5）不等对方说完，就挂断电话；在电话礼仪中，尊者先挂电话；(6）整个通话过程无一句礼貌用语。

理论拓展

Business Telephone Etiquette
商务电话礼仪

Some people just don't know how to speak on the phone. You can hear every breath they're taking and the crunch-crunch of their afternoon corn chips, or they have the receiver so far away from their mouths that they sound like they're talking to you from the slopes of Mount Kilimanjaro[1]. Some people also don't know how to listen on the phone. They respond "Uh-huh" to whatever you say while you hear the clicking of their busy fingers on the keyboard in the background, or they talk so much that you can't get a word in edgewise. These typical scenarios are common, but shouldn't be this way! If you use the information in the following sections, you'll be a polite speaker and listener on the phone in no time.

So many people work in front of a computer screen all day that it's easy to forget the usual social graces—which include things they learned as children, such as how to answer and place a call. Every time you make or receive a telephone call at work, you're representing your company. And, many times, the first contact a person has with a company is over the phone, so the impression you make on the phone may be a lasting one. Therefore, you want to sound professional. Now for some basic telephone manners:

Prepare for the phone call before you make it. Have some idea of what you're going to talk about. Have a pen and paper handy[2].

Make notes if necessary, especially if you're forgetful. Planning is better than having to make a second call. When you call someone, introduce yourself the right way:

1. Say, "Hello."
2. Identify yourself and your affiliation[3].
3. Ask for the person to whom you would like to speak.

Here's an example: *"Hello. This is Tom Canon from Canon Technologies, calling for Ms. Hillander concerning next spring's conference. Is she available?"*

Always state the reason for your call. Don't feel put off if you're asked to state the purpose of your business.

If Ms. Hillander is available, you will be transferred to her. When she answers, repeat your name and affiliation, state your business, and give an estimate of the time you think the call will take, as in this example:

"Hello, Ms. Hillander. This is Tom Canon from Canon Technologies, calling about next spring's conference in San Francisco. Do you have ten minutes to talk about marketing strategy?"

That's all you need. You've said who you are and what you want to talk about. Now you pass the ball into the other person's court and let her respond.

If the person you are calling is not available, whether you're leaving a voice mail or a message with a real person, give your name, your company's name, your telephone number, a time you can be reached, and a brief message. Refrain from leaving a **monologue**[4] to replace the conversation you would have had. If you're leaving a voice mail, repeat your phone number and speak slowly.

When your conversation is finished, end it cordially and quickly. A business call is not a social call, so you don't need to drag the conversation out beyond the business at hand. If you know the other person well, however, you may end the conversation with a few questions about something personal, such as "I was glad to hear your mother is back from the hospital" or "How did Sarah's soccer game go?"

Keep the following guidelines in mind during a phone conversation:

—Answer as promptly as possible.

—Exercise patience on the phone, and let other people finish their sentences.

—Focus on listening.

—Speak so as not to be misunderstood.

—Listen to what the other person is saying.

—Don't interrupt and speak over and while the other person is speaking.

—Confirm you're listening with periodic oral sounds, such as "ah-hah," "yes," and the like.

—Don't chime in to interject your own comments and opinions.

—Be sure to speak directly into the mouthpiece, slowly and clearly. Articulate properly, for example, "yes" instead of "yeah."

—Your posture when you speak on the phone strongly affects how you sound to the person on the other end and the energy that comes across on the telephone. Don't slump in your chair; sit up straight. Also, smiling while you speak can actually make the tone of your voice more pleasant.

—If you dial an incorrect number, apologize before you hang up. This is also considerate if you get someone's voice mail.

Watch out for these mistakes:

—Never sneeze, belch, blow your nose, snort, or cough into a phone. Of course this can be unavoidable, so always turn your head away from the phone and offer an apology.

—Never use phone calls as an opportunity to get caught up with paper-shuffling.

—Never eat, drink, or chew gum while you're on the phone.

—Never answer the phone abruptly by simply saying "yes."

—Never use slang terms or words that are inappropriate in business, such as "honey," "dear," and "sweetheart."

(From https://www.linkedin.cn/)

Notes

1. Mount Kilimanjaro：（非洲的）乞力马扎罗山
2. handy：手边的，就近的
3. affiliation：附属机构，隶属机构
4. monologue：（戏剧）长篇独白；滔滔不绝地讲话

Group Discussion

How to be a good telephone communicator?

要点小结

本节的目标任务是希望学习者了解商务电话联系礼仪的基本方式和要求。电话联系礼仪是人们在进行电话交流时所应当遵循的礼貌和仪态，是公共关系礼仪的重要组成部分。因此，在接电话、代接电话、打电话、挂断电话时都应注意使用得体的礼貌用语。

Task 3　Meeting Etiquette
会面礼仪

商务谈判活动中，作为公司代表，要给客户留下好的印象，会面礼仪显得尤为重要。只有先规范会面礼仪，接下来的谈判及其他一系列商务活动才能有效、顺利地进行。

案例学习

An American businessman went to Brazil to discuss business and hired a local assistant and interpreter. The negotiation was very hard and two parties finally came to a deal through efforts. The American was so excited that he gave an "OK" gesture habitually by putting his thumb and forefinger into a circle with other three fingers to show that he was satisfied with the negotiation. However, the Brazilians were all stunned and looked at him angrily. The moment was extremely awkward.

案例思考

1. Why were the Brazilians stunned and angry?
2. Do you know the meaning of "OK" gesture in different cultures? Give some examples.

案例解析

无论在什么场合，手势动作都要非常谨慎地使用。因为手势动作虽然表意十分丰富，在语言表达不顺畅的时候，能辅助我们表情达意。但是，由于国家、民族、风俗习惯的不同，同一个手势却会有不同的含义。正如美国人在表示满意、赞赏时喜欢用“OK”的手势，可是在南美，尤其是巴西，如果做此手势，女性会认为你在勾引她，而男性则认为你在侮辱他，马上会做出戒备的姿态。

理论拓展

Business Greeting Etiquette
商务会面——问候礼仪

In business, who you know matters and first impressions are the longest lasting. That's why it's so important to make the best impression when greeting someone by using the proper business greeting etiquette, which will help guarantee you start your relationship right every time. Of course, because greeting etiquette around the world and even among different industries varies, be prepared to adjust your greeting slightly based on circumstance when necessary.

Standing Is Proper Greetings Etiquette

Standing when you meet someone both shows respect and physically puts you eye-to-eye, helping you to establish eye contact. If you're unable to stand for some reason, for example, you're trapped in the corner of a long booth and getting up would be impractical, offer an explanation. In this case, saying something along the lines of "excuse me for not getting up, but this seat doesn't exactly make for easy maneuverability[1]."

Smile and Make Eye Contact

Greeting etiquette when entering a room or when someone else enters a room dictates you smile and make eye contact with those you are meeting. This bit of body language starts a proper business greeting even before you make physical or verbal contact. These two gestures say that you are happy to see the person and interested in talking to them.

Introduce Yourself and Shake Hands

Don't wait for someone else to make introductions if you're approached by someone you don't know. Be sure to give enough information to let the person know why you two should be talking. For example, say, "Hi, I'm Daniel Rivers, I'll be handling your account for Business Corp," not just, "Hi, I'm Daniel Rivers."

As you give your greeting, extend your hand. Don't shake so hard you'll hurt the other person's hand. Keep your wrist firm, not limp as this makes the other person feel like they're shaking hands with a noodle and subconsciously makes them think you seem weak and unimportant. A handshake should last as long as it takes to state both of your names, any longer makes things feel awkward.

While women from some cultures do not shake hands, business women in America do and most professionals who do business with Americans understand that as well. Don't ever act awkward about shaking hands with a woman, however, if a woman from another culture doesn't shake hands back, gracefully pull your hand back and chalk it up[2] to cultural differences.

Always Listen to Names

It's easy to tune out when someone says their name, but in business, names are power. Always focus when someone introduces themselves and make an effort to remember his name. If you didn't catch someone's name, ask him politely to repeat it. Once you're sure of the name, make an effort to say it back to him, for example, "Nice to meet you, Mr. Smith, now let's talk about your business."

There was a time when it was important to distinguish between a Miss or a Mrs., but a woman's marital status should be irrelevant to your business purposes. As a result, it's preferable to always refer to a woman as "Ms."

In most industries, you should use the formal title and last name of the person you are meeting unless they tell you to use the first name. If the person is a doctor or has another formal title, use that title before their last name. If you work in a creative industry where the use of first names is standard, you can use the person's first name, but you may want to revert to the last name again if she continues to use your last name. When working with someone from another culture, use their last name unless they ask you to do otherwise.

(From https://bizfluent.com/)

Notes

1. maneuverability：灵活性，可操作性
2. chalk it up：记录下来

Pair Work

Practice greetings and making introductions to each other if you were meeting for the first time in business.

Business Card Etiquette
商务名片发送礼仪

Business is a sphere of communication and people's activity that requires businessmen the highest level of social awareness, politeness and courtesy. A business card is an inexpensive, internationally recognized means of representing yourself to business associates and of conveying contact information to them. A well-designed and professionally printed business card makes a good impression, the way you present your card and receive other's cards also says a lot about you. Be sure to follow the proper etiquette for exchanging business cards so that you make the most positive and lasting impact possible.

Preparations

Never leave your office without a case filled with ten or twenty of your own business cards. Do not stuff them in your pocket, purse, or brief case, since loose business cards can get damaged. Buy a nice and simple case to hold your business cards and the cards you receive from others.

Right Protocol[1]

In many cases, you can ask for a card from someone you just met. Usually they will offer you theirs as well. If they do not offer theirs, you should not always ask. If they outrank your business status, wait for them to offer their business cards to you. If their level of title is the same or lower than yours, use your own discretion in the situation. The only exception for this protocol is whenever you are at a networking function; it is expected that you will exchange cards with everyone you meet.

Only One Card

It is important to keep the exchange personal by only giving and receiving one business card. If you give one person multiple cards, you are presuming that they will pass it on. For your first meeting, it is best to stick with the one-on-one interaction.

Respect

When you hand your card to someone or when someone gives you their card, handle the cards with care. Hold the edges of the card with the front facing up. When you are given a card, look it over and read it. Take some time and make a remark about the design or logo. After you read the card, carefully place it in your card case. Thank the other person for their card.

When exchanging business cards, details are important. Not only are you making a professional impression when you use good etiquette, you also prevent offending a new contact. In some countries, business cards are thought to be an extension of the giver. If you treat all business card exchanges as such, you will be sure to make every first meeting positive.

(From http://lydiaramsey.com/)

Note

protocol：此处同“etiquette”，意为“礼仪”，指名片交接中应该注意的相关事项。

Group Work

Divide the class into groups, each group should design and make a simple business card, then each student in the group practices business card exchanging with others.

Business Etiquette for Handshakes
商务握手礼仪

Business usually begins and ends with a handshake. It is commonplace across many cultures. A handshake is more than just a greeting. It is also a message about your personality and confidence level. A handshake leaves a very definite and often lasting impression, and in the business world a handshake is the only truly appropriate physical contact for both men and women.

A proper handshake, not only gives off good body language, starts a meeting off with energy and shows your enthusiasm, but could influence an important business decision, such as whether you strike a big deal or get a new job; While a poor handshake, such as one that lasts too long, can make the other party uncomfortable or even weaken a relationship.

So, being familiar with the following universal rules of handshakes will help you immensely:

Begin with an Oral Introduction of Yourself

Before extending your hand, introduce yourself. Extending your hand should be part of an introduction, not a replacement for using your voice. Extending your hand without a voice greeting may make you appear nervous or overly aggressive.

Pump Your Hand Only 2-3 Times

A business handshake should be brief and **to the point**. Consider a handshake a short "sound bite" greeting, not a lengthy engagement. Holding on for more than three or four seconds can make other people feel uncomfortable.

Shake from Your Elbow

If you shake from the shoulder, using your upper arm instead of just your forearm, you risk jolting your handshake partner. The idea is to connect, not be **overbearing**.

Do Not Use a Forceful Grip

A handshake should be a friendly or respectful gesture, not a show of physical strength. An uncomfortable handshake is never a pleasant experience for anyone. Imagine you are opening a door handle and use about the same level of grip in your handshake.

Avoid Offering a "Fish Hand[1]"

A limp hand is never a good idea when it comes to a business handshake. Do return the grip, but do not get into a power struggle, even if the other person squeezes too hard.

Forget "Lady Fingers"

This is not a Southern Cotillion[2], this is business. Offering only your fingers to shake may be appropriate in some social settings, but in business settings you are an equal, not a "lady". Extend your entire hand, and be sure to grasp using your entire hand as well.

One Hand Is Better than Two

Avoid the urge to handshake with two hands. It is always better in business introductions to use only one hand—your right hand—for the shake. The use of two hands with strangers is seen as **intrusive**, and too personal. In fact, a two-handed shake is called the "politician's shake[3]," because it appears artificially friendly when used on people you barely know.

Shaking a Sweaty Hand

If you shake hands with someone who has sweaty palms, do not immediately wipe your hands on your clothing, handkerchief, or tissue. This will further embarrass the other person, who is probably already aware they have sweaty hands. You can discretely wipe them on something after you are out of site, and wash them later.

Ending a Handshake

End the handshake after 3-4 seconds, or 2-3 pumps. In order to avoid creating an awkward moment, your shake should end before the oral introduction exchange does. Without conversation taking place during the entire handshake, it becomes too intimate, and can feel more like hand holding.

Ingredients of a Good Handshake

Hold the person's hand firmly.

Shake web-to-web, three times maximum.

Maintain constant eye contact.

Radiate positive **aura**.

Knowing how to shake hands in a business setting is important, but so is knowing when, and when not to shake hands. Here are guidelines to help you put your best hand forward.

When to Shake Hands in Business

- New business contacts, staff, coworkers, or others you are meeting for the first time;
- A former business or casual acquaintance, especially if it has been a while since you last saw him;
- Concluding a business transaction or meeting;
- Congratulating someone else for an award, event, or accomplishment;
- When leaving a business event, including social settings where business contacts or acquaintances are involved.

When Not to Shake Hands

The first rule of thumb in handshaking is simple: Never offer your hand first, at any time, or in such a way, that makes the other person feel inconvenienced or uncomfortable.

With this rule in mind, it is not a good idea to be the one to initiate a handshake:

- With someone of higher status (let them approach you or make the first gesture);
- To break an awkward moment of silence when being introduced to someone new (a proper handshake should also involve conversation);
- If you have nothing to say to the person (a handshake is an invitation for conversation or desire for social interaction);

● Someone whose right hand, arm, or shoulder, is clearly injured, or they need their hand to support their weight with a cane or crutches;

● If the other person's hands are full and a handshake would require them to shift items from one hand to another, or to have to put things down.

(From http:www.thebalance.com/)

Notes

1. fish hand：此处同“limp hand”，指握手时软弱无力。

2. Southern Cotillion：沙龙舞，一种类似四对舞伴方块舞的交际舞，流行于美国南部的成人礼舞会。

3. politician's shake：在西方，参加竞选的政客会用右手握住对方的右手，再用左手搭在互相握住的手背上，试图让接受者感受到他的热情真挚与诚实可靠，故被称为“政治家的握手”。

Group Work

Divide the class into groups, and each student in the group practices handshaking with each other to learn how to make a good business handshake.

要点小结

本节的目标任务是希望学习者了解商务会面礼仪的几个基本要求，诸如如何称呼对方、如何进行介绍、名片的交换和使用以及握手的问题等。商务交往中会面礼仪很重要，它能够影响客户对你的第一印象，这对谈判的成功与否有着很重要的意义。

Task 4 Business Welcoming and Seeing-off Etiquette
商务迎送礼仪

迎送礼仪是商务谈判中最基本的礼仪之一。这一礼仪包含两方面：一方面，对应邀前来参加商务谈判的人士，在他们抵达时，一般都要安排相应身份的人员前去迎接；另一方面，谈判结束后，要安排专人欢送。

案例学习

Lantian Electric Power Company reached an agreement with US PALID Company after negotiations, and the two sides agreed to sign formal documents on July 5. At nine am that day, the general manager of PALID Company came to the headquarters of Lantian Electric Power Company in a car on time. The office director Mr. Chen awaited and he saw a female guest sit in the co-pilot seat, then he opened the door with elegant posture for the female guest, and politely greeted her. Then, Director Chen went to the right rear door quickly with the similar action to welcome the guest, but unexpectedly, the female guest had already opened the back door and greeted the male guest in the rear. At the moment, Director Chen showed his greetings hurriedly, but he obviously felt the two American guests were a little bit unhappy.

案例思考

Do you think there are any problems in the welcoming etiquette of Director Chen?

案例解析

迎来送往是一种很常见的社会交往活动，对应邀前来参加商务谈判的人士一般都要安排相应身份的人员前去迎接，即迎送人的身份与地位与来者相差不多，以对口对等为宜。本案中，中方派办公室主任迎接美方公司总经理，接待身份明显不对等。此外，迎送人员还应了解和掌握一些必要的乘车礼仪及座次排序，例如迎接来访者时，如遇到对方有专职司机，则对方的重要人物一般坐在后排右侧，前排副驾驶则是随行人员。本案中，中方接待人员弄错了美方公司总经理的乘车座次，造成了场面的尴尬。而且，迎接人员应事先了解来访者的有关资料和基本情况，掌握对方的姓名、职务及相貌特征，以便迎接时应用。

理论拓展

Etiquette to Welcome Business Clients
商务客户接待礼仪

Everyone knows good first impressions are essential to forming long-term relationships, so it's important to make every office visitor feel welcome. Whether you're hosting clients or greeting interviewees, you need to make sure those first interactions with your company are flawless—from the moment your visitor steps through the door into your reception area to the moment they leave.

Things like a warm welcome, a tidy reception area, and a streamlined check-in go a long way.

Here are some tips for making sure you properly welcome your business clients when they visit your office.

Training

Train all employees that all visitors are their personal customers, even if they do not have a functional role with that visitor. This means making eye contact, smiling, saying hello, and asking any unattended visitors if they can help. This alone can make a huge difference between having a terrible experience and a potential customer feeling welcome enough to consider doing business with your company.

Remind the Reception Staff to Be Attentive

The most important employees in the office are the reception staff. What are they communicating when someone walks in? Even if they're busy answering phones, they can still make friendly eye contact, use hand gestures to indicate they'll be right with the visitor and offer assistance immediately after getting off the phone. Be sure to instruct your reception staff not to be constantly looking down at their phones, as this can be a huge turn off when a guest is patiently waiting, trying not to be rude.

Creating a Personalized Greeting

Have a lobby board that says, "Welcome, Joe Smith from XYZ Company." This incredibly simple gesture takes you no more than a couple of minutes to put together and pays dividends[1] by showing your visitors that you consciously thought about them before their arrival. And if it's a potential client you're having in, this small welcome gesture that shows how much you care about their experience, which can make the difference between their choice to do business with you or a competitor that does give them a memorable experience.

The Importance of Maintaining a Clean, Welcoming Environment

Maintain a clean workplace in every area a visitor can see, especially near the entrance. Have someone other than yourself look at your work entrance and critique[2] it from the point of view of a potentially valuable customer who comes in to visit. Is the paint chipped? Is the carpet worn? Are two-year-old tattered[3] magazines strewn around the visitor lobby? Make it part of someone's job to assure that the visual aesthetics[4] of your workplace shine through and reflect the professionalism you want to convey for welcoming in clients and prospects.

Offering Self-Serve Refreshments[5]

Invest in a nice coffee and water system that isn't buried in the kitchen area. Put it where customers can find it and serve themselves while they wait or prepare for their meeting. Have some fresh fruit or healthy, wrapped snacks available (not cheap, stale candy).

For bonus points after your client leaves, consider sending all of your most important visitors a thank you card or small gift to show them that you appreciated them taking the time to come into your office and visit. While this is yet another small gesture, it can go a long way towards wowing[6] a client and giving them a reason to choose you over the competition. Remember, whether your company is large or small, every one of your employees is selling, all of the time.

(From https://www.thebalancesmb.com/)

Notes

1. dividends：分红，红利
2. critique：评论，评判
3. tattered：破旧的，破烂的
4. visual aesthetics：视觉美学，视觉审美
5. self-serve refreshments：自助茶饮（茶点）
6. wowing：称赞，欢呼

Group Work

How to welcome clients who visit your working place?

要点小结

本节的目标任务是希望学习者了解商务谈判迎送礼仪的基本要求。迎来送往，是商务谈判礼仪中最基本的形式和重要环节，是表达主人情谊、体现礼貌素养的重要方面，需要引起接待各方的重视。

Task 5 Business Seating Etiquette
座次安排商务礼仪

成功重在细节，商务谈判时，合适的座次安排，在彰显你方得体的谈判礼仪的同时，更体现出你方的企业形象。因此，商务谈判中，一定不要忽视座次安排这个小小的细节。

案例学习

Dongfang Company reached an agreement with British CRIS Cooperation after rounds of negotiations. Dongfang Company was responsible for the arrangement of the signing ceremony. They chose a big meeting room as the signing location and placed flowers inside, laid dark green cloth on the rectangular signing table, set national flags of two countries—British flag on the left side and Chinese one on the right. They put the two copies of the signing text in black plastic folders, and placed pen, ink absorption stationery on both sides respectively... It seemed everything was all right. To their surprise, the British guests seemed to be very unhappy when they came into and scanned the signing hall. They were even unwilling to sit and seemed to have changed their minds.

案例思考

Is there any problem on the arrangement of signing activity? Please state your opinion.

案例解析

商务谈判中以礼待人，不仅体现自身的教养与素质，而且还会对谈判对手的思想、情感产生很大的影响。可以说，商务礼仪是谈判的润滑剂。

中国传统的礼宾位次是以左为上，右为下，而国际惯例的座次位序则是以右为上，左为下；在商务谈判时，应按国际通行的惯例来做，签字仪式应该遵循“主左客右”的原则，否则，哪怕是一个细节的疏忽，也可能导致功亏一篑、前功尽弃。

理论拓展

The Etiquette for Business Sitting Arrangements
商务座次安排礼仪

Where you seat people or where they sit on their own can affect the outcome of a communication encounter. There is a “seating” language. If you, like many people are not aware of it, read on. You can create the illusion of power or equality in your relationship-building efforts by where you sit and where you seat others at meetings, conferences and after-hours events. The choice is often yours to make!

Power Position

The power position in a meeting being held at a rectangular table is always in the center facing the door, where the person can see who is coming and going. The second most important position is to the person’s right, the third to his/her left.

Cooperative

Let’s assume that person A is calling the meeting. The most cooperative position is next to him/her (B) because there are no barriers between them. People who already know each other frequently assume this position in business and social situations. While it is acceptable and recommended, business people meeting each other for the first time rarely use this position.

The next most cooperative position is C, which has the corner of the table between the two. Business people often use this arrangement at a first meeting or until they get better acquainted.

It is recommended for a job interview. It allows two people to be close while still having the corner of the table as a safety zone.

Competitive

The most competitive position to A is D, which is directly across from the A. The table is a barrier between them, and people may become competitive and defensive when seated across from each other. If you have a choice, like in a restaurant, sit in the corner position or ask for a booth. Don't set up a competitive situation unnecessarily. It can hamper an otherwise potentially positive relationship-building situation.

When seated in the competitive position, a person also becomes defensive about his/her personal territory (or half of the table). Don't accidentally push items into someone else's space, as it is as much an invasion at dinner as if you had reached into their space and touched them.

Autonomous[1]

A fourth position (E) is autonomous. It's across the table, and in the position next to competitive. It is where you sit when you need to share a table, and you do not want to be involved with the other person. You might choose it at a library or in a self-serve restaurant. You may have to share space, but not necessarily conversation.

Meetings

You can direct or control responses in a meeting through seating arrangements. Putting chairs in a circle encourages equal contributions. A horseshoe[2] or "T" will recognize and emphasize people at the head of the table. Theater seating or side-by-side says, "You are here to listen, not to talk."

In a training situation, you can use circles for small group discussions, a horseshoe for workshops led by internal or external experts and theater seating for a keynote[3] presentation. When you add a raised speaking platform, you are giving special status to the speaker, as well as setting up more of a barrier between him/her and the audience. Interaction is reduced; in fact, people usually wait to be called upon.

(From http://www.sideroad.com/)

Note

1. autonomous：自主的，自主选择的
2. horseshoe：这里指马蹄形状的会议桌
3. keynote：主旨讲演，报告

Group Practice

Practice the above-mentioned seating arrangements with your classmates.

要点小结

本节的目标任务是希望学习者了解商务谈判落座礼仪的基本要求。在各类商务谈判

中，作为商务礼仪中很重要的一部分，座次安排是非常有讲究的。落座是指谈判双方进入谈判会场后就座的姿态和形态。如何落座，可以在一定程度上反映出谈判者的地位和信心，反映出一个谈判集体的团结力、控制力和组织能力。

综合实训

Task 1

1. Read the following articles and finish the practices.

Article 1

Gestures, Eye Contact and Space

Gestures that have positive connotations in one culture have negative meanings in another. For example, the V for victory gesture is positive in the United States and in many cultures; in England, however, when the palm is facing in the gesture has a crude connotation. The thumbs-up signal is another positive gesture in North America but is rude in Australia and West Africa. Likewise, the OK sign, though positive in the United States, is viewed as obscene in Brazil. In Belgium and France, the meaning is "worthless" or "zero," while in Japan, the gesture means money. The beckoning gesture (finger upturned, palm facing the body; the hand is waved back and forth) should be used with discretion; it is offensive to Filipinos, Mexicans, and Vietnamese. The gesture is used to summon people considered inferior, such as prostitutes. Because cultures vary widely in their use of gestures, learning a culture's common gestures is recommended before visiting the country. At the very minimum, it is important to know that people of China, England, Japan, Germany, and Switzerland use few gestures, while people of France, Greece, Italy, Spain, as well as people in Middle Eastern countries and most countries of Central America, are expressive in their gesturing. Watch what gestures the people in the country use; avoid the use of gestures unless the meaning is known.

Eye contact is important in the U.S. and Canadian macro-cultures; eye contact implies attentiveness, respect, truthfulness, and self-confidence. However, a steady, unbroken gaze makes most U.S. people uncomfortable. People of France, Germany, the Middle East, and some Latin American countries favor prolonged eye contact. On the other hand, people in many Asian countries, specifically China and Japan, are uncomfortable with direct eye contact and tend to direct their gaze just below the other person's chin.

Space and touch are two important types of non-verbal communication that are closely related. For example, U.S. people need their space; they also prefer to avoid touching, with the exception of shaking hands. Likewise, Canadians and the Dutch value their personal space and do not touch during greetings and conversations. People of Japan and Southeast Asia stand even farther apart than U.S. people and are uncomfortable with touching. On the other hand, people of Latin America, the Middle East, and some Asian countries, and districts e.g., the

Republic of Korea, stand close while talking; they often touch each other during greetings and conversations. People from cultures that need a lot of space should not step back when interacting with people from cultures who prefer to stand close to avoid giving offense.

Practice:

1) According to the article, finish the link task. (Countries or regions listed to the right may be used more than once or not at all.)

________ The OK sign means worthless or zero.	A. Canada
________ The beckoning gesture is considered offensive.	B. China
________ Prolonged eye contact is preferred.	C. France
________ Standing close during conversations is customary.	D. Germany
	E. Japan
	F. Mexico
	G. Netherlands
	H. the Republic of Korea
	I. the United Kingdom

2) Divide the class into groups, each student in the group learns and practices the correct gestures, eye contact and space requirements in different countries.

Article 2

Elbow Bump (碰肘) Etiquette

Greetings are used in the community every single day. Greeting people can be confusing, especially during cross-cultural communications. Will a simple handshake do? Should you give a hug or offer a kiss on the cheek? People in different countries have their own greetings. While the goal is to have a positive interaction, different cultures and traditions as well as societal expectations demand certain methods of greetings. Common forms of greetings include handshakes, hugging, kissing, bowing down, verbal greetings, footshakes and elbow bumps, just to name a few.

The elbow bump is an informal greeting where two people touch, bump, or tap, elbows. It has gained in popularity because it respects the privacy customs of nearly all cultures, and has excellent hygienic qualities.

It is said that the elbow bump got renewed interest during the avian flu (禽流感) scare of 2006, the 2009 swine flu (猪流感) and the 2014 Ebola (埃博拉病毒) outbreak, when health officials supported its use to reduce the spread of germs.

With the coronavirus pandemic, on some occasions elbow shakes have replaced handshakes or kisses, in a bid to try and minimize the spread of the virus. Now the elbow bump has become an etiquette during the new coronavirus (新型冠状病毒，世界卫生组织命名为 COVID-19). However, some experts claim they should also be avoided as the recommended 1.5-metre distance would not be maintained in the interaction.

Questions:

1) What is "elbow bump"?

2) Why do some people touch/bump/tap elbows instead of a handshake or kiss?

Task 2

1. Work in pairs

Student A

1) You arc Hull Anderson. Now you telephone Chanel at BBS Training:

- Request the details of next course on telephone communication skills.
- Ask her to send the information by email.
- Tell her you'll send 10 members of your staff to this course.
- Ask what discounts can be given on group bookings.

2) You work for BBS Training. Someone calls to speak to your colleague Luis but she is on business today. Take a message using the form below.

To: ________________	**Date:**________________
From: ______________	**Company:**______________
Tel: ________________	

Message

____

____

____

____

Student B

1) You work for BBS Training. Someone calls to speak to your colleague Chanel but she is in a meeting. Take a message using the form above.

2) Your name is Shell Surlase. You telephone Luis at BBS Training:

- Cancel your booking for the seminar of sales skills on June 13th.
- Apologize for the cancellation.
- Request the details of next similar seminars after June 13th.
- Ask when the money for the canceled seminar will be refunded.

Task 3

1. Decide the following cases true or false, and state your reasons.

1) Your boss, Ms. Alpha, enters the room when you're meeting with an important client, Mr. Beta. You stand up and say "Ms. Alpha, I'd like you to meet Mr. Beta, our client from San Diego."

2) In the business arena, it is not necessary for men or women to stand for handshaking.

3) In a business greeting, if someone forgets to introduce you, it is appropriate to move on with the conversation without saying anything.

4) When shaking hands, a man should wait for a woman to extend her hand.

5) You meet the CEO of a corporation, after the brief talk, you give your business card.

2. Divide the class into groups, and discuss the case study in class.

After Frank Lewis, the manager of a large U.S. bookstore, hired Wu Ching, a newcomer from China, as a clerk, he invited her to join him for coffee and try to get to know her better. Throughout their conversation, Frank noticed that Wu Ching always looked down at the floor and never gave him eye contact. He interpreted this as inattention and lack of respect.

Task 4

Divide the class into groups and role-play the following situation.

A business delegation consisting of 3 members led by CEO Mr. George Wash will come to visit your company and talk about the future cooperation. You are the general manager of Dongfang Electric Company, now you need to go to the airport to meet the delegation with the director of sales department and your secretary.

Task 5

Divide the class into groups, and finish the following tasks according to the following situation.

Your company is going to negotiate the purchase of a kind of electric watch with ABC Company. ABC Company is sending 4 members for the negotiation including the general manager, marketing director, financial director and secretary. And the general manager, sales director, technical director, office staff and translator are the negotiating members in your company. After the negotiation, both sides agree to sign the contract.

1) Place a negotiation room, and arrange the seats of both sides properly.

2) Design a signing room, place the signing table and seats arrangements; and simulate the signing ceremony.

实践语句

1. I hope this meeting is productive.
我希望这是一次富有成效的会谈。
2. I'm sure there is some room for negotiation.
我肯定还有商量的余地。
3. We are always willing to cooperate with you and if necessary make some concessions.
我们总是愿意合作的，如果需要还可以做些让步。
4. If you have any comment about these clauses, do not hesitate to make.

对这些条款有何意见，请尽管提，不必客气。

5. We'd like you to consider our request once again.

我们希望贵方再次考虑我们的要求。

6. We hope that the next negotiation will be the last one before signing the contract.

我们希望下一次谈判将是签订合同前的最后一轮谈判。

7. Oh, I'm sorry, I misunderstood you. Then I go along with you.

哦，对不起，我误解你了。那样的话，我同意你的观点。

8. We can get the ball rolling on this deal by talking to the company's vice president.

关于这笔生意，我们可以先找这家公司的副总谈。

9. If you think you have a better idea than this, shoot.

如果你觉得还有比这更好的意见，尽管直说吧！

10. I'd be happy to answer any questions you may have.

我乐意回答贵方提出的任何问题。

11. When it comes to income agreements, we're on common ground.

就收入方面的协议而言，我们持有相同的意见。

12. Your demand is too high, but if we can reach some middle ground we might have a deal.

你的要求太高了，不过，如果我们能折中，或许可以成交。

13. It's about the best we can do.

这是我们所能做到的极限。

14. We did the best that we could to give you a low price.

我们已经尽力给了你们较低的价格。

15. Here is a little something for you. I hope you'll like it.

这是给你的一件小礼物。我希望你喜欢它。

16. On behalf of our company, I'd like to present you a gift, Mr. Bush. It's a sample guitar for you from our Chinese branch.

布什先生，我谨代表我们公司向您赠送这件礼物。这是中国分公司生产的吉他样品。

核心词汇

aura	*n.* 气氛，氛围
intrusive	*adj.* 受到侵犯的
monologue	*n.* 长篇大论
overbearing	*adj.* 傲慢的，骄傲自大的
refreshments	*n.* 茶点，点心
to the point	直截了当的

Unit 12 Cultures and Taboos in Business Negotiations

商务谈判中的文化与禁忌

任务目标

1. Knowing cultural differences in business negotiations
2. Understanding taboos of different negotiators
3. Learning strategies to cope with cultural differences and taboos

文化禁忌是指在某个民族或宗教传统文化里禁忌的一些事物、行为或言语。禁忌成为人们交际活动，尤其是跨文化商务交际的一大障碍。在国际商务谈判中，应加强跨文化谈判的意识，了解不同文化背景的谈判者在需求、动机、信念上的不同，学会了解、接受和尊重对方的文化。每种文化都有其各自的禁忌，中国文化也不例外。我们应学会正确表达自己的意愿，尽量缩小和避免文化差异带来的负面影响，适当地调整自己的谈判方式及策略以达到预期目的，取得谈判的成功。

Task 1 The Influence of Cultural Differences on Business Negotiation

文化差异对商务谈判的影响

文化对谈判的影响是广泛而深刻的。不同的文化将使人们相互疏远并形成沟通中难以逾越的障碍。因此，谈判者要尊重、接纳彼此的文化，而且要透过文化的差异，了解对方行为的真正意图，并使自己被对方所接受，最终达成一致的协议。

案例学习

An American company called HSO, which is an electronic equipment manufacturer, sent the representatives to Tokyo to negotiate a sale with a Japanese electronic production company. In thc first two days when the representatives from the American company arrived in Japan, they were showed around some interesting places for relaxation by the representatives from the Japanese company. In the third day, the negotiation meetings began. But actually, the Japanese company spent a lot of time talking about some issues unrelated to the sale. The American representatives didn't know why the Japanese company talked about so many things unrelated to business.

案例思考

What causes the differences in the business negotiation between the two companies?

案例解析

这是一个由于文化差异而造成的双方谈判沟通失败的案例。案例中，日本公司更愿意将时间花在建立关系上面，而美国公司则倾向于在谈判伊始讨论销售事宜。双方有不同的时间概念以及面向任务的不同态度。日方公司代表是关系导向型的，而美国人则是任务导向型的。在谈判中，日本公司倾向于花时间先与对方建立良好的关系，而美国公司倾向于尽早实现目标任务，而不是花很长时间建立关系。

理论拓展

Cultural Differences in Cross Cultural Negotiations
跨文化谈判中的文化差异

Culture profoundly influences how people think, communicate and behave, especially in the form of international businesses, whether in the form of trade, investment or business relations. The type of transactions you make and the way you negotiate also affect the type of people you interact with, as well as the quality of your relationships with other people.

The great diversity of cultures around the world makes it difficult for negotiators, no matter how competent and experienced they may be, to fully understand all cultures they can encounter. Cultural differences, such as family businesses, religions and ethnic groups, can create barriers that hinder or completely block the negotiation process. Therefore, learning the opponent's culture and having a good understanding of how cultural differences affect negotiation will be critically important if one wants to succeed in cross-cultural negotiations.

1. Eye Contact

In the US, UK and much of northern Europe, strong, direct eye contact conveys confidence and sincerity. In South America it is a sign of trustworthiness. However, in some cultures such as the Japanese, prolonged eye contact is considered rude and is generally avoided.

2. Personal Space & Touch

In Europe and North America, business people will usually leave a certain amount of distance between themselves when interacting. Touching only takes place between friends. In South America or the Middle East, business people are tactile and like to get up close.

In Japan or China, it is not uncommon for people to leave a gap of four feet when conversing. Touching only takes place between close friends and family members.

3. Time

Western societies are very "clock conscious". Time is money and punctuality is crucial. This is also the case in countries such as Japan or China where being late would be taken as an insult.

However, in South America, southern Europe and the Middle East, being on time for a meeting does not carry the same sense of urgency.

4. Meeting & Greeting

Most international business people meet with a handshake. In some countries this is not appropriate between genders. Some may view a weak handshake as sign of weakness whereas others, such as the Japanese, would perceive a firm handshake as aggressive.

How should people be addressed? Is it by first name, surname or title? Is small talk part of the proceedings or not?

5. Gift-Giving

In Japan and the Republic of Korea gift-giving is an integral part of business **protocol**, however, in the US or UK, it has negative connotations.

Where gifts are exchanged should one give lavish[1] gifts? Are they always reciprocated[2]? Should they be wrapped? Are there numbers or colours that should be avoided?

6. The Basis of the Relationship

In much of Europe and the US, business is contractual in nature. Personal relationships are seen as unhealthy as they can cloud objectivity[3] and lead to complications.

In South America and much of Asia, business is personal. Partnerships will only be made with those they know, trust and feel comfortable with. It is therefore necessary to invest in relationship building before conducting business.

7. Information at Negotiations

Western business culture places emphasis on clearly presented and rationally argued business proposals using statistics and facts. Other business cultures rely on similar information but with differences.

For example, visual and oral communicators, such as the Turks, may prefer information presented through speech or using maps, graphs and charts.

8. Negotiation Styles

The way in which we approach negotiation differs across cultures. For example, in the Middle East rather than approaching topics sequentially negotiators may discuss issues simultaneously. South Americans can become quite vocal and animated[4]. The Japanese will negotiate in teams and decisions will be based upon consensual agreement.

In Asia, decisions are usually made by the most senior figure or head of a family. In China, negotiators are highly trained in the art of gaining **concessions**. In Germany, decisions can take a long time due to the need to analyse information and statistics in great depth. In the UK, pressure tactics and imposing deadlines are ways of closing deals whilst in Greece this would backfire[5].

(From https://www.commisceo-global.com/)

Notes

1. lavish：奢侈的，大方的
2. reciprocate：回报，报答
3. cloud objectivity：此处指影响商务活动的客观性
4. animate：兴奋的，有活力的
5. In the UK, pressure tactics and imposing deadlines are ways of closing deals whilst in Greece this would backfire：在英国，施压战术和设定最后期限是完成交易的方法；然而在希腊，这将适得其反。

Group Discussion

How to behave in a cross-cultural negotiation?

要点小结

本节的目标任务是希望学习者了解文化差异对商务谈判的影响。在国际商务谈判中，除了掌握基本的谈判技巧外，了解文化差异对谈判活动可能造成的影响并做好充分的准备也十分重要。

国际商务谈判不仅是经济领域的交流与合作，而且是各国文化之间的碰撞与沟通。

来自不同国家、不同地区的谈判人员在语言沟通、思维方式、决策过程和谈判风格等方面有着显著差异，正是这种文化上的差异，稍不注意就可能导致谈判陷入僵局甚至失败。总的来说，文化差异对谈判的影响主要体现在语言沟通技巧的运用、非语言——肢体语言的使用、谈判风格等几个方面。

Task 2 The Strategies of Dealing with Cultural Differences in Business Negotiation
商务谈判中应对文化差异的策略

面对不同文化的交流和碰撞，谈判者应及时调整谈判策略，把握谈判的主动权。

案例学习

Rainbow Inc., an American company, had a proposal to import Chinese Green Tea from Leshan Export Company. The two companies had a negotiation about the quotation of the Green Tea. The sales managers of both companies were the chief negotiators for the two negotiation teams. The American negotiators made a counter-offer of $6.5 for the quotation of $9.5 offered by the Chinese side. The counter-offer was in fact the target price set by the American company, whereas the Chinese side was attempting to obtain a higher price in the negotiation. The Chinese side tended to strive for a higher price than the American company's target price due to the cost of time, while the American side considered the negotiation to be time-consuming, trying to make the bargaining time shorter. One of the negotiators in the Chinese company said that the American negotiators offered the target price directly at the beginning of the negotiation, and the Chinese company offered the first quotation that was not the target price. The Chinese negotiators tended to take a long time to negotiate, but the American negotiators preferred their target price to be the final quotation for their company and they would not make a deal with the Chinese company if the price offered by the Chinese company was higher than their target price. The Chinese negotiator also said that the Americans communicated with them in a very direct way throughout the negotiation process. For example, the American negotiators frankly told their counterparts that the target price was the exact quotation they could accept, whereas the Chinese negotiators tended to communicate in an indirect way that they wanted to negotiate progressively to reach an agreement. But they were not sure if the quotation of $6.5 offered by their **counterpart** was their target price, and they still negotiated for a higher price than $6.5. In the end of the negotiation, the Chinese company accepted the American company's quotation of $6.5.

案例思考

What can you learn from the case?

案例解析

在谈判过程中，美方谈判代表很好奇为什么中国的同行在谈判桌上花了大量时间讨价还价，但最终还是接受了他们的还价；而中方谈判人员也想知道为什么美国人谈判如此直接，一开始就报出了自己的目标价格。从这个案例可以看出，中美双方在诸如交际方式、时间观念等方面存在差异。一般说来，美国人习惯于直面问题本身，而中国人则倾向于用间接的手段处理问题。在商务谈判中，美国人一向直截了当地表达自己的观点，而中国人喜欢委婉的陈述。这些文化差异造成了双方谈判的困难。在跨文化商务谈判中，我们应该及时了解双方的文化差异，熟悉对方的文化特点，有效地开展商务谈判。

理论拓展

Managing Cultural Differences in Business Negotiations
商务谈判中的文化差异管理

Imagine that you're about to engage in an international negotiation with someone from a different culture. How would you go about it? In all likelihood, you would focus on managing cultural differences by studying the other party's culture, customs, and tendencies. You might try to answer questions such as, Should I bow upon meeting my counterpart? Should I bring a gift? Should we meet over dinner and get to know each other, or get right down to business? What is considered rude in their culture, that is acceptable in mine?

It's important to educate yourself about your counterpart's culture so that you don't risk offending him/her or seeming unprepared. At the same time, it would be a mistake to focus too narrowly when preparing for cross-cultural communication in business. Research on international negotiation can help us think more broadly when it comes to managing cultural differences.

Putting Too Much Stock in Stereotypes[1]

One common risk of studying up on a counterpart's culture is that it can lead us to expect that person to behave like a walking, talking stereotype. For example, relying on stereotypes gleaned[2] from international negotiation how-to books, you might expect your German counterpart to be exceedingly rigid and punctual. Or you might expect a Mexican negotiator to communicate expressively and devote a lot of time to rapport-building.

Such stereotypes may or may not turn out to apply to any given individual. Moreover, our culture is just one contributor to our identity and behavior. Our profession, personal history, ingrained personality, and experiences also define who we are and how we negotiate. Yet we tend to focus on an unfamiliar counterpart's culture because it is often her or his most obvious feature. International conflict and misunderstanding can be the inevitable result, and you want to make sure you are able to manage cultural differences if you ever want to get anywhere in negotiations.

Culture and Confusion

In fact, negotiators tend to over-rely on stereotypes when managing cultural differences in international negotiation, University of Waterloo professor Wendi L. Adair and her colleagues have found. In a study of American and Japanese negotiators, the researchers found that study participants typically adjusted their negotiating style too far toward the other party's culture. That is, they expected their counterpart to negotiate as they imagine he would at home, not anticipating that he would likely try to adjust to the foreign context as well. Ironically, this mutual adjustment led to cultural clashes when negotiators were trying to share information and persuade one another.

To take an example, suppose that a Brazilian and a German are about to negotiate. From her research, the Brazilian may expect that the German will want to immediately get down to business. Meanwhile, the German may think that the Brazilian will want to spend some time building rapport. If the Brazilian tries to hurry the talks along to meet what she perceives to be the German's expectations, the German may feel rebuffed[3] and disappointed.

Moving Beyond Stereotypes to Managing Cultural Differences

Here are three guidelines for managing cultural differences and reducing cultural barriers to negotiation:

1. Research the whole person. In addition to learning about a negotiating partner's culture, try to get to know him as an individual. Where has he worked? What are his skills? What is his reputation like as a negotiator? You might answer such questions by consulting his LinkedIn[4] profile, speaking with people in your network or his, and getting to know him over the phone or in person. You'll probably discover that your counterpart has been formed just as much or more by his personality, experience, and profession as by his nationality.

2. Negotiate like a diplomat. To look further beyond stereotypes, consider the broader context of your negotiation. Harvard Business School Max H. Bazerman notes that this is a core skill of experienced diplomats. Thinking several steps ahead, diplomats tend to consider broad issues related to a negotiation, such as the changing politics and laws of a region, the likely response of community groups and activists to your decisions, and so on, Bazerman has observed. All of us can practice thinking broadly in international negotiation—and move beyond stereotypes in the process.

3. Take the pressure off. Interestingly, negotiators are more likely to adhere to cultural stereotypes when facing demands on their attention, including time pressure, Columbia University professor Michael W. Morris has found. In one study, for example, American participants facing time pressure were more likely than participants from the Republic of Korea to blame the individual rather than the situation for a problem—an American negotiating bias[5]. Unfortunately, when we resort to stereotypical behavior, careful analysis tends to fall by the wayside. To encourage deeper thinking, lessen the stress surrounding your negotiation by taking frequent breaks, getting to know one another, and making sure deadlines aren't too tight.

(From https://www.pon.harvard.edu/)

Notes

1. stereotypes：固化的思想、看法
2. glean：收集，搜集
3. rebuff：断然拒绝，回绝
4. LinkedIn：中文名为领英，是全球最大的职业社交网站，2003 年 5 月正式上线，坐落于美国加州硅谷。在海外，LinkedIn 只是一个找工作的平台，而对于广大的外贸企业来说，LinkedIn 是一个巨大的潜在客源地，近 8 成的国内外贸企业将 LinkedIn 视为搜集潜在客户名单的重要来源。
5. bias：偏见，成见

Group Discussion

In cross-cultural negotiations, how to reduce the impact brought by cultural differences?

要点小结

本节的目标任务是希望学习者了解和掌握商务谈判中应对文化差异的策略。国际商务谈判是一种复杂的跨国界、跨文化的商务活动。谈判者应学会观察，注意彼此间的文化共性，淡化双方的文化差异，以取得跨文化谈判的成功。

因此，我们在谈判中要主动地了解中西方文化差异，发现导致彼此误解或对立的真正原因，想方设法找到建设性的沟通渠道，促进谈判向成功的方向发展。

Task 3 Taboos of Different Negotiating Rivals
不同谈判对手的禁忌

与不同文化背景的人谈判时，一定要懂得并遵循他们的规矩，触犯了禁忌，不仅会引起误解，而且会导致谈判的失败。

案例学习

A US company, the United Co. sent vice president Harry to exploit the market in Europe.

Harry's first stop was London, where he made brief talks with local bankers—by phone. In Paris, he booked lunch in the Silver-tour Hotel, and greeted his guest, the president of an industrial engineering company, "Jacques, call me Harry please." In Germany, Mr. Harry was like a motor. He made a harangue on marketing, supplemented by chart and audio-visual materials, so as to show how excellent he was in business-dealing. On the flight to Milan, he talked with a Japanese businessman. He threw his business card on the tray; when they said goodbye to each other, he shook hands and held the Japanese's right arm. Later, when he met with an Italian businessman, he wore his comfortable corduroy sport coats, khaki pants and sneakers. Everyone knows that Italians are relaxed, isn't it?

Six months passed, and the United Co. received nothing except a pile of bills. In Europe, no one is crazy about Harry any more.

案例思考

Why did Harry achieve no result in his trip in Europe?

案例解析

美国人哈利的欧洲之行之所以失败，主要是因为他不了解谈判对手的禁忌。例如，英国人通常不用电话做生意；法国人对陌生人非常正规，不喜欢太快地亲近，不愿意被陌生人直呼其名；德国人不喜欢夸张和卖弄，喜欢与内敛沉稳的商人做生意；意大利人对时装非常敏感，他们穿着漂亮并崇尚创造，对别人不得体的衣着会感到不解；日本属于“无碰触文化”，随意地碰触会被认为是失礼和狂妄自大。最终，哈利的自以为是自食苦果。

理论拓展

Understanding Different Styles in Cross-Cultural Negotiation
理解跨文化谈判中的不同风格

Understanding the local negotiation style is key to getting the business outcome you want.

If you've ever tried to buy a carpet in a Turkish bazaar[1], you'll know the ritual. The seller mentions a ridiculous price. You (if you are bold enough) make a ludicrously[2] low offer. The seller expresses outrage. You **haggle**[3] for a while. If your nerve is strong, you walk away. If the seller still has some **leeway**[4] in their selling price, they'll chase after you, with a better "final price". Then you leave with a new carpet.

This is one of the most extreme forms of negotiation. But understanding the local culture and bargaining style will help you get the best price for your carpet. The same applies to any cross-cultural business transaction. Of course, every individual is different, but cultures around the world certainly display an element of consistency in their negotiating style.

Australia

Hype-fueled arguments and high-pressure techniques will not impress Australians and are most likely to provoke some caustic comments. Derisory[5] remarks about others or competitors can be viewed also with suspicion or as not being "fair play"; this is a nation that favors the underdog[6]. What is said will be taken literally, and Australians expect you to take what they say literally as well. Storming off in a mock fit of indignation will make you look foolish[7]. Australians do not have the same tradition of bartering as, for example, their Asian neighbors, and expect an offer to include only a small margin for compromise and focus on a win-win outcome.

Canada

Canadians usually aim for a win-win outcome, in which information sharing and problem solving lead to gains for both parties. Expect negotiating style to be polite, direct and efficient and for hard fact to be seen as more important than the relationship.

China

Chinese are renowned for their tendency to be tough, canny[8] negotiators. Large groups are always used for negotiations, never individuals, with one spokesperson per group. Chinese negotiations are characterized by a soft sell and a hard buy; initial offers will be extreme and generous concessions need to be made. Watch out for certain tactics. These may include controlling the meeting venue and schedule; withholding information; threatening to do business with a competitor; displays of mock anger (here saving "face is so important"). Your counterparts may invoke the "guanxi argument", too, calling in favors from their business network which, for the purpose of the deal, includes you. Be thoroughly prepared, patient, reserved and always dignified.

Norway

Norway is almost the complete opposite. Negotiating meetings are **collaborative**, direct and efficient. Do not play games. Avoid hype[9] or threats and on no account go in with a high-low gambit—starting with a ridiculous price and expecting to reduce it. The Norwegians (and other Scandinavians) will aim for **consensus** in the group. Your goal should be a win-win outcome.

United Arab Emirates

In the Arab world, negotiations are driven by two things: price and personal relationships. Although selling benefits are critical, they are not the primary factor. Expect a negotiating meeting to be fluid, with constant interruptions. Although much of the emphasis of the discussion will be on your relationship and happy future together, it will still all come down to price. Know your bottom line and don't waiver[10]. Know when to walk away—your counterpart will often call you back. A seller will start off very high with a much, much lower actual price in mind. Keep a few cards up your sleeve for last-minute concessions. Arabs expect a win-lose outcome to negotiations and you must show that you are prepared to give a little.

USA

Americans tend to prefer a zero-sum[11] result approach and information is used as power. Each side has a limit and it is hoped that common ground will be found where these bargaining zones overlap. The transaction is the focus; speed, cost and efficiency are useful bargaining chips. An action plan is desirable; Americans do not like vagueness.

Zambia

Zambians, along with several other southern and east African cultures, aim for a win-win outcome. So if your potential partner demonstrates flexibility and willingness to commit, try to do the same yourself. Expect a degree of haggling, which is part of everyday life. Instead of giving you a price, your counterpart may put you on the spot by asking what you want to pay, which can un-nerve[12] the inexperienced negotiator. A starting price on any deal may be unrealistically high but the goal of any deal is to get this to a level that is acceptable to both parties.

(From https://theculturemastery.com/)

Notes

1. bazaar：集市，市场
2. ludicrously：荒唐地，可笑地
3. haggle：讨价还价
4. leeway：余地，退路
5. derisory：嘲笑的，嘲弄的

6. underdog：弱者，失败者

7. Storming off in a mock fit of indignation will make you look foolish：假装愤然离去会使你看起来很愚蠢

8. canny：精明的，谨慎的

9. hype：大肆宣传，炒作

10. waiver：放弃

11. zero-sum：零和博弈，与非零和博弈相对，是博弈论的一个概念，属非合作博弈。它是指参与博弈的各方，在严格竞争下，一方的收益必然意味着另一方的损失，博弈各方的收益和损失相加总和永远为“零”，故双方不存在合作的可能。

12. un-nerve：使失去勇气

Group Work

Work together and try to find more country tips of different styles in cross-cultural negotiation.

要点小结

本节的目标任务是希望学习者了解在跨文化商务谈判中，要提前做好充分的准备。针对不同的谈判对手，了解其文化背景以及相关禁忌，切勿由于疏忽大意而造成谈判中的不愉快，并导致生意失败。

谈判对手一般可以分为三种类型：进取型：以取得成功为满足；关系型：以与别人保持良好关系为满足；权力型：以与别人和对谈判局势施加影响为满足。

Task 4　Cultural Differences and Negotiating Styles
文化差异与谈判风格

文化差异从谈判目标、个人风格、交流方式、时间观念等方面影响商务谈判的风格。了解这些差异有助于我们领悟不同国家商务谈判风格差异产生的深层原因，以减少跨文化商务谈判进程中的误解和障碍。

案例学习

An American oil company manager, Carl, met with an Arab representative Ali from OPEC for the agreement on the final details of Sales Contract. When they were talking, the Arabian Ali gradually got close to the American Carl, only 15cm from each other. At that time, Carl was not too familiar with customs in the Middle East, so he moved back. Ali hesitated and frowned, then went nearer to Carl. Carl got nervous and took a further step back. At this moment, Carl found his assistant was anxiously staring at him, shaking his head and motioning. So Carl understood his hint and stood still at once. Then they settled the deal in a way Carl felt the most awkward.

案例思考

How could they finally come to an agreement?

案例解析

在商务交谈中，阿拉伯人往往会坐或站立得离对方很近，有时甚至把手放在交谈者的肩上，用手拍肩臂或触碰。在案例中，Carl 两次退步是很危险的动作，意味着对阿拉伯人的不尊重。助手的示意，指明 Carl 不应该退步避开，这才使双方最终达成了协议。在与特别注重习俗、有着虔诚的伊斯兰教信仰的阿拉伯人进行谈判时，谈判者对他们的风俗应尊重，尽可能适应他们，理解他们，才能够得到他们的尊敬和友好之情，使谈判取得较好的效果。

理论拓展

Cross-Cultural Negotiation Styles
跨文化谈判风格

Cultural differences play a significant role in negotiation styles. Both spoken and **non-verbal** communication can impact a delicate negotiation between two or more parties. Taking the time to learn about cultural differences and business etiquette is an important part of preparing for any important business negotiation.

Time Considerations

One basic difference between cultures is the way time is perceived. A culture's relationship to time defines it as either a monochronic or a polychronic culture[1]. Characteristics of a monochronic culture include a preference and expectation for schedule adherence, meeting agendas, scheduled breaks and detailed communication. Countries considered to be monochronic are countries such as the U.S., Switzerland, Scandinavia and Germany. Japan also falls in this category. In contrast to the monochronic cultural perspective on time, polychronic cultures start and end meetings spontaneously, take breaks as necessary and are comfortable with a less structured meeting where dialogue and information flows freely. Countries identified as polychronic include France, Italy, Greece, East African countries and Mexico.

Formal Versus Informal Negotiation Styles

Many negotiations are less than successful, ending abruptly when one party decides they are being rushed or disrespected. Different cultures' expectations can differ radically about the **formality** of the negotiation process. For instance, if an American called a Japanese negotiator by his first name at a first meeting, the Japanese businessperson would be offended. In the U.S., a person's first name is often used as a sign of friendliness. This is representative of the type of misunderstanding that undermines many negotiation efforts. A formal style of negotiation includes using a person's titles and refraining from conversation directed toward a person's family or private life. Anecdotes are considered too informal for people to introduce into the conversation. The Germans and the Japanese are thought to be more formal than Americans.

Negotiation Objectives

Business people from different cultures have varying objectives when they participate in a negotiation. This is a very important distinction that should be understood prior to attending a meeting. Americans attend negotiations seeking an agreement, often in the form of a contract. The Spanish also strive to obtain a contract as a sign of successful negotiation. Conversely, in Latin American countries, parties focus on developing the relationship. Similar to the Latin American culture, the Japanese are likely to focus more on the relationship being forged and less on the details.

Eye Contact

Interpreting behavior is always a challenge in an important negotiation. Understanding both verbal and non-verbal communication is helpful for interpreting the actions of someone from a different culture. A good example of non-verbal communication that can be significant is eye contact. In the U.S., Canada and Arab countries, direct eye contact is considered a sign of trustworthiness. Where misunderstandings could crop up[2] is how differently Asian countries view eye contact. In Asian society, looking down is considered a sign of respect.

(From https://bizfluent.com/)

Notes

1. monochronic or a polychronic culture：单一时间文化或多元时间文化

2. crop up：突然出现，发生

Group Discussion

What about the negotiation styles of Chinese people in Time Considerations, Negotiation Styles, Negotiation Objectives and Eye Contact, etc.?

要点小结

本节的目标任务是希望学习者了解不同文化背景下谈判者谈判风格的差异。在商务谈判中，要想取得实质性的成果，了解各国不同的文化背景以及各国谈判人员在谈判中表现出的言谈举止，处事方式的不同，就显得尤为重要，这样不仅可以消除商务谈判中可能产生的误解，而且可以使谈判过程更加顺利。

综合实训

Task 1

1. Read the following case and finish the practices.

An American company called HSO, which is an electronic equipment manufacturer, sent the representatives to Chengdu to negotiate a sale with a Chinese electronic production company. In the first two days, when the representatives from the American company arrived in China, they were showed around some interesting places for relaxation by the representatives from the Chinese company. In the third day, the negotiation meetings began. But actually, the Chinese company spent a lot of time talking about some issues unrelated to the sale. The American representatives didn't know why the Chinese company talked about so many things unrelated to business.

Practices:

1) Divide the class into groups, imitate the negotiation situation in the above case, then try to continue the negotiating process, and see what result you'll get at last.

2) How do cultural differences affect a business negotiation? Please talk about it.

Task 2

1. Practice the following case and learn the differences in cross-cultural negotiation. Think about what lessons the Chinese team should learn? How do they cope with this tough situation?

A negotiating team from China went to the Middle East for a project contract negotiation.

While chatting, one of the Chinese members commented unconsciously on Islam, which offended the negotiating rival. When it came to substantive issues, the members from the Middle East did not show any sign of concessions and revealed their intention to pull out of the negotiation, so the negotiation was fruitless in the end.

2. Group the class and discuss the cultural differences between China and the United States. Then design a negotiation situation and talk about how to reach a win-win agreement despite of cultural differences during the Sino-US negotiation.

Task 3

1. Divide the class into groups, role-play the following situation. Provided you go to European countries to promote the products as a Chinese sales representative, how do you behave while meeting people from different countries?

A US company, the United Co., sent vice president Harry to exploit the market in Europe. Harry's first stop was London, where he made brief talks with local bankers—by phone. In Paris, he booked lunch in the Silver-tour Hotel, and greeted his guest, the president of an industrial engineering company, "Jacques, call me Harry please." In Germany, Mr. Harry was like a motor. He made a harangue on marketing, supplemented by chart and audio-visual materials, so as to show how excellent he was in business-dealing. On the flight to Milan, he talked with a Japanese businessman. He threw his business card on the tray; when they said goodbye to each other, he shook hands and held the Japanese's right arm. Later, when he met with an Italian businessman, he wore his comfortable corduroy sport coats, khaki pants and sneakers. Everyone knows that Italians are relaxed, isn't it?

Six months passed, and the United Co. received nothing except a pile of bills. In Europe, no one is crazy about Harry any more.

Task 4

1. Read the following case and finish the practice.

An American oil company manager, Carl, met with an Arab representative Ali from OPEC for the agreement on the final details of Sales Contract. When they were talking, the Arabian Ali gradually got close to the American Carl, only 15cm from each other. At that time, Carl was not too familiar with customs in the Middle East, so he moved back. Ali hesitated and frowned, then went nearer to Carl. Carl got nervous and took a further step back. At this moment, Carl found his assistant was anxiously staring at him, shaking his head and motioning. So Carl understood his hint and stood still at once. Then they settled the deal in a way Carl felt the most awkward.

Practice

Provided you are a Chinese exporter discussing with an Arab importer on silk goods.

Imitate the situation showed in the above case and learn the different negotiating styles in different countries.

2. Case study

（1）日本商人在同外商进行初次商务交往时，喜欢先进行个人的直接面谈，而不喜欢通过书信交往。对于找上门来的客商，他们则更倾向于选择那些经熟人介绍来的，因此在初访日商时，最好事先托朋友、本国使馆人员或其他熟悉的人介绍。日本商人善于把生意关系人性化，他们通晓如何利用不同层次的人与谈判对方不同层次的人交际，从而探明情况，研究对策，施加影响，争取支持。

问题：

- 上述案例突出说明了哪种文化因素会影响国际商务谈判的风格？
- 日本商人的谈判风格是什么？
- 日本商人的谈判禁忌有哪些？

（2）某国商人见面与离别时，都面带微笑地与在场的人们握手；彼此问候较随便，大多数场合下可直呼其名；对年长者和地位高的人，在正式场合，使用“先生”“夫人”等称谓，对于婚姻状况不明的女性，不冒失地称其为夫人。在比较熟识的女士之间或男女之间会亲吻或拥抱。在交谈时习惯保持一定的身体间距，彼此站立间距约 0.9 米，每隔 2～3 秒有视线接触，以表示兴趣、诚挚和真实的感觉。

问题：

- 上述案例中的商人最有可能是哪一国籍的？
- 该国商人在谈判中的价值观怎样？
- 该国商人的谈判风格是什么？

实践语句

1. We'll come out from this meeting as winners.
这次会谈的结果将是一个双赢。

2. I hope this meeting is productive.
我希望这是一次富有成效的会谈。

3. Frankly, we can't agree to your proposal.
坦白地讲，我无法同意您的提案。

4. No, I'm afraid you misunderstood me. What I was trying to say was...
不，恐怕你误解了。我想说的是……

5. Oh, I'm sorry, I misunderstood you. Then I go along with you.
哦，对不起，我误解你了。那样的话，我同意你的观点。

6. **A:** I'm sorry to say that the price you quote is too high. It would be very difficult for us to push sales if we buy it at this price.

B: Well, if you take quality into consideration, you won't think our price is too high.

A: Let's meet each other half way.

A: 很遗憾你们报的价格太高，如果按这种价格买进，我方实在难以推销。

B: 如果你考虑一下质量，你就不会觉得我们的价格太高了。

A: 那咱们就各让一步吧。

7. People judge you by your appearance, whether you like it or not.
无论你喜欢还是不喜欢，人们都会从你的外表来进行评判。

8. This outfit is not appropriate, it's too provocative.
这套衣服不太适合，太过暴露。

9. What time are you available tomorrow for our meeting?
明天你什么时间有空，我们见面谈谈？

10. I'm so sorry for forgetting our appointment.
非常抱歉，我忘记了我们的约会。

核心词汇

collaborative	*adj.* 合作的，协作的
concession	*n.* 让步，妥协
consensus	*n.* 一致，共识
counterpart	*n.* 对应的人或物
formality	*n.* 手续，仪式
haggle	*v.* 讨价还价
non-verbal	*adj.* 非言语的
protocol	*n.* 礼仪
stereotype	*n.* 老套，刻板，陈词滥调

References

[1] 陈文汉. 商务谈判实务 [M]. 北京：人民邮电出版社，2011.
[2] 丁建忠. 商务谈判教学案例 [M]. 北京：中国人民大学出版社，2005.
[3] 方明亮，刘华. 商务谈判礼仪 [M]. 北京：科学出版社，2011.
[4] 黄伟，钱莉. 国际商务谈判 [M]. 北京：冶金工业出版社，2012.
[5] 蒋磊. 国际商务英语谈判 [M]. 北京：对外经济贸易大学出版社，2014.
[6] 雷娟，全婧. 商务谈判 [M]. 西安：西安交通大学出版社，2011.
[7] 廖国强，王朝晖. 国际商务礼仪 [M]. 北京：对外经济贸易大学出版社，2018.
[8] 刘春生. 国际商务谈判 [M]. 北京：对外经济贸易大学出版社，2013.
[9] 刘园，姜和. 国际商务谈判 [M]. 北京：外经济贸易大学出版社，2013.
[10] 罗伊 • J. 列维奇，布鲁斯 • 巴里，戴维 • M. 桑德斯. 国际商务谈判：英文版 [M]. 6 版. 北京：中国人民大学出版社，2014.
[11] 马润泽. 经济全球化背景下国际贸易争端的解决 [J]. 商场现代化，2015 (5)：8-9.
[12] 宋格兰. 国际商务谈判 [M]. 北京：高等教育出版社，2012.
[13] 汤秀莲. 国际商务谈判 [M]. 北京：清华大学出版社，2009.
[14] 童成寿. 商务英语谈判 [M]. 北京：对外经济贸易大学出版社，2015.
[15] 王方. 商务谈判实训 [M]. 大连：东北财经大学出版社，2009.
[16] 夏美英，徐珊珊. 商务谈判实训 [M]. 北京：北京大学出版社，2013.
[17] 杨洁等. 体验商务英语听说教程 [M]. 北京：高等教育出版社，2006.
[18] 余慕鸿，章汝雯. 商务英语谈判 [M]. 北京：外语教学与研究出版社，2005.
[19] 张立玉. 商务谈判英语 [M]. 武汉：武汉大学出版社，2009.
[20] 张立玉. 实用商务涉外礼仪 [M]. 北京：北京理工大学出版社，2009.
[21] 仲鑫. 外贸函电 [M]. 北京：机械工业出版社，2010.
[22] 周庆. 商务谈判实训教程 [M]. 武汉：华中科技大学出版社，2011.